UNJUST DEBTS

UNJUST DEBTS

How Our Bankruptcy System
Makes America More Unequal

MELISSA B. JACOBY

THE
NEW
PRESS

NEW YORK
LONDON

Requests for permission to reproduce selections from this book should
be made through our website: https://thenewpress.com/contact.

Published in the United States by The New Press, New York, 2024
Distributed by Two Rivers Distribution

ISBN 978-1-62097-786-6 (hc)
ISBN 978-1-62097-864-1 (ebook)
CIP data is available

The New Press publishes books that promote and enrich public
discussion and understanding of the issues vital to our democracy
and to a more equitable world. These books are made possible by
the enthusiasm of our readers; the support of a committed group of
donors, large and small; the collaboration of our many partners in the
independent media and the not-for-profit sector; booksellers, who often
hand-sell New Press books; librarians; and above all by our authors.

www.thenewpress.com

Composition by Dix Digital Prepress and Design
This book was set in Sabon LT Pro

Printed in the United States of America

2 4 6 8 10 9 7 5 3 1

For my parents, who taught me the value of a book,

and

for W.M.C.W.

CONTENTS

INTRODUCTION

This book is a story of falling out of love. With a law.

The story almost never got off the ground. For my last year of law school, I signed up for a course about bankruptcy. I had second thoughts while out with friends the night before the fall semester started, on a roof deck at a TGI Fridays. The professor held high expectations and a preference for early-morning teaching. Did I want to spend my last year of school working so hard, on a subject my friends considered dull, dry, and just about money?

I set the alarm, walked to school to check out the first class, and, until now, never looked back. I learned that the federal Bankruptcy Code intersects with the lives of more people in the United States than virtually any other law does. The system's instruction manual enacted by Congress, the Bankruptcy Code, was a jigsaw puzzle. Fitting the pieces together helped me see the big picture: restoring economic opportunity in a capitalist society.

The potency of bankruptcy also held my attention. I learned that every contract in America contains an invisible caveat:

different enforcement rules apply if one of the parties files for bankruptcy. Whatever might have happened under ordinary law, bankruptcy could change the outcome like the flip of a switch. But this legal equivalent of a shiny set of power tools existed for a reason, or so I thought. To my student self, the bankruptcy system looked like a useful form of social insurance, a safety valve giving people the freedom to try, fail, and try again. I was taught that bankruptcy could deliver life-changing relief, reduce stress and suffering, and promote innovation and economic participation.

That class and that professor, Elizabeth Warren, changed my life. As graduation crept closer, she encouraged me to apply to work for a federal bankruptcy court, an institution I had only recently learned existed, in Chicago, a city I had never visited. After taking the bar exam required for new lawyers, I drove overnight in a rented van to start my professional life as a law clerk for the Honorable Robert E. Ginsberg.

Working with Judge Ginsberg gave me a front-row seat in the most bustling type of federal court in America. The year was 1994 and bankruptcy filings were skyrocketing. In the federal courthouse, a tall black box designed by Ludwig Mies van der Rohe, I watched and learned as Judge Ginsberg distinguished between better and worse legal arguments, better and worse lawyering, better and worse cases.

The court was a forum of last resort for families that

experienced bad things in volume: layoffs and shortened work hours, crumbled marriages, miscarriages and failed adoptions, flimsy health insurance and medical crises. I was struck by how people had tried everything, for better or worse, before resorting to bankruptcy. One laid-off hospital worker had used credit card cash advances to gamble on a riverboat, intending to bridge the financial gap until he got his job back.

Bankrupt businesses also landed in Judge Ginsberg's courtroom. They were nightclubs, hardware store chains, suburban home developers, paper goods manufacturers, and a security guard company responsible for airports and National Football League stadiums. Were they strong enough to reorganize, or should they shut down? Every day, I rushed to the courthouse to learn what would happen next.

As bankruptcy filings rose along with debt levels and economic insecurity, the consumer credit industry lobbied Congress to make personal bankruptcy relief harder and more expensive to access. It wasn't wrong to want to improve bankruptcy law. My job after the Chicago court involved policy work to do just that. There was plenty to fix, for sure. And, although we did not yet have the research to articulate all the problems, the personal bankruptcy system already was treating Black and white filers differently, reinforcing the effects of race discrimination in credit markets and elsewhere.

But increasing fairness and efficiency were not what the

credit industry was after. Its message was simple—bankruptcy law should not reward irresponsibility and bad decisions—and yet its requested fixes were horribly complicated. To anyone reading the fine print, it was clear that the goal was to make a mess, to squeeze extra profits from the least of us, whatever the causes of financial distress or the effects on everyone else. Insistent, but patient, the lobbyists got much of what they wanted by 2005, when Congress made hundreds of changes to bankruptcy law on a largely bipartisan basis.

The responsibility message not only was misleading, but destined to be unevenly applied. The American legal system tends to be more deferential to artificial persons like big corporations than to humans of modest means. Although the 2005 legislation included some changes to business bankruptcy, the consumer credit industry reforms did not try to make big enterprises take personal responsibility for bad decisions by restricting their bankruptcy access. The consumer credit industry was not focused on whether enterprises used bankruptcy to halt jury trials triggered by hazardous products or child sex abuse. The consumer credit industry was unconcerned with whether cities minimize the legal consequences of police brutality against their Black and brown residents by filing for bankruptcy. The consumer credit industry was not trying to stop businesses from using bankruptcy to sell companies quickly, shedding responsibilities to provide health care for retirees in hazardous industries or to remedy employment discrimination.

In other words, at the same time bankruptcy has fallen short in providing basic debt relief for struggling families, lawyers for big enterprises and other powerful parties have transformed bankruptcy into a legal Swiss Army knife. They bring into the system all sorts of policy problems beyond its domain and institutional capacity, even climate change if you can believe it.

Even though some of these examples remain rare (for now), the bankruptcy system, as specialized as it seems, affects nearly everyone. About one in ten living American residents has been through bankruptcy at least once. Big enterprises go bankrupt in smaller numbers, but each case can directly affect hundreds of thousands of people, and many millions more indirectly.[1]

Though I have become concerned about the broader impact of the bankruptcy system, the nation's bankruptcy courts, helmed by merit-selected judges, remain a source of inspiration. Their commitment and work ethic are a model for other courts. But individual judges do not have the tools or the authority to address the forces that make the bankruptcy system undercut equality and liberty. Bigger rethinking is in order.

Some contributors to the system's shortcomings stem from

broader forces in American law. American law has a one-track mind when it comes to remedies. If people prove in a civil lawsuit that they have been injured by a hazardous product, were unconstitutionally beaten by the police, or suffered unlawful discrimination, the judgment rarely results in an admission of wrongdoing, or a process of reconciliation. Payment of money is typically the best-case scenario in a civil lawsuit—or its frequent supplement or replacement, a settlement—no matter what the harmed party prefers, no matter what remedy would incentivize better behavior in the future. The preference for using money to compensate for harm has some justifications, such as the limitation on courts' ability to oversee other kinds of remedies. But the current use of the bankruptcy system shows the consequences of this preference. As America translates policy problems into money, liability for those problems becomes debts that lawyers will be tempted to sweep into bankruptcy. Survivors of wrongdoing are recast as creditors, indistinguishable from credit card issuers or sellers of basic commodities. When everything becomes just about money, other objectives of the legal system get deprioritized, such as deterrence, accountability, and restoring agency to harmed parties.

Treating all legal responsibilities as no more or less than money obligations that can be addressed in bankruptcy remains a policy choice, not an inevitable outcome. Giving the concept of a debt the broadest possible sweep leads the bankruptcy system to interfere with the pursuit of other public policies, subordinating those policies to objectives like maximizing economic value—an aspiration easier to utter than to measure. Especially when it comes to restructuring for-profit and nonprofit entities, bankruptcy's powerful tools are better suited to obligations arising from contracts than to those arising from pretty much anything else.

We also should recognize the hazards of intentional legal complexity, a prominent challenge in the world of bankruptcy. I sometimes show students a cartoon of one man in a suit saying to another, "We need some new jargon. The public is starting to understand what we're talking about!" Lawyers and their clients can profit from making these laws sound too hard for the rest of us to understand, suggesting that we should leave these complex matters to them, the experts. Some may earnestly believe that their decisions and strategies make the world better. They tend not to be the ones facing the consequences, and have already moved on to other projects, when they turn out to be wrong.[2]

Chapter 1 of this book begins with bankruptcy for individuals and the hurdles to the system delivering basic debt relief. It highlights the scrutiny financially distressed individuals undergo, especially after the big system overhaul in 2005.

Synthesizing an established body of research using a wide

range of methods and sources, chapter 2 talks about racial disparities in personal bankruptcy. It illustrates how facially neutral bankruptcy laws generate suboptimal experiences and outcomes for Black filers.

Chapter 3 introduces how bankruptcy law treats fake people, such as corporations, differently than it treats the individuals discussed in chapters 1 and 2. Like many areas of law, bankruptcy law gives enterprises the benefit of personhood. But artificial persons filing for bankruptcy, especially if they are bigger in size, are far less likely to encounter the value judgments that lower-income individuals face before, during, and after they file. For example, fake people can cancel legal obligations—including those that arise from bad behavior—that humans cannot. In addition to reflecting bias, bankruptcy undercuts efforts to deter, remedy, and punish serious corporate misconduct.

Chapter 4 shows how artificial person bankruptcies provide additional pathways for undercutting liberty and equality. A special kind of bankruptcy law for cities weakens legal and constitutional responsibility for police misconduct and other violations of civil rights. Congress originally made bankruptcy accessible to cities to change payment terms on municipal bonds with the support of the majority of bondholders. The law has broadened considerably since then. In this new world, police officers get a prominent seat at the negotiating table; residents who allege violence at the hands of the state do not.

The rest of this book explores the transformation of corporate reorganization law for businesses and nonprofits. Chapter 11 of the Bankruptcy Code is a package deal of benefits and obligations. The package was designed to promote the instrumental objectives that flow from keeping a viable but heavily indebted company alive. As seen in chapter 5, financial institutions, private equity firms and other buyers of and investors in distressed companies extract the perks of Chapter 11 for their own benefit while abandoning the larger objectives of the national bankruptcy system. Chapter 5 also illustrates how the funding of the bankruptcy system contributes to these patterns.

In the contexts discussed in chapter 6, enterprises use Chapter 11 to halt litigation and cap liability for alleged wrongdoing rather than to restructure debts. Companies shift people who have suffered from hazardous products or survived child sex abuse out of the civil justice system and into Chapter 11, where debtor companies and co-defendants have significant extra leverage and control. Citing economic efficiency and the opportunity to "unlock value," these enterprises seek to permanently limit their responsibility, protecting not only the entity that filed the bankruptcy petition but also solvent third parties who may have committed wrongdoing of their own. Chapter 6 traces bankruptcy's evolution into the business of tort liability management.

Chapter 7 dives further into the details of bankruptcies filed to stop lawsuits and cap liability for hazardous products and child sex abuse. The concept of "mass torts" notwithstanding, one cannot evaluate the system's fairness and effectiveness without considering its impact on the real individuals whose remedies have been forever altered. Recognition of the spectrum of injuries and strength of proof is also necessary to illustrate why claimants with serious injuries might find the system unfair, even if they vote in favor of a bankruptcy plan.

The conclusion to this book invites consideration of structural change, with modesty about the capacity of a national bankruptcy system. The system needs to be a fair and effective, but targeted, tool to relieve overindebtedness. It should not be a legal Swiss Army knife tackling a world of policy problems that tax the system's institutional competence and lead to regressive effects. The stories in this book lead back to bankruptcy's broad definitions of *debt* and *claim*—key to recruiting so many kinds of policy problems into bankruptcy—and whether the system might be fairer and more consistent with democratic values if it had a narrower scope.

Two key words embedded in this book's title are *just* and *debts*. The multiple meanings of *just* lead to a common end.

Just connotes justice. *Just* also is a limiter, signifying "only." The American economy, families, and communities benefit when the bankruptcy system provides robust cancellation of obligations the average person recognizes as debts. On that central objective, the system has fallen short. Meanwhile, too many system activities bear distant relation to canceling or restructuring debts as traditionally understood, and are disrupting other societal objectives and foundational legal principles, including separation of powers and federalism. If this book has a policy prescription, it is to reduce the footprint of the bankruptcy system. To contribute to a more just legal environment and society, the bankruptcy should focus on *just debts.*

1

Bankruptcy for Real People

Sylvia does not answer the phone when you try to reach her on her sixtieth birthday. Her voice mail is full each time you call. Maybe the messages are from other friends and family. More likely they are threats and warnings from companies hired to collect debt.

Sylvia has had a tough five years. She missed a lot of work caring for her sick mother. She got fired after her boss lost patience with her pattern of absences. Her firing resulted in a loss of employer-based health insurance. As she depleted her meager savings, she used credit cards for necessities. After her mother died, Sylvia found a new job at a much lower salary and with fewer employee benefits. She buried the credit cards in the back of a kitchen drawer and chipped away at the debt as best she could. The debt grew rather than shrunk because of compounding interest and fees.

That Sylvia's debt is unpayable does not make it unprofitable to the consumer credit industry. Lenders often make money because of, and not in spite of, high rates of default. When Sylvia's creditors give up on their own collection efforts and sell her debts to third parties, the prices her creditors receive for the sale of those debts will likely be only a fraction of the principal debt's face value, but they may have already profited from interest and fees. Almost anything the debt buyers collect will be a win for them too.

What lies ahead, then, for Sylvia's sixties and seventies, and beyond? The debt collectors will call and call. If they file and win lawsuits, they may be able to garnish Sylvia's bank accounts and automatically subtract money from Sylvia's paychecks, depending on where she lives. If the debts still are not fully satisfied as court judgments near expiration, collectors will file paperwork to extend the right to enforce the obligations. When Sylvia dies, some collectors may reach out to Sylvia's family members and coax them to repay the principal, fees, and interest, not mentioning that her family has no legal responsibility to do so.

Unless Sylvia wins the lottery or has a surprise rich relative about to impart a big inheritance, these are zombie debts. They will hang over Sylvia for the rest of her life and will affect her decisions, her transactions, her friendships, her family.

If Sylvia's story has too little blood for your taste, watch the South Korean limited series *Squid Game*. Characters have amassed overwhelming debt trying to make ends meet and have no exit from that burden. They sign up to compete in high-stakes versions of schoolyard games like tug-of-war and red light, green light. The winner can pay off debts. The rest of the contestants die. When I agreed to watch the show at the encouragement of my teenage niece, I had no idea it would be so relevant to my research.

American bankruptcy law is supposed to make *Squid Game* unnecessary. The system's superpower is canceling debts. If Sylvia takes the steps the law requires, and if a court grants Sylvia a "discharge," the debts become legally unenforceable. They are canceled. Voice mail empty.

Sylvia is not a real person, but her story reflects decades of research on the humans who pass through the bankruptcy system day after day, year after year, decade after decade. If you need an image of a bankruptcy filer when reading more general descriptions of personal bankruptcy or when we work through some of the more exceptional stories, come back to Sylvia—she will keep you grounded.

The federal government has the authority to cancel Sylvia's debts because the U.S. Constitution says so. The Constitution's Bankruptcy Clause is just a few words. Article 1, section 8 gives Congress the authority "to establish . . . uniform laws on the subject of bankruptcies throughout the United States." The clause is in the original 1787 Constitution, but its reasoning is largely lost to history except for the intention to give Congress the power to override inconsistent state laws. Apparently, drafters worried that states would write debtor-creditor laws that would prioritize their own residents over those of other states.

For a long while, Congress didn't make much use of this authority. Early bankruptcy laws fell in and out of fashion, passed only to be quickly repealed. That changed when Congress passed the Bankruptcy Act of 1898, which stuck around for eighty years. Economic historians tell us that by the 1920s, bankruptcy was accepted as part of the American legal system by both Republicans and Democrats; by 1950, bankruptcy was "an essential part of the American social safety net."[1]

In the 1970s, a bipartisan group of lawmakers used Congress's constitutional power to develop the Bankruptcy Code, which President Jimmy Carter signed into law in 1978. That law forms the backbone of today's bankruptcy system. The Bankruptcy Code established pathways to debt relief for individuals as well as for entities such as for-profit companies, nonprofit organizations, and cities. In all these contexts, Congress broadened what counted as a "debt" that the system could address and potentially cancel, probably not foreseeing the potentially far-reaching effects of that decision.

The Bankruptcy Code outlines two main options for

individuals like Sylvia: Chapter 7 and Chapter 13, each named after its location in the statute. As originally designed, Chapter 7 was supposed to offer swift relief and cancel most unsecured debt. *Unsecured* means obligations to pay that are not backed by property, such as a car or house.

Chapter 13 has always been a longer and pricier road to debt relief. In Chapter 13, Sylvia would have to commit all disposable income to a repayment plan for three to five years. If she owns a home or car and defaulted on a home mortgage or car loan, Chapter 13 has some tools to help with that. If she finishes the repayment plan, Chapter 13 offers slightly broader debt relief than Chapter 7 does. If she doesn't finish—and most people don't, as you will see—Sylvia likely will not get any debt relief. Or a refund on the fees she paid to file the case or payments made to date.

Chapter 7 probably is the preferable path for Sylvia. Protections will start from the moment Sylvia files a petition with the court, whether digitally or in person, and pays a filing fee to the government. Sylvia's creditors immediately will be subject to an "automatic stay." That is a major legal protection that prohibits creditors from calling Sylvia, sending letters, or otherwise trying to collect payment on debts or recover her property. The automatic stay stops foreclosure on a house and repossession of a car, at least temporarily. It is a breathing spell for a financially distressed person. It also protects creditors from one another; collection is no longer a matter of a race among claimants, with the winner taking all.

To get the full benefit of Chapter 7 bankruptcy, including permanent debt relief, Sylvia must forfeit financial privacy. In addition to the bankruptcy being listed on her credit report, Sylvia must disclose all sorts of information and calculations that will be available to the public (other than sensitive information like her Social Security number). Before she files, Sylvia must fill out many forms and disclosures, under penalty of perjury. If she does not provide the required information, the court will dismiss her case. Hiding information or assets not only risks losing a shot at bankruptcy relief but can be a federal crime punishable by time in prison. The forms that Sylvia completes also determine whether she is entitled to Chapter 7 relief at all or whether she should be sent into a repayment plan or ejected from the system altogether.

Once Sylvia has filed her bankruptcy petition, the government will appoint a trustee to scrutinize her case and disclosures. The Chapter 7 trustee is a private individual, usually a lawyer, appointed in most states by a division of the U.S. Department of Justice to fulfill this official responsibility. The trustee is charged with ensuring that Sylvia has followed the rules. The trustee would like to sell Sylvia's property to pay creditors and himself, but Sylvia probably does not have enough property to make doing so worthwhile.

How will the trustee know what Sylvia owns? The trustee will start with the disclosures Sylvia made under penalty of perjury. To ensure accuracy, Sylvia needs to think broadly about her property interests. They might be tangible and touchable, like a car or computer. But intangible property must be listed too. Things like cryptocurrency or money in a bank account or the right to collect money from someone else are all property that must go on the list.

Sylvia also gets to take the first step of declaring what property is *exempt*. That means if the property fits certain categories and is worth less than any listed dollar limits, the law will protect the property from creditors and let Sylvia keep it. For example, everyone will be better off if Sylvia gets to keep pots and pans for cooking and clothes to wear to work. Even though bankruptcy law is national, the amount of property Sylvia can protect depends on her state of residence. Some exemption laws are far more generous than others, in terms of both categories of property and the dollar limits.

Even before the big legal overhaul of personal bankruptcy law in 2005, but especially after it, Chapter 7 has been sufficiently complicated that Sylvia probably will want to hire a law firm to represent her. That will make filing bankruptcy a lot more expensive, but it also will increase the odds that she will get some debt relief.

As noted before, Chapter 13 conditions debt relief on

completing a multiyear repayment plan. Sylvia's income will determine both how long she must pay (three years versus five) and how much money she must devote to the plan. The government will appoint a trustee to collect every penny Sylvia's plan promises and will distribute the money to creditors. Whether Sylvia is having trouble with a home mortgage or car loan will also shape the details of her repayment plan and allocation of payments.

Because Chapter 13 is meant to ensure Sylvia devotes all disposable income to repaying her creditors, it presents opportunities for scrutiny of Sylvia's personal financial circumstances and choices. For a lower-income person, disposable income means every dollar "not reasonably necessary" for household maintenance. That makes every small choice a potential discussion point—veterinary expenses, the Netflix streaming service, dry cleaning bills, fast-food meals. In the 1990s, some trustees tried to prevent debtors from tithing at their churches so they could pay creditors more. Congress fast-tracked a change to the Bankruptcy Code to put an end to that practice.

Scrutiny of personal bankruptcy filers is typically motivated by money—pay creditors more—but not always. Paul filed for Chapter 13 to save his Kentucky home from foreclosure. At the time, Paul was spending $190 a month for cigarettes. He disclosed this expense under penalty of perjury. Paul's lawyer told me that the presiding judge offered to approve Paul's proposed plan to save his home *if* Paul promised to give up smoking. Paul's lawyer explained that the judge's intervention seemed more focused on the health hazards of tobacco than on the cost of the habit. Didn't Paul want to live long enough to watch his kids grow up? Paul's story is unusual because of the non-financial objection to an expense, but it reflects the everyday surveillance on which Chapter 13 debt relief hinges. For individuals, bankruptcy seems to couple the privilege of debt relief with the insistence that debtors' lives are free of even minor indiscretions. As discussed in chapter 3 and onward of this book, the expenses and choices of big enterprises tend not to be similarly judged.[2]

Scrutiny of financially struggling individuals has been part of the law for a long time. This impulse was supercharged when a national narrative of personal responsibility collided with a rising bankruptcy filing rate in the 1990s. This collision enabled a popular political donor, the consumer credit industry, to work both sides of the aisle to frame the very existence of personal bankruptcy as a serious policy problem and to pitch complicated restrictions on bankruptcy relief as the obvious solution.

From Fixing to Defending the Bankruptcy System

When the annual bankruptcy filing rate exceeded 1 million filings in the 1990s, the consumer credit industry used the opportunity to press Congress for restrictions on personal bankruptcy relief. The industry contended that abuse of the bankruptcy system cost every American family $400 a year. That statistic was bogus. The figure matched a rough estimate of debt discharged in *all* bankruptcies in a particular year, not just the small percentage of cases that some contended were inappropriate. Even if America had *no* bankruptcy system of any kind, that debt was largely uncollectible. Maybe you don't need solid evidence in your corner if you have Federal Reserve Board chair Alan Greenspan, who lamented in the press that "personal bankruptcies are soaring because Americans have lost their sense of shame."[3]

The narrative of waning personal responsibility was already in the national spotlight because of debates over welfare reform that exploited race stereotypes. With that backdrop, characterizing financially distressed families as spending beyond their means, slacking off in the workforce, and seeking a bailout from the federal government via the bankruptcy system may have seemed like a natural next step. A more accurate framing of the rising bankruptcy filing rate came from what political scientist Jacob Hacker later called the Great Risk Shift:

individuals increasingly bore the risks of job insecurity, health insurance fragmentation, wage stagnation, and more.[4]

After seeing specific examples of the causes and consequences of debt in Judge Ginsberg's busy Chicago bankruptcy court, I ended up with an even more immersive crash course on a national scale. In 1995, Chief Justice of the United States William Rehnquist appointed Judge Ginsberg to a new National Bankruptcy Review Commission. Congress created this commission as part of the 1994 bankruptcy reform bill. Some observers said the commission's creation was an effort to defer the consumer credit industry's demands for major personal bankruptcy restrictions. President Clinton, leaders of the House and Senate, and Chief Justice Rehnquist were charged with selecting the nine commissioners. I first extended my clerkship to help Judge Ginsberg on commission business along with helping on cases. Then, in mid-1995, the commission hired me as a staff attorney. The commission had appointed Elizabeth Warren, at this point a Harvard Law School professor, to lead their research, outreach, and development of recommendations. I would work directly with my former professor, the person who had first led me into this field.

Warren was especially alarmed about financial distress and household debt burdens. But she also knew that it would be counterproductive to respond by restricting access to the bankruptcy system. Warren analogized personal bankruptcy to a hospital emergency room. The existence of hospitals does not incentivize people to get ill or injured. Warren also witnessed that the very industry that was seeking to restrict bankruptcy access was the one reaping historic profits from encouraging high-cost borrowing. Outstanding credit card debt had exceeded the $1 trillion mark. Other consumer loans were also having a moment. Lenders marketed mortgages for loans that intentionally exceeded home values, a popular figure being 125 percent. Far from incentivizing homeowners to pay down debt to build equity, lenders were inviting people to put their homes at greater risk.

Some lenders were not particularly discerning screeners of potential borrowers. While I was working for the government commission, at a fraction of peers' big law firm salaries, a shiny hot-pink flyer landed in my mailbox: "Turn Your Stucco into Sand," it said. The proposal was that I mortgage my house to go on a beach vacation. I did not have a house. The offer had been sent to my tiny rental apartment, with not an inch of stucco to leverage, to someone with many student loans to repay. But the bigger message was clear: if you weren't stretching your finances by taking vacations, you weren't doing your life right.

The fact that a lender invites you to borrow money to go on vacation does not mean that you should accept the invitation. It nonetheless was frustrating to see the very same industry that publicly lamented high bankruptcy filings be so heavily invested in creating the conditions for overindebtedness. Meanwhile, the academic research suggested that credit use patterns connected far more to Hacker's Great Risk Shift— that is, to fill the gaps in paying for fundamental household expenses—than to living a freewheeling life on other people's money.

From windowless offices deep within a federal building next to Union Station in Washington, DC, the commission staff logged thousands of pieces of correspondence from individuals and organizations opining on the bankruptcy system. We plowed through published court decisions and legal and economic research. We traveled around the country to study how the bankruptcy system operated. We planned and held twenty-one public meetings and regional hearings. Lawyers and lobbyists for almost every conceivable constituency testified about what was right and what was wrong with the bankruptcy system. Judges shared how they managed their cases and courtrooms, whether in El Paso or Detroit, Tacoma or Baltimore.

The final report logged in at over one thousand pages and bore an uncanny physical resemblance to the Yellow Pages telephone directory that since has fallen out of favor (at least one of its manufacturers, R.R. Donnelly, has gone through bankruptcy). The report set forth 170 recommendations for reform, including 32 proposals directed at personal bankruptcy. In the fall of 1997, we hand delivered this big softcover book around Washington, DC, including to Chief Justice Rehnquist at the Supreme Court and to members of Congress.

In this report, a majority of the commissioners expressed alarm at the dramatic rise of consumer credit but did not accept the framing of household financial problems offered by the credit industry and Greenspan. Led by former congressman M. Caldwell Butler, a Republican, the majority rejected the consumer credit industry's call for more roadblocks to debt relief, including the industry's proposed means testing of individual bankruptcy filers. In congressional testimony, my former boss, Judge Ginsberg, called the credit industry proposals expensive and radical given the paucity of evidence of personal bankruptcy abuse.[5]

That said, commissioners did not simply support maintenance of the status quo. The system needed not only to *be* fair to all parties affected by the system but to *seem* fair to those parties and to the public. To ensure the system's integrity, the commission recommended that Congress restrict the ability of individuals to file for bankruptcy multiple times, clarify how to treat obligations such as home mortgages, more sharply delineate debts that bankruptcy could not cancel, impose more uniform rules on creditor repayment that created work incentives, introduce random auditing of bankruptcy files, and improve data collection so that the system could be better monitored over time.

The dissenters on the commission, not any more politically aligned than the majority, embraced consumer credit industry proposals, including means testing of personal bankruptcy filers. The dissenters included Jeffrey Hartley, a Democrat and lawyer who previously had worked with U.S. senator Howell Heflin, and the Honorable Edith Hollan Jones, a conservative jurist of the U.S. Court of Appeals for the Fifth Circuit, sitting in Houston, Texas.

This split notwithstanding, the commission report was full of ideas that most or all members supported. The group had no lawmaking power of its own, so bankruptcy reform headed back to the House and Senate. Believing that the House Judiciary Committee needed a staff lawyer to work on meaningful bankruptcy reform, Warren and several commissioners said I should seek the job.

Their idea to get me hired by the committee had shortcomings. For example, the job did not exist. If and when the House Judiciary Committee needed to expand its staff, it was far from clear I would be the right fit. The committee's jurisdiction covered many topics far outside my expertise. Bankruptcy was hardly the main event.

Still, I followed instructions, one of which was to find a

way to talk to Representative George Gekas, who chaired the
key subcommittee that would lead any work on bankruptcy
reform. Representative Gekas and I were both lawyers. We
both came from Pennsylvania. I tracked down the congressman at a peach festival at a church in Harrisburg, where he
was playing the piano.

Given that Representative Gekas did not stop playing that
piano, not even for one moment, while I made my pitch, it was
not a shock when the House Judiciary Committee declined to
hire me. And it was probably for the best. The reform debates
would prove to be a fight about money and power in Washington, not about how the law worked in real life. Enjoying
close reads of the Bankruptcy Code was the wrong skill set.
Despite all the research and the commission's detailed findings, lawmakers on both sides of the aisle seemed ready to
accept that declaring bankruptcy was too easy. If nothing else,
that framing could forestall consideration of a more challenging problem: staying financially afloat in America was so hard.

While restricting access to personal bankruptcy seemed
inevitable, the credit industry did not get its proposals over the
finish line until 2005. Bumps in the road included First Lady
Hillary Rodham Clinton worrying aloud that the bill would
hurt women and children trying to collect child support from
a dad who was a debtor in bankruptcy. Meanwhile, women-
headed households had become the largest demographic group

using bankruptcy, further encouraging advocacy groups to take an interest in this legislation.[6]

As often happens in Washington, debates about research and merits were less potent in slowing the path of this legislation than were hot-button amendments. Some Democrats said that if this bill was about abuse of the bankruptcy system, it needed to prevent people from using bankruptcy as an end run around liability for abortion clinic violence. Randall Terry, founder of the abortion opposition group Operation Rescue, filed for bankruptcy after a court ordered him to pay money damages arising from his activities at abortion clinics. He explained his bankruptcy by pronouncing, "I will never let a cent of my money be seized to support the killing of the unborn."[7]

At first, the abortion amendment slowed the bill's progress. With a quickly developed interest in bankruptcy policy, the U.S. Conference of Catholic Bishops opposed the legislation. To get their bill back on track, the consumer credit industry recruited conservative lawyer Kenneth Starr to assure anxious Republicans that the proposed abortion amendment would have "little practical effect."[8]

Abortion clinics fell out of the legislation and the Bankruptcy Abuse Prevention and Consumer Protection Act, carrying the cumbersome acronym BAPCPA, added hundreds of new pages to bankruptcy law that leaned largely in one direction: making personal bankruptcy harder to access and

relief less available. Although the majority of the National
Bankruptcy Review Commission had concluded that means
testing personal bankruptcy filers was unnecessary and counterproductive, Congress did it anyway. Financially strapped
individuals would need lawyers more than ever to navigate
bankruptcy law, and those lawyers would charge higher fees
for their services, given all the new requirements. Some legal
aid offices that represented low-income people for free had to
stop doing bankruptcy work altogether. The law had become
too complicated for non-specialists.

The 2005 amendments also aimed to make the government
fee for Chapter 7 access higher than the fee for Chapter 13
repayment plans. Unlike other social insurance systems that
spread their costs across the public, bankruptcy is funded
largely by people who need debt relief. Lawmakers across the
ideological spectrum have emphasized "the importance of the
goal that the bankruptcy system is self-funded, at no cost to
the taxpayer." If you harbor the belief that individuals bear
fault for their debt problems, it might seem like cosmic justice that they need to find the money to finance a bankruptcy
case. You must pay not to pay. There is no constitutional right
to bankruptcy access for low-income people. In the 1970s, a
divided U.S. Supreme Court held that the government deny
financially distressed people bankruptcy access if they could

not pay the fee even if the whole point of the system was that these individuals don't have enough money.[9]

Although the 2005 law mostly made bankruptcy harder and more expensive for individuals, it also authorized courts to waive bankruptcy filing fees for people with incomes falling below 150 percent of the poverty rate and for whom paying the filing fee in installments was infeasible. In a system that operates off the backs of financially distressed people, however, the incentive to collect the fees is strong. In an early study, very few bankruptcy filers—under 2 percent—even requested a fee waiver, and courts rejected nearly 30 percent of the requests they did receive.[10]

The price tag of the 2005 amendments for financially distressed individuals increased further because the law imposed other fee-based requirements. Individual bankruptcy filers had to buy and complete credit counseling briefings and financial education courses. A person whose bankruptcy is triggered by bad financial planning and a person whose bankruptcy is triggered by a hurricane and cancer have the same obligation to pay for and complete these steps.

And that takes us back to Sylvia, with the voice mailbox full of collection calls and no real possibility of repaying her debts. After 2005, people like Sylvia would likely put off bankruptcy for longer, struggling to make minimum payments in the meantime. Not the best outcome for Sylvia, the economy, or society. For the consumer credit industry, excellent news.

Before and after 2005, American bankruptcy law contained both a Chapter 7 and a Chapter 13 for individuals. Before and after 2005, the basic elements applied: an automatic stay to stop collection, a virtual basket of the debtor's property to be monitored and examined and property exemptions that the debtor can keep to be determined, and the possibility of debt relief. Before and after 2005, Chapter 13 allowed creditors to keep nonexempt property and required a commitment of all disposable income. But this basic description belies the dozens, if not hundreds, of small ways the system became more complicated and less generous. And, inevitably, how the system became far more expensive to use.

Changing the costs and benefits of the system did not make financial distress disappear, of course, as the hospital analogy would suggest. Between 2010 and 2020, more than 15 million individuals filed for personal bankruptcy.[11]

Getting up to speed on these changes to the Bankruptcy Code involved a huge amount of work. The burden on courts and lawyers was higher because the statutory amendments were poorly drafted (almost certainly intentionally) and destined to invite disputes. Courts had little time to spare in getting up to speed because the system was about to get pulled into the fallout of the 2007 home mortgage foreclosure crisis, which then morphed into a broader financial crisis. Hundreds of thousands of families filed for bankruptcy to stop foreclosures on their homes, while others sought debt relief in the aftermath of layoffs and related dislocations.

Although the 2005 amendments made the system more complicated and expensive across the board, filers' experiences, both before and after the changes, almost certainly depended on demography. Picking up on themes raised in earlier research, academic studies of people who sought bankruptcy relief in 2007 and after left little doubt: not only were Black bankruptcy filers overrepresented in the bankruptcy system but their experiences diverged from those of their white counterparts. The next chapter takes a closer look at how one national system, whose governing statute appears race neutral, treats people so differently.

2

Race Disparities in Bankruptcy for Real People

One thousand. That was the number of job applications the Durham, North Carolina, resident, a middle-aged woman, had recently submitted. Let's call her Linda. When Linda wasn't job hunting, she was cutting grass, doing odd jobs, taking on renters, and asking family members for help. When that wasn't enough, she filed a Chapter 13 bankruptcy petition to try to save her home from foreclosure. She explained her situation under oath, on the witness stand, in a federal courthouse.

You may or may not have considered Sylvia's race, in chapter 1, but for this chapter it matters that Linda is Black. Without a steady job, Linda would have a hard time keeping her home, even if she had a competitively termed mortgage. But as discussed in this chapter, the home mortgage industry has not treated Black and white people alike.

Although the 2005 amendments to the Bankruptcy Code complicated the path to debt relief for all individuals, individuals experience the system differently depending on their race. The tension points are many—from the type of bankruptcy lawyers recommend, to the circumstances under which filers can keep assets, to the system's dictates on what obligations personal bankruptcy can cancel.

The Filing Decision

The federal government does not ask bankruptcy filers to share their racial identity. Still, in the twentieth and twenty-first centuries it has become clear that the racial composition of people in bankruptcy has not mirrored that of the general population. According to economic historians, the overrepresentation of Black people in the bankruptcy system, and particularly in the precursor to Chapter 13 repayment plans, was documented in the 1960s. Studying people who filed for personal bankruptcy in 2001, Elizabeth Warren reported that Black people were over three times more likely to file bankruptcy than white families. The divide grew for homeowners; Black homeowners were resorting to bankruptcy at a rate more than five times that of white homeowners.[1]

Since then, researchers have done more not only to document the racial disparities but also to flesh out (and rule out) explanations for them. For decades, the ratio of Chapter 7 and Chapter 13 filings has varied dramatically depending on location. In some places, Chapter 13 repayment plans dominate the courts. In others, they are the exception rather than the rule. That means the cost of filing, and the likelihood of receiving debt relief, has varied as well. Chapter 13 is more expensive than Chapter 7 and defers debt relief until the end of a lengthy repayment plan that many filers never reach. If they do not finish their plans, filers typically get no permanent debt relief.

The Consumer Bankruptcy Project, an ongoing study of personal bankruptcy, helped document the racial filing gap because it matched filing data with questionnaires that collected race information. The first national round, using filing data from 2007, found that African American debtors were about twice as likely to file for Chapter 13 than were other debtors. The racial filing gap could not be explained by obvious financial or legal variables.

To supplement these findings, the authors of the study, Jean Braucher, Dov Cohen, and Robert Lawless, also surveyed bankruptcy lawyers. They asked lawyers to opine on the appropriate chapter a hypothetical family should use. Each lawyer was queried about a family with the same details except for the debtors' names and their church. Some lawyers received a hypothetical with the debtors identified as Reggie and Latisha, who belonged to the Bethel AME Church. Other lawyers were prompted to consider Todd and Alison, who belonged to the First United Methodist Church. In a third hypothetical, lawyers got the facts without any debtor or church names that might signal racial identity.

The attorneys were more likely to recommend Chapter 13—the more expensive option, with lower odds of relief—to Reggie and Latisha, the Black couple, than to Todd and Alison or to a couple lacking demographic characteristics. Lawyers recommended Chapter 13 about 47 percent of the time for Reggie and Latisha but 32 percent of the time for Todd and Alison. The study was published in a selective peer-reviewed journal and featured on the front page of the *New York Times* in 2012. America's largest association of bankruptcy professionals, the American Bankruptcy Institute, held an event about the findings and published articles about them in its widely circulated research journal.[2]

Lawyers may be on the front lines of the filing decision, but they are less keenly aware of these patterns of discrimination than one might expect. In another study of personal bankruptcy lawyers surveyed in 2011, the lawyers overstated the proportion of white filers and understated the proportion of Black filers in Chapter 13 bankruptcy. The authors hypothesized that lawyers predict demography backward based on stereotypes about "which groups comprise the most responsible citizens."[3]

Researchers have not let up exploring these questions and the disparities persist. In a study of cases pending between 2012 and 2016 using a different methodology from the earlier examples, race was a driving factor in the overrepresentation of Black bankruptcy filers in Chapter 13 cases. In research on filings from 2013 to 2019, Black filers were way overrepresented in Chapter 13 and underrepresented in Chapter 7. Thirteen percent of the American population identifies as Black; 43 percent of Chapter 13 filers identified as Black.[4]

Being in Chapter 13 automatically lowers the odds of debt relief relative to being in Chapter 7 for everyone, but being a Black person in Chapter 13 lowers those odds even more. Historically, only about one-third of Chapter 13 filers finish repayment plans and receive debt relief accordingly. Controlling for other factors, Black families complete payment plans and receive debt relief at *half* the rate of other Chapter 13 filers.[5]

In yet another twist to the impact of the 2005 amendments, recall that the amendments implemented a controversial formal screening of Chapter 7 filers. With lower incomes and higher debt loads on assets like homes and cars, Black families might seem less likely to be screened out of Chapter 7 than their white counterparts. But the actual means test application had less of an effect on limiting access to debt relief than did the big increase in cost of Chapter 7 representation that the 2005 amendments wrought.

In short, bankruptcy affects white and Black households differently, starting even before they enter the system. That disparity is shaped by attitudes about how much they should pay for debt relief and how high a priority it is that they actually receive it.

Homes and Cars

Homeowners are less common in bankruptcy than in the general American population, but Linda was among those who filed for Chapter 13 bankruptcy hoping to hold on to real estate after defaulting on her mortgage. Because bankruptcy does not print money, someone out of work may not be able to save their home in Chapter 13 however competitive their mortgage terms may be. But there are plenty of reasons to wonder whether Linda's home mortgage fit that description and what the terms would have looked like had she been white.

The homeownership rate among Black families is significantly lower than the rate among white families in the general population. Black people historically were excluded from programs designed to help white people buy homes and build wealth with solid fixed-rate mortgages. In a society with entrenched income and wealth gaps, Black borrowers face more barriers to accessing sustainable mortgage loans and encounter much higher costs of credit than do white borrowers with similar financial characteristics.[6]

Sociologist Jacob Faber found that Black borrowers were significantly less likely to be approved for a home mortgage than white borrowers were, controlling for relevant financial factors. His research showed that low-income white borrowers had a greater approval rate than the highest-income Black borrowers, whose incomes were seven times larger. Black and Latinx borrowers were about three times as likely as white borrowers to receive high-cost loans.[7]

In and around the 2007 mortgage crisis, many people struggling with their mortgages were ready to negotiate a workout, and willing to make significant sacrifices if it meant they could keep their homes. It is well documented that workouts save the mortgage industry from the significant costs of foreclosing on homes. Mortgage payments can be made more feasible even without reducing the principal obligation. For example, interest rates and loan duration could be reconsidered. Workouts have been common for commercial borrowers and their lenders for a long time and bankruptcy law offered businesses an assist if their lenders resisted: businesses can restructure the terms of loans secured by buildings or other assets over their lenders' objections.

Departing from the treatment of commercial property, bankruptcy law does not allow homeowners to unilaterally change the terms of mortgages on their principal residences. Chapter 13 does offer the chance to resume mortgage payments on the exact terms of the contract while simultaneously making up missed payments. This tool could be useful for people with well-priced mortgages and sufficient income. If one has faced discrimination in the mortgage market that has translated into a higher-cost product, catching up on missed mortgage payments while also resuming regular monthly payments is likely unaffordable, especially if one also has lower wages. This concern is not theoretical. Being Black and filing for bankruptcy to save a home correlates with lower rates of Chapter 13 plan completion.[8]

Insulating home mortgages from modification in bankruptcy has long been justified by preserving access to the home mortgage market. But this objective benefits some groups of borrowers far more than others. If Black debtors have more costly mortgages than do white people with similar financial characteristics, they will not have the same ability to make up missed payments in Chapter 13. If their homes go into foreclosure because bankruptcy's home-saving rules do not work for the mortgages marketed to Black families, their neighbors' homes will decline in value. The ability of Black families to build wealth and borrow will also decline. Seemingly technical rules about debt restructuring and aspirations for credit market preservation do not affect everyone equally.[9]

Whereas homeowners are underrepresented in bankruptcy relative to the general population, car ownership among bankruptcy filers is more common. Indeed, most bankrupt households have cars when they file. Many, though not all, have car loans, and the terms of those loans can vary greatly. Expensive subprime loans, with longer repayment periods, have become prevalent, as have defaults.

Any kind of bankruptcy can stop a car repossession in the short term because of the automatic stay that halts all collection as discussed in chapter 1. That is not, however, a long term solution. Chapter 13 allows debtors to modify some terms of car loans, although it exacts a high price from people in terms of money and autonomy.

People generally want to keep cars not because they are stable stores of wealth but because they have no other feasible transport. The majority of car-owning Chapter 13 filers have a car loan to manage. The median debtor owes more on their car loan than the car is worth. They promise to pay a lot in Chapter 13 in the hopes of keeping their mobility.

What about the cars of Black Chapter 13 filers? The car loans held by Black filers similarly exceed the value of their cars. Nonetheless, law professors Pamela Foohey and Robert Lawless and sociologist Deborah Thorne found that African

American households are more likely than white households
to be "driven to bankruptcy." That does not mean they see
Chapter 13 as a well-matched solution to the financial challenges Black households face. The personal bankruptcy system
does not have the capacity to "solve the racial disparities in car
prices, auto loan rates, ticketing, and repossessions." [10]

That reference to "ticketing" indicates that cars connect
with racial disparities in bankruptcy through a different kind
of obligation: government fees and fines. Having fiscal problems of its own, the City of Chicago tried to raise revenue by
fining residents with the least political clout. The underlying
infractions involved parking tickets, failure to display parking stickers, and driving with suspended licenses on account
of unpaid parking tickets. The city granted itself the power to
seize its residents' vehicles for minor infractions like unpaid
parking tickets. To retrieve the car, the owner must show up
ready to pay thousands of dollars.

Could bankruptcy help people get their cars back from the
city? Lawyers thought Chicago would return the cars promptly
if the owners filed for Chapter 13 and promised to pay the fees
over time in a repayment plan. This approach to car recovery would not come cheap, adding several thousand dollars of
lawyers' fees and every penny of disposable income for three
to five years to the cost of being united with their vehicles.
Financially strapped Chicagoans on the South Side took the

lawyers' advice: academic research has tied Chapter 13 filing rates to Chicago's practice of targeting predominantly Black neighborhoods for the pursuit of fines.[11]

The strategy not only was expensive, but it ultimately proved ineffective. The city refused to return the cars as a matter of course, and took its fight all the way up to the U.S. Supreme Court. The Supreme Court held that Chicago did not have to return the cars unless debtors initiated and prevailed on a separate lawsuit (a *turnover* action). But again, Chapter 13 filers did not get back the money they paid to file the case when this use of bankruptcy did not work out.[12]

Keeping Other Assets

The fate of homes and cars is inevitably shaped by the presence of *security interests*. As the basic structure of a home mortgage demonstrates, families sometimes make the following deal when they borrow and pledge the home as security (*collateral* for the loan): if they default on this loan, the lender has special legal rights to take away this property and terminate the borrower's ownership. What about property that is not encumbered by security interests? *Property exemptions* determine what families can keep in bankruptcy or under state debt collection law, even if they owe money on credit cards or other debts not backed by collateral. Here again, bankruptcy law has a "racial benefits gap," in the words of law professor Mechele Dickerson.

Most people who file for bankruptcy don't have much. And they have exhausted resources trying everything under the sun to manage their financial problems in the meantime. But protection of even limited assets can make a big difference. Remember Sylvia, who needed clothes for work and pots and pans to cook? It would be counterproductive to strip such assets from someone in financial distress, and doing so would not yield much if any money for creditors. Exemptions can be more generous than these basics, however. Exemptions can enable modest wealth accumulation that can be drawn on for retirement, unemployment, illness, and injury. So it matters what assets the law says someone like Sylvia can keep.

Professor Dickerson found that the pattern of asset protection in exemption law mapped onto what white people were more likely to own, such as homes and retirement savings. In other words, the Bankruptcy Code exemptions were optimized for white families. Some of us just complain about the law, but Professor Dickerson offered a detailed blueprint for how to fix this racial benefits gap. For example, she proposed that lawmakers rethink how they treat property interests like real estate leases.[13]

The timing should have been perfect. When Professor

Dickerson's article was released into the world, Congress was still considering a big bankruptcy bill. Yet, when that bill became law in 2005, on a largely bipartisan basis, it showed no signs of addressing racially disparate effects.[14]

Student Loans

Vera Frances Thomas's bankruptcy made the local newspaper. The headline and photo told readers that this sixty-two-year-old African American woman had no home, no car, and no job. The article describes her assets as modest enough to fit inside a midsize sedan. She had been diagnosed with diabetic neuropathy that made many types of work infeasible. Still, Vera Frances Thomas was not at rest. Like Linda at the outset of this chapter, Vera Frances Thomas had applied for job after job, for two years straight, to no avail.[15]

Debt relief for individuals is supposed to be possible only if the debtor is "honest but unfortunate." Thousands of courts and commentators have cited a 1934 U.S. Supreme Court decision involving a man named William Hunt that included that language. No one seemed to doubt Vera Frances Thomas fit the description of "honest but unfortunate." The bankruptcy system granted her relief from her existing credit cards and medical bills. But before she had become ill, Vera Frances Thomas had enrolled in community college courses and taken out student loans for the tuition. Bankruptcy notwithstanding, Vera Frances Thomas would remain liable for these student loans for the rest of her life.

Student loans are an especially big deal in bankruptcy because so many people who file for bankruptcy have attended college without receiving a degree. Having "some college" has long been more common in bankruptcy than in the general population. Paying little attention to this detail, Congress repeatedly has made it harder to get relief from student loans for everyone who files for bankruptcy. Under current law, to have any chance of relief from student loans, the debtor must file a separate lawsuit and prove, by a preponderance of the evidence, that repayment of the loans would constitute an *undue hardship*. Vera Frances Thomas filed such a lawsuit.

What counts as an undue hardship? Congress put the term in the statute but did not explain it, so courts must figure it out. The bankruptcy judge presiding over Vera Frances Thomas's case in Dallas could not decide on his own what it meant. He was bound to follow the law of the U.S. Court of Appeals for the Fifth Circuit. The Fifth Circuit defined undue hardship far more narrowly than the average person might imagine: the debtor had to prove total incapacity to earn a living, now and in the future. With that kind of direction, the presiding bankruptcy judge had *never* relieved a debtor of student loans over the objection of a student lender. Not even once. And notwithstanding her circumstances, Vera Frances Thomas would not be the first.

Might learning about Ms. Thomas help the Fifth Circuit modernize its thinking? Her lawyer took the case to the Fifth Circuit to find out. The answer was no. Judge Edith Hollan Jones, one of the members of the National Bankruptcy Review Commission in the 1990s, authored the decision. Because Vera Frances Thomas *might* have some medical improvement some day and *might* get hired to do *some* paid work in the future, she was disqualified from student loan relief under the undue hardship standard.[16]

The Fifth Circuit decision does not mention that Vera Frances Thomas is Black, and the court's total incapacity standard sounds race neutral. But restricting student loan cancellation does not affect people equally because student loans do not burden everyone equally. More Black students borrow, borrow greater amounts, and owe the debt for longer than do white students. Not only are Black women more likely to have student loan debt but they are more likely to incur this debt from attending for-profit schools that may not generate a degree or viable job prospects.[17]

The American bankruptcy system makes everyone pay not to pay. The baseline race disparities in student loan burdens make the student loan exception to discharge hit Black people particularly hard. In parts of the country where courts have adopted a somewhat more capacious definition of undue hardship than the Fifth Circuit has given us, the racial wealth gap, income inequality, and heavier loan burdens might increase the odds that debtors will be able to prove undue hardship if they try. But it takes a lot of resources to even try to win that argument. Financially distressed Black families already have trouble paying bankruptcy lawyers for basic representation, let alone for taking them through an extra fact-intensive trial. Vera Frances Thomas lost her quest to get student loan relief, but she stands out for having a lawyer willing to pursue the fight at all.[18]

Fees and Fines

Parking tickets, mentioned in the discussion of cars, have other fees-and-fines siblings that are meant to raise revenue. Let's add fines for jaywalking, mismatched curtains, spitting, removing trash from a can, sitting in a public place, and declining to mow the front lawn. These kinds of fines, directed toward lower-income communities of color, received overdue scrutiny when the Obama-era Department of Justice investigated the city of Ferguson, Missouri.[19]

The bankruptcy system treats those fines as if they were of top public importance. If government fine practices reinforce inequality, as is often contended, bankruptcy's treatment of those fines are destined to do the same. The Bankruptcy Code has long protected the government's moneyed interests by making it hard for individuals to get relief from taxes or other obligations. It has long been the law that individual debtors cannot get relief from "a fine, penalty, or forfeiture payable to and for the benefit of a governmental unit, and . . . not compensation for actual pecuniary loss."

In the 1986 case *Kelly v. Robinson*, the U.S. Supreme Court read this language broadly. That case involved a criminal judgment against Caroline Robinson for wrongful receipt of state welfare benefits in Connecticut, rather than for a Ferguson-type fine, but the holding is not so limited. In 1980, as part of her sentence, the state ordered Robinson to pay $100 a month for five years. In 1981, Robinson filed for Chapter 7 bankruptcy and disclosed the $100 monthly obligation. The federal bankruptcy court granted a discharge and Robinson made no more payments, taking the view that the discharge had canceled this obligation. The state of Connecticut saw things differently, taking the view that Robinson still owed the money, bankruptcy notwithstanding.

Writing for the majority, Justice Lewis Powell agreed with Connecticut and held that Robinson was still on the hook for the monthly payments. Although the Bankruptcy Code said that the obligation should be discharged if it is compensation for pecuniary loss, the majority opinion gave no weight to that language.[20]

Courts and commentators generally read *Kelly* with the breadth the Supreme Court majority seemingly intended: individual debtors in bankruptcy cannot get relief from monetary obligations to the government, period. But the limitation in the statutory language relating to compensation for loss remains helpful to a certain class of debtor who has engaged in a certain kind of wrong.[21]

A lawyer named Anthony J. Kassas fit that description. The state of California took away Kassas's license to practice law for his involvement in a fraud scheme involving financially distressed homeowners back when Vice President Kamala Harris was attorney general of the state. Kassas owed over $60,000 to the state for the cost of disciplinary proceedings. In those proceedings, the California Supreme Court ordered Kassas to pay the clients he defrauded, an amount over $200,000. And Kassas was supposed to reimburse the state for restitution made to individual victims. That amount turned out to exceed $2 million.

You know where this is going: Kassas filed for Chapter 7 bankruptcy and received a discharge. How did that experience change Kassas's financial responsibilities for his wrongdoing?

He remained liable for the costs to the state of the disciplinary proceeding, the $60,000. The bankruptcy court held the fees-and-fines rule did not make the obligation to pay $200,000 to his defrauded clients survive bankruptcy because Congress said the exception to discharge for government fees is limited to amounts payable to and for the benefit of the government. An appellate court went further: bankruptcy also relieved Kassas of the obligation to compensate the state bar over $2 million for restitution it made to Kassas's clients.[22]

How does Kassas's victory on appeal help low-income people facing Ferguson-type fees and fines or Chicago's South Side parking infraction problems? It doesn't.

Here again, government fee practices that focus on low-income communities of color may amplify the overrepresentation of Black people in Chapter 13. That is because the fine print of the Bankruptcy Code suggests that completing a Chapter 13 payment plan may bring more debt relief from fees and fines than could be achieved in Chapter 7. To get there, though, a debtor must commit all disposable income for three to five years, paying thousands of dollars to lawyers in the meantime, in the hope of completing the plan, which is not the norm. At that point, relief from the fine will be determined by whether the fine was considered part of a criminal sentence—itself a murky issue.[23]

Liability for Willful and Malicious Injury

Now you know that an individual stays liable for a fine for an overgrown lawn even after bankruptcy, but another, a dishonest lawyer, does not have to pay back the clients he hurt. What if a debtor is a government officer liable to a Black resident for violating her constitutional rights? Or is a white supremacist ringleader who has engaged in domestic terrorism? Those kinds of situations don't come up frequently, but they offer some jarring lessons about the bankruptcy system's values when they do.

Concluding this chapter's disparity tour is the realization that Congress made it easier to cancel debts that arise from the violation of someone's civil rights than obligations to pay jaywalking fines. A white supremacist ringleader who has engaged in domestic terrorism gets less up-front screening in personal bankruptcy than, say, Sylvia from chapter 1.

Legal obligations arising from terrible conduct may survive bankruptcy, but Congress implemented an entirely different procedure that requires considerably more resources from parties injured by that conduct. Student loans presumptively survive bankruptcy unless the debtor proves undue hardship through a separate lawsuit. For the most part, government fees and fines imposed on individuals survive bankruptcy, period. But an obligation that arises from a willful and malicious injury is dischargeable unless the injured party has the resources to be proactive. The injured party must file a separate lawsuit. In that lawsuit, the plaintiff must prove that the debt arose from a "willful and malicious" injury. If the plaintiff already has secured a judgment, and that judgment includes the willful and malicious elements, the court may be able to use that prior judgment to find that the debt survives. But if the judgment does not clearly spell out those elements, or if a judgment had not yet been reached, the road to resolution will be longer. Assuming one has the time, money, and legal knowledge to go this route, justice can be further delayed as parties dispute procedural issues like which court should preside over this matter.[24]

Examples from published cases are rare but go back decades. In Knoxville, Tennessee, in 1979, Gerald Bruner was asleep in his car, but not for long. Police officer Steve Tinder woke him, ordered him out of his car, and struck him on the back of his head. Bruner tried to flee but was intercepted by other officers, including Gregory Taylor. A neurosurgeon determined that because of the confrontation, during which he sustained another blow to the head, Bruner had a skull fracture and brain injury, which resulted in permanent brain damage and epilepsy. Bruner sued for violation of his constitutional rights and won. Afterward, in 1985, one of the officers, Taylor, filed for bankruptcy. When Bruner said Taylor should not get debt relief from this obligation, the court said bankruptcy law required another trial to make extra sure that the resulting debt really met the "willful and malicious" standard. Taylor would get a fresh start unless Bruner could prove that Taylor not only intended to beat Bruner but also intended the result.[25]

Case law also shows how bankruptcy might be used to scale down the remedy for a civil rights obligation. In 1982, a longtime Chicago police officer named Stephen Todd stopped Glenn Weeks, ordered him to exit his car, put a gun to his head, and chased, beat, and detained him. Weeks won a lawsuit in federal court for a violation of his constitutional rights. A jury awarded punitive damages and Todd's wages were garnished. Todd filed for bankruptcy. Weeks complained to the bankruptcy court that Todd should not be let off the hook for hurting him. The court sided with Weeks, but only to a point. It was not per se illegitimate to use bankruptcy under these circumstances, said the court, but Todd should try to pay a little bit more to show he was pursuing bankruptcy in good faith.[26]

In 1998, the U.S. Supreme Court reinforced the divide between the treatment of government fines and the treatment of tort liability in personal bankruptcy. Like in the fees-and-fines context, the facts of the case the Supreme Court took up were very different from the contexts in which the holding would apply. In *Kawaauhau v. Geiger*, the debtor was a doctor whose error had resulted in the amputation of a patient's limb. The patient argued that the doctor's medical malpractice constituted willful and malicious injury. After all, the doctor intentionally gave the patient inadequate care. Not so, said the Supreme Court. Unanimously, the court held that the debt survives bankruptcy only if the plaintiff proves the debtor intended the *injury*, not just the act that led to the injury.[27]

That ruling probably makes sense in a medical malpractice context, but it applies in all cases involving the willful and malicious exception, including police brutality and sexual harassment. The holding also increased the likelihood an injured party would have to pursue and win a second trial if the perpetrator filed for bankruptcy.

The possibility of escaping tort liability creates some strange incentives to file for bankruptcy. David Ayers spent twelve years in prison for a murder he did not commit. In 2013, a jury found that Ohio police officer Denise Kovach had violated Ayers's constitutional rights. The city of Cleveland encouraged Kovach to file for bankruptcy and assisted her in hiring a bankruptcy lawyer. A few months after Kovach filed for Chapter 7, the court, with no actual knowledge of this history, entered an order canceling Kovach's debts as a matter of course.[28]

That was not the end of the story because Ayers eventually found out about the bankruptcy, but Kovach still ended up with a financial fresh start. Although Ayers was Kovach's most

significant creditor, Ayers did not receive notice of the bankruptcy while it was happening. Kovach also had failed to list
the right to be indemnified by the city of Cleveland as an asset.
When Ayers complained to the bankruptcy court, the court
reopened the bankruptcy to take a look. The court held that
Ayers could pursue Cleveland for its obligation to indemnify
Kovach. Because of the bankruptcy, however, Kovach would
be off the hook.[29]

When the consumer credit industry pressed Congress to
tighten the bankruptcy rules, it was interested in restricting
access for individuals who used its financial products, not in
screening individuals for bad behavior. Slipping through the
cracks may be what Nathan Damigo was aiming for when he
filed a Chapter 7 bankruptcy. Damigo was the founder of Identity Evropa, a white supremacist organization. He went on to
help organize the violent and tragic events in Charlottesville,
Virginia, in August 2017. Neo-Nazis, members of the Ku Klux
Klan, and white supremacists converged on Charlottesville on
the weekend of August 11, 2017, for a Unite the Right rally.
They advertised the threat of violence when they encouraged
their supporters to join them, and the event was ultimately one
of domestic terrorism.[30]

People harmed in Charlottesville filed a civil lawsuit against
Damigo and Richard Spencer, several divisions of the Ku
Klux Klan, and other neo-Nazi organizations. Ostensibly in

the hopes of avoiding legal and financial responsibility for the consequences, Damigo rang in the new year in 2019 by filing for Chapter 7 bankruptcy in California. He lived with his grandparents and had limited assets. As for debts, the paperwork showed almost nothing—far less than what the typical individual bankruptcy filer owed. Damigo had a $1,200 balance on a Chase credit card. Consistent with bankruptcy's very broad definition of claim, Damigo listed as creditors people who accused him of violating their rights in Charlottesville. Damigo also listed *potential* litigants as creditors, most notably the family of Heather Heyer, who was killed in Charlottesville.[31]

Unlike a local fine or student loan, liability for willful and malicious injuries is canceled unless someone notices and files a separate lawsuit within the bankruptcy. In Damigo's case, someone did notice: one of the big law firms representing plaintiffs in the Charlottesville litigation happened to have a bankruptcy department. To even preserve the possibility that Damigo would remain accountable for the horrors of Charlottesville, the lawyers took three steps. First, they filed a separate lawsuit within the bankruptcy alleging that the liability to certain plaintiffs resulting from the Charlottesville litigation arose from willful and malicious injury. Second, they asked the bankruptcy court to pause that lawsuit, pending resolution of the Charlottesville litigation (including, apparently, appeals). The hope was that the findings from the Charlottesville litigation would be sufficient to establish a "willful and malicious" injury, or at least some of the elements. Third, they filed a separate action to make sure the Charlottesville litigation in Virginia could continue against Damigo even though he was in bankruptcy (that is, they sought to lift the *automatic stay*).[32]

Those steps required resources, persistence, and specialized bankruptcy expertise. All were undertaken to increase the odds that bankruptcy did not undo the work of the civil justice system. When the appeals in the Charlottesville litigation have been resolved, the lawyers will have to return to the California bankruptcy court to finish the work. In the meantime, if you look up the bankruptcy of Nathan Damigo in public court records, you will find a court order granting a fresh start.[33]

The bankruptcy system is full of people like Vera Frances Thomas, Linda, and Sylvia. It is not loaded with white supremacists accused of committing domestic terrorism. But the difference in treatment of liabilities sends a message, even if each of the rules—student loans, fees and fines, willful and malicious injury—had some basic rationale.

The more profound, disparate impact, however, comes from the overrepresentation of African American people in Chapter 13 and the basic treatment of assets and more frequent debts like student loans, car loans, and mortgages. In a country still combating the long aftermath of slavery and Jim Crow, it should not be surprising that debtor-creditor laws are not as race neutral as they seem on their face.

Bankruptcy cannot raise wages or equalize the cost of goods and credit, but it can, and should, stop piling on and exacerbating the effects of existing inequality. Rolling back the 2005 amendments, by itself, would not be enough to address the roots of race disparities that almost certainly preceded that legislation.

Our next step in this journey through the bankruptcy system is to compare the treatment of individuals relative to that of artificial persons. The following chapters introduce the experiences of for-profit companies, nonprofit entities, and municipalities that file for bankruptcy. Corporations and other artificial persons are legally autonomous, separate from the humans that created them, because the law says so. Nothing requires that fake people be treated more favorably than real people, in bankruptcy or elsewhere. The fresh start concept was meant for real people, not fake people such as corporations. And yet, as we will see in chapter 3 and beyond, enterprises receive more advantages in the bankruptcy system than do humans. It isn't that bankruptcy for bigger businesses is easy. Still, as you are about to see, it sure is different.

3

Bankruptcy for Fake People

In the book *Freaky Friday*, a mother and daughter switch bodies and learn what it is like to walk in the shoes of the other. The book generated multiple films, perhaps the best-known version starring Jamie Lee Curtis and Lindsay Lohan. A *Freaky Friday* setup for the bankruptcy system might involve a lawyer swap. One lawyer, a solo practitioner, earns less than $2,000 for each Chapter 7 personal bankruptcy case, start to finish, and under $4,000 for each Chapter 13 case, start to finish. The other lawyer, a partner at an international law firm, typically bills $2,000 for each hour he spends representing multinational corporations in a Chapter 11 bankruptcy.

In theory, the lawyer swap should be no big deal. The same national legal and court system applies to all of these cases. Both people are bankruptcy lawyers, even if one has fancier suits and shoes than the other. The *Freaky Friday* swap will reveal that these lawyers do not have the same job at all. The system perceives these lawyers and their clients' financial problems in profoundly different ways, depending on whether their clients are real or fake people.

Some lawyers laugh nervously when I refer to fake people. The term is descriptive. In law, the term "person" encompasses more than humans. The law makes corporations people. Limited liability companies are people. So are other associations that are treated as autonomous under American business law. "Artificial person" may sound less cheeky than "fake person," but both phrases lead to the same place.

Fake personhood is the building block of enterprise of all sizes. I can run and own a design shop without creating a separate company, but the law offers incentives for me to file papers with the state to create a separate person—Melissa's Design, LLC. Giant companies tend to create many separate entities, resulting in complicated organizational charts.

Nonprofit and public enterprises also are people. Churches and charities. Hospitals and soup kitchens. Cities. Even sewer systems.

These types of fake people can file for bankruptcy under some circumstances. People in America regularly interact with enterprises that have been through bankruptcy. Major airlines have been through bankruptcy, along with the private company that offers passengers a swifter trip through the airport security line by collecting biometric data. As have hotels and car rental companies. Restaurant chains. Orchestras and museums and churches and organizations that arrange children's activities. Perhaps even your favorite sports team.

This chapter will focus particularly on examples from the for-profit business world. Companies are the most common type of fake people that file for bankruptcy. That will entail introducing some features of Chapter 11 of the Bankruptcy Code, designed to allow and promote the reorganization of financially distressed companies.

A Cleaner Slate?

It should be fresh in your mind that bankrupt individuals, however honest but unfortunate they are, cannot cancel all obligations. Government fees and fines are protected from discharge in personal bankruptcy cases. Cancellation of student loans is at least an uphill battle—and in the states covered by the Fifth Circuit (Texas, Louisiana, Mississippi), which governed Vera Frances Thomas's bankruptcy, an unwinnable one. As for obligations arising from bad deeds, perpetrators might get debt relief if their victims don't know to be proactive about protecting their rights or are unable to meet the burden

of proof. But if injured parties prove that the obligations constitute fraud or willful or malicious injury, perpetrators cannot
get debt relief for those obligations.

The list of obligations that Congress said human debtors
might have to repay, bankruptcy notwithstanding, runs much
longer than the examples highlighted in chapter 2. Over time,
Congress has added to the Bankruptcy Code almost twenty
exceptions to discharge for individuals and, as we have already
seen, some courts interpret those exceptions broadly, further
limiting debt relief. The rationales for the obligations vary.
Some of the exceptions have nothing to do with how "honest
but unfortunate" the debtors are, and everything to do with
protecting the public fisc. Other exceptions relate to debtor
wrongdoing. One way or another, the no-discharge list nar-
rows the boundaries of the fresh start for individuals.

Although I would rewrite this no-discharge list if I could—
the National Bankruptcy Review Commission I worked for in
the 1990s tried to do just that—exceptions to discharge can
be perfectly defensible, policy-wise. The bankruptcy system
can fulfill important legal and economic functions by canceling ordinary consumer debt without wiping the slate clean of
obligations incurred through misconduct, for example.

Nonetheless, any no-discharge list that applies to humans
needs careful crafting because of the virtues of the fresh start.

Debt cancellation relieves suffering, promotes class mobility, and reduces the need for other state supports. The justifications for debt relief are not promoted by one political party and denounced by the other; the 1978 Bankruptcy Code was a strongly bipartisan partisan effort.

If a *Freaky Friday* swap results in the big-business restructuring lawyer representing a lower-income individual, that lawyer will have relatively little experience with the no-discharge list because the list does not apply to fake people in Chapter 11. Enterprises that persuade a majority of their creditors and a court to support their Chapter 11 plan can cancel almost everything, even debts arising from willful and malicious injury or fraud. Although both real and fake people must pay debts backed by collateral due to security interests in order to keep those items, as we saw in chapter 2, businesses have more latitude than individuals do to change the terms of the loans, including reduction of the principal amounts, in many more instances than humans can.[1]

If permitting a fresher start for fake people than for real people seems odd to you, I agree. After all, humans who start one company can turn around and start another one. In the state of Delaware alone, hundreds of limited liability companies are created *every day*, through the submission of some forms and fees. Yet, when Congress has considered keeping

Chapter 11 debtors on the hook for more obligations in the aftermath of big corporate scandals, the reaction from the bankruptcy world would make you think Congress had proposed something controversial.[2]

Debt cancellation rules do not have to be the same for fake people and real people. It is not constitutionally required. But is it good policy to give broader relief to a corporation that has engaged in wrongdoing than to humans under any circumstances?

It is not a novel concept in American law to consider fake people culpable for independent wrongdoing. Corporations cannot be incarcerated, but they can be accused and convicted of crimes. Companies can be held directly responsible for employment discrimination and other wrongs. Insurers issue policies to protect corporations for wrongdoing because the legal system attributes those wrongdoings to the enterprise as well as to individuals.

In addition, keeping companies on the hook for debts to the government would seem to have even stronger fisc-protecting benefits than those gained from Ferguson-type fees and fines in low-income communities of color. The Bankruptcy Code contains no ban on relief from fees and fines for a fake person so long as those obligations fit under the bankruptcy law's very broad definition of *claim*.

The justifications for the Bankruptcy Code giving fake people broader debt relief than it gives humans tend to be tied to the virtues of reorganizing a business through Chapter 11. To see the logic, it is time for more details about that style of bankruptcy.

Imagine a pottery company that has fallen on hard times. It makes decent products, employs people fairly, and has a promising future if it can rework some of its debts. The company is probably worth more alive than dead. Of the company's 1,000 creditors, 850 are willing to work with the company and agree to a new payment schedule. The remaining 150 creditors do not think highly of the company and don't care if it survives. Left to their own devices, the dissenters will press for full payment of their own debts, come what may. In Chapter 11, with the support of most of the creditors, the pottery company can bind the dissenting creditors to a new deal. If the reorganized company thrives, it will keep people employed and retain customer and supplier relationships.

How does this basic logic of Chapter 11 connect to disparate discharge policies for businesses and individuals? In one prominent Chapter 11 case involving A.H. Robins Company, which will get more attention later in this book, courts reasoned that holding a company responsible for bad behavior might result in smaller payouts to other creditors, would "inhibit the effectiveness of Chapter 11," and would create undesirable uncertainty that would lead parties with resources to forego investing in a reorganized company.[3]

I struggle with this logic because personal bankruptcy also has instrumental economic and third-party objectives. It is no small thing that bankruptcy, if done right, relieves suffering for individuals, many of whom are raising young children. But personal bankruptcy also promotes entrepreneurship, as just one example of how the bankruptcy of an ordinary person can have a positive economic effect for those around them, just like fake people such as corporations can.

Also, the pro-reorganization reasoning for the distinction between the discharge policies for businesses in Chapter 11 and those in personal bankruptcy can be hard to operationalize. Where does the logic end? A company would have a better shot of reorganizing and staying financially afloat if it were allowed to rob a bank. Or flout environmental laws. Or require employees to work for free.

Another argument I have heard for broad debt cancellation in business cases is that it promotes the equal treatment of creditors. Again, I do not know why this factor should be more important in business cases than in personal bankruptcy cases. But it almost does not matter, because if one measured business bankruptcy on its equal treatment of creditors equally, the system would get a low grade, as later chapters of this book explore. For now, just know that businesses in Chapter 11 routinely have latitude to choose the winners and losers among

creditors in their cases. Bankruptcy can be a profitable experience for some creditors, but not all of them.

Whether a distinction in business and individual discharge
policy strikes you as defensible, it remains a form of legal bias,
albeit one that the U.S. Constitution tolerates. The distinction
has other costs, including sending the message that fake people
are not independent, culpable actors. That message puts bankruptcy on a different path from the one for laws that take institutional culpability more seriously.

Although the Bankruptcy Code's lengthy no-discharge list
does not apply to fake people, courts sometimes rule that companies remain on the hook for obligations they would prefer
not to honor by finding that those obligations are outside the
definition of a claim under bankruptcy law. For example, the
Environmental Protection Agency requested, and a district
court ordered, that a formerly bankrupt firm named Apex
Oil Company clean up toxic waste in the village of Hart-
ford, Illinois, under the federal Resource Conservation and
Recovery Act. The company appealed the order to the U.S.
Court of Appeals for the Seventh Circuit, headquartered in
Chicago, arguing that its Chapter 11 bankruptcy more than
two decades earlier relieved the company of this obligation.
The Seventh Circuit held that Apex Oil had to perform the
obligation because it fell outside the definition of a claim in

bankruptcy. The federal environmental statute spoke in terms only of injunctive relief, not money. But because this decision is arguably inconsistent with the Bankruptcy Code's very broad definition of claim, which does not defer to whether another statute contemplates a monetary alternative, other courts would likely see the issue differently.[4]

The system is not lacking in ways to address the various kinds of wrongdoing in Chapter 11 business cases, even without a no-discharge list. Tools abound—in theory. For example, parties can ask a court to subordinate the claims of creditors with unclean hands (including company insiders) to the claims of others harmed by the activity. This power is called *equitable subordination*. The Bankruptcy Code also contains grounds to file lawsuits against third parties who might have colluded with the debtor somehow or might have extracted value that left other creditors worse off. Yet, the discharge policy distinction still sends a troubling message about the differential treatment of real and fake people. In addition, these other tools are underused, especially in bigger cases. One big reason is money. As discussed in chapter 5, the public does not finance the use of integrity-promoting tools in Chapter 11, and private parties that have the money to finance these activities often have incentives not to do so.

A measure that would be quite responsive to wrongdoing by the bankrupt company is one you have seen in all personal bankruptcy cases so far: the government appoints a trustee to take charge. Here comes a second big distinction between real people who file Chapter 7 or Chapter 13 and fake people who file for Chapter 11 even when they have little prospect of reorganization.

Govern Thyself

When Vera Frances Thomas filed for personal bankruptcy under Chapter 7, she gave up money and financial privacy and the right to govern her own affairs. Linda, who entered Chapter 13 bankruptcy to try to save her home, gave up the same, plus all disposable income, for an even longer time. In every personal bankruptcy case under these chapters, the system appoints a trustee, effective immediately.

Automatic trustee appointment applies to business cases that land in Chapter 7, too, but a lawyer who specializes in big corporate restructurings would not enjoy a *Freaky Friday* swap that takes him into Chapter 7. The corporate lawyer's preferred chapter is Chapter 11, whether or not the corporate client has much of a chance at reorganization. In addition to the loss of control debtors and professionals experience in Chapter 7, the rules for compensating professionals are different in Chapter 7, and far less generous to lawyers, than they are in Chapter 11.

Lawyers' wallets notwithstanding, Chapter 7 can be an important creditors' remedy when a business has disappointed its creditors. Consider the company that put on the ill-fated Fyre Festival. Billed as a "cultural experience of the decade" for millennials, the event was held on a private island in the Bahamas and promised top musical talent, immersive experiences, and discussions with thought leaders. It did not go as advertised. The organizers collected a large amount of money from investors and eager attendees. Arriving guests found FEMA tents instead of luxury villas, gravel pits instead of sandy beaches, luggage dumped from shipping containers rather than handled by white glove concierge service, and sad cheese sandwiches instead of cuisine created by celebrity chefs. Fyre Festival mastermind William (Billy) McFarland went to prison.

Fyre Festival ended up in Chapter 7 because its creditors put it there—a rare example of an *involuntary bankruptcy*. The trustee selected by the government watchdog tracked down assets on the creditors' behalf. For example, the trustee sued model and influencer Kendall Jenner because Fyre Festival had paid Jenner $275,000 for a single Instagram post that touted the festival and strongly suggested that she and her then brother-in-law Kanye West would be there. (They were not.) Jenner settled the lawsuit with the trustee by paying $90,000.[5]

Overall, a Chapter 7 trustee can investigate the company's

business practices, sell the company's assets, and pay creditors from whatever is collected. Trustees may dig into company records and file lawsuits against the company's allies. In absolute terms, creditors' recovery in the Fyre Festival bankruptcy remained small: just pennies on each dollar of debt. On the other hand, that recovery was more than most spurned claimants would have received from their own collection efforts.[6]

The trustee's ability to investigate and file lawsuits and turn assets into cash for creditors depends on the resources available. The public does not fund the integrity-promoting efforts of the bankruptcy system, and thus all too often these efforts are underutilized. Maybe that should change, but in the meantime, lawyers in a variety of fields are willing to work on contingency; that means trustees may be able to finance a worthwhile investigation and get paid if the investigation succeeds.

When a company files Chapter 11, the government does not appoint a trustee at the outset, or typically at all. Chapter 11 was designed to boost the odds that a company will reorganize and continue to operate, under ordinary management. Not ousting a company's leadership was supposed to incentivize companies to try to reorganize before it is too late to turn things around.

It is possible to appoint a trustee (or a related concept, an *examiner*) in Chapter 11, but that is unlikely to occur, even if the odds of reorganizing are slim and even if a quick sale of the company is all but certain. As chapter 5 will explore, many incentives, including bankruptcy's funding structure, operate to discourage frustrated creditors from trying to oust management.

Every rule has exceptions, so let us look at an example of a Chapter 11 case with a trustee. Bikram Yoga, founded by Bikram Choudhury, fueled the hot yoga craze in America. The company was on the defendant side of lawsuits for sexual harassment and wrongful employment termination. Choudhury transferred assets to far-flung places and fled the country. Bikram Yoga filed for Chapter 11 in Los Angeles. The company had installed a new executive to run things during the bankruptcy (the now-common *chief restructuring officer*), but the government watchdog worried this person was too close to Choudhury. The bankruptcy court granted the watchdog's motion for a Chapter 11 trustee. If you review the court docket of this case, you can see the methods and efforts of the trustee, lawyer Robbin Itkin, to comb the nation and the world for company property and sell it for the benefit of creditors.[7]

A higher-profile example reflecting the more typical Chapter 11 practice—no trustee—involves the Weinstein Company, an entertainment firm that produced movies and television, among other things. The company filed for Chapter 11 in Delaware in March 2018, six months after a *New York Times* investigation on sexual harassment, assault, and cover-ups in the company went viral.

At the very first hearing in the company's bankruptcy, the company's lead bankruptcy lawyer, Paul Zumbro, assured the court that the company already had fired Harvey Weinstein from his executive position. Individualizing the wrongdoing, Zumbro stated that the Weinstein Company had immediately initiated an independent investigation into "Harvey's behavior" back in the fall. (Documents filed in the case indicate that the company had quickly suspended that investigation for lack of funds.) This individualization of the harm came barely a month after New York's attorney general announced the results of its investigation into Weinstein Company violations of human rights law, antidiscrimination law, denial of equal protection under state civil rights law, and illegal business conduct. Female employees not only were expected to recruit women for sexual encounters but also were assigned stereotypical female chores and pressured to keep silent about their experiences. The attorney general's complaint alleged that those in power at the Weinstein Company repeatedly failed to investigate red flags and "deliberately looked the other way or took actions that enabled [Harvey Weinstein] to retaliate against employees who complained of misconduct." [8]

Private lenders remained willing to lend money to the Weinstein Company during its bankruptcy, but the money could be used only to prepare for selling the company to a private equity firm, including to pay lawyers and financial advisors. The loan could go into default if anyone even suggested trustee appointment, which could derail a fast-track sale.

Who, then, was to run the company during the bankruptcy? *Robert* Weinstein, Harvey's brother and longtime business partner, would serve as chief executive officer and chair of the board during the most consequential phase of the bankruptcy. The company also brought in a chief restructuring officer, who would do most of the talking for the company but served at the direction of the board. Robert had been in business with his brother since the 1970s. They had started with concert promotion and moved on to buying and distributing independent films. The brothers were entangled in settlements and cover-ups around the world. In court, however, Zumbro described Robert as a dedicated leader of the company who with other board members had "devoted themselves to navigating [the Weinstein Company] to the soft landing that its creditors, employees, and other claim holders deserve."[9]

While the board, helmed by Robert, remained in control of the company, the board members also were named defendants for their role in the company's handling of sexual harassment and employment discrimination. As indicated by the New York attorney general investigation, the evidence was mounting that the Weinstein Company was propped up for years by those willing to tolerate toxic culture in the hope of a better return on investment. Other private lawsuits alleged that the company and Robert had violated New York City human rights and employment discrimination law. For example, the lawsuit of Sandeep Rehal alleged a pervasive and severe sexually hostile work environment, and her claim against Robert Weinstein survived a motion to dismiss in New York State court.[10]

Apart from these allegations of an illegal workplace, there were other reasons to doubt that the Weinstein Company should govern itself in bankruptcy. Commercial creditors expressed bitter complaints about the Weinstein Company's management unrelated to its toxic culture for women. The company had been in financial trouble on and off since its inception. Its own descriptions of its path to bankruptcy in court papers reflected chaos: many vacant positions, lack of internal legal counsel, refusal by others in the industry to engage with the company, and loss of half of the board. The buyer of the Weinstein Company called the company "one of the worst-managed companies I've ever seen. They had no financial controls, no legal controls. . . . It was an 'inmates ran the asylum' type of scenario." The buyer had his own reasons for puffery, of course, but the description is consistent with other accounts of the state of the company.[11]

Notwithstanding this context, the Weinstein Company got to control its own bankruptcy in ways that far more responsible personal bankruptcy filers in Chapters 7 or 13 never can. Not a single party asked the court to appoint a trustee, convert the case to Chapter 7, or dismiss the case altogether. As already reviewed, the lack of a request is not a sign that all was well in the company. It is a sign of an open secret: the parties controlling access to money for the company will not tolerate a trustee looking over their shoulder.

Lawyers in big cases seem genuinely surprised when a court grants a request to impose a trustee—either in Chapter 11 or by converting the case to Chapter 7. Forever 21, a fast-fashion retailer, filed for bankruptcy in 2019, prior to the retail bankruptcy spike from the COVID-19 pandemic, owing vendors of its merchandise hundreds of millions of dollars. Forever 21's lawyers were from the law firm Kirkland & Ellis, which dominated the market for big company representation in Chapter 11.

Kirkland & Ellis was close to a rare *Freaky Friday* moment when the government watchdog asked the court to convert its Forever 21 case to Chapter 7, and the court granted the request. As a practical matter, conversion would not change the fate of the company. Forever 21 had sold its assets. It had no remaining employees. No reorganization was even possible. The only thing left to do was to figure out how to wrap up the case. Chapter 11 generally permits plans of liquidation. The government watchdog said staying in Chapter 11 was not appropriate for Forever 21, however, because the company's bankruptcy was not in compliance with the Bankruptcy Code. A Chapter 11 plan must repay in full vendors who supply goods *during* the bankruptcy. Those claims have special priority under bankruptcy law. Forever 21 could not meet this requirement and thus should exit Chapter 11.

Not satisfied with the court's ruling to move the case to Chapter 7 where a trustee would take over, Forever 21 implored the court to reconsider. Forever 21 compared its "inherently challenging" retailer bankruptcy with President John F. Kennedy's space program, including using the former president's quote: "We choose to go to the moon in this decade and do the hard things, not because they are easy, but because they are hard." What great world-altering outcome could come from letting this already-dead fast-fashion retailer continue to run itself without trustee interference, in a Chapter 11? Forever 21 wanted more time and leverage to persuade creditors that they should be happy with a fraction of the recovery that bankruptcy law promised them. Forever 21 complained that being precluded from having the chance to propose a Chapter 11 plan was "unjust." [12]

At a court hearing on Forever 21's motion in the fall of 2020, Forever 21's lawyer did not mention moon landings but otherwise went all in: "I'm not a proponent, myself, personally of words like 'unlikely' or 'impossible.' I think you simply never know and if you can't give it a shot and fail then you will never have tried."[13]

A fast-fashion retailer being sent to Chapter 7 after spectacularly shortchanging its suppliers is an unlikely candidate for the most "unjust" treatment. But Forever 21 prevailed, and Kirkland & Ellis got to control the bankruptcy until the end, without a trustee.

For human debtors, bankruptcy relief is inextricably linked with loss of autonomy, the belief that they must succumb to an extra overlay of government supervision. Forever 21 is emblematic of how big businesses and the most elite law firms expect to run the show, even when they are not following the basic Bankruptcy Code requirements. Big enterprises that are unable to reorganize—which was the point of allowing management to stay in control in Chapter 11 in the first place—are nonetheless entrusted with the privilege of charting their own course, huddling with moneyed interests to plan the strategy.

Timing and Conditions of Debt Relief

Debt relief for fake and real people is conditioned on different events. For individuals in Chapter 13 repayment plans, debt relief is conditioned on finishing the plan after devoting every penny of disposable income, subject to trustee supervision. If they do not finish, and most do not, Chapter 13 filers typically get neither debt relief nor a refund for the cost of the process. Their debts remain, plus interest on the debt that accrued in the meantime. Given that people often exhaust all other options before they seek bankruptcy relief, it is hard to know what their next move should be. One hopes it is not as dire as *Squid Game*, but it may be another Chapter 13 filing, which means more fees and more supervision.

By contrast, Congress instructs courts to give businesses a discharge upon Chapter 11 plan *approval*, rather than upon completion however many years later (Chapter 11 has no time frame for business restructuring plans). Is that because businesses always finish their Chapter 11 plans? They do not. As discussed in chapter 7, some of the very largest Chapter 11 filers do not finish their plans, often culminating in a return trip to bankruptcy court.

Companies that file for bankruptcy, however many times, also do not have to pay to be schooled on credit and financial management, whatever mistakes they have made. As we have seen, the 2005 amendments to the Bankruptcy Code make only individual debtors pay for credit counseling briefings before they file the case and financial literacy lessons on the back end of the case or else they cannot get debt relief.

Sharing

Big companies that file for bankruptcy also get more runway than humans when it comes to disclosure of information. Bankruptcy protection starts immediately upon filing a petition because of the automatic stay, which immediately stops all creditor collection. The trade-off for this protection is supposed to be extensive, and *prompt*, disclosure of information. Individuals who fail to submit the paperwork will see their cases dismissed. The request to delay mandatory disclosures is so routine in big Chapter 11 cases that it is genuinely a surprise if the disclosures are filed on time. The disclosures sometimes do not even come in until the debtor has asked the court to rule on matters of major consequence.

Individual debtors are not allowed to have a lot of secrets if they want debt relief, but secrets have become so second nature in big business bankruptcy that companies may balk when asked to make their information as public as it was supposed to be. For example, the gun and bullet maker Remington Outdoor Company filed Chapter 11 not once but twice in recent years. The second time, the company wanted to sell itself very quickly. Grieving families who had sued Remington after their children and other loved ones were murdered in Sandy Hook, Connecticut, had questions. They wanted more information about the company's finances and time to study the company's proposal. Remington's lawyer protested: "[J]ust because we filed for bankruptcy doesn't give [the Sandy Hook families] a right to sort of walk around and look and snoop around our business." [14]

That response should surprise the average personal bankruptcy lawyer: for better or worse, snooping around in the debtor's business is exactly what bankruptcy is and does. It is a trade-off for the extraordinary relief the system offers. Trustees, courts, and creditors may ask an individual about tobacco, pet care, entertainment, and house cleaning services. They may demand to know why debtors let adult children live with them and share their meals. They ask why the debtor isn't seeking a higher-paying job and the exact function of airplane tickets the debtor bought on a credit card two months before the bankruptcy. This scrutiny may or may not generate a few more dollars of creditor repayment, but in personal bankruptcy it has become part and parcel of the bankruptcy bargain. Not so for big business bankruptcy.

A Spectrum of Enterprise

So far, this chapter has given examples of the ways bankruptcy treats fake and real people differently. But enterprises come in a lot of shapes and sizes. The jobs of lawyers in smaller businesses and bigger bankruptcies look similar, but they still are far from the same. Smaller business cases are perceived more like real people.

Even if incorporated, smaller businesses often are tied to real humans' blood, sweat, and tears, not to mention the object of their financial devotion. They may have paid the fees and filled out the forms to set up a separate fake person, but smaller businesses reflect the entrepreneurial spirit of specific humans, both when they go right and when they go wrong.

The following story shows how closely connected a family and a business can be, while also driving home differences in treatment of debtors of various types and sizes. Ample Hills Creamery, a beloved ice cream company, was founded by Brian Smith and Jackie Cuscuna in Prospect Heights, Brooklyn. If ever you need an example of how being beloved does not guarantee financial security, here it is. Expansion plans, including buying a new factory, generated a lot of debt the company could not repay. When Ample Hills filed for bankruptcy in 2020, the founders lost their company. Because they had signed personal guarantees on business loans and their company had fallen behind on certain taxes, Brian and Jackie remained on the hook for many of the obligations of their business.

The founders' personal bankruptcy filing made clear just how much the owners had devoted personal resources into Ample Hills. Despite the fame of their ice cream, Brian and Jackie had little in terms of savings, investments, or assets.

They did not own a home and lost their lease, requiring finding somewhere else to move their family of four. Because federal law protects many obligations individuals owe to the government, Brian and Jackie remained responsible for the taxes their business had not paid, their own personal bankruptcy notwithstanding. Brian and Jackie got less of a fresh start in bankruptcy than do most major corporations that reorganize in Chapter 11.

The 2005 amendments that brought more scrutiny of personal bankruptcy filers also ushered in an era of distrust of the smallest businesses. Earlier legislative hearings set the scene. In 1998, a prominent corporate restructuring lawyer named Stephen Case testified in Congress about a grade school friend. All grown up, that friend was running a small business that had filed for Chapter 11. The premises were dangerous for workers, said Case, and the business was not paying its taxes. According to Case, his friend's story offered an example of a much larger phenomenon of businesspeople "recklessly using Chapter 11 to perpetuate a dead business." [15]

Rallying around such images, the 2005 amendments coupled the crackdown on personal bankruptcy with a crackdown on small business reorganization. These rules would not apply to a company with as much debt as Ample Hills Creamery, but they would apply to the great majority of small businesses that sought the chance to reorganize. Small businesses were required to submit more information than big businesses. The government watchdog had greater rights to inspect these smallest Chapter 11 businesses and to demand more frequent meetings with management. If the business could not manage all these extra requirements, not only would the case be dismissed but the business also would not be able to file a second Chapter 11 petition with full bankruptcy protection anytime soon.[16]

In 2019, the pessimism about the future of small businesses reflected in the 2005 amendments gave way to a shift in perspective. Building on years of research and reform proposals, Congress enacted a new subchapter of Chapter 11 that reinfused small business bankruptcy law with a pro-reorganization philosophy that large businesses have long enjoyed. Among bankruptcy judges and professionals, there is cautious optimism that this new part of Chapter 11, *Subchapter V*, better reflects national policies supporting small businesses.[17]

This new small business reorganization law has a quid pro quo that lawyers for big companies would not tolerate for their own clients: a trustee. Subchapter V trustees have a different job description from other trustees, as they do not displace management. Yet, the installation of a trustee at all reflects the perception of small businesses as more closely tied to human foibles than to those of corporate America.

————

The bigger and more powerful they are, the more elite lawyers they can hire, the more likely that bankrupt fake people get privileges that would not be extended to the average human who files for bankruptcy. Bankruptcy lands in a different place from criminal, constitutional, and other major areas of law by all but disclaiming the corporation's capacity as a culpable actor and by associating misconduct with individual bad actors. The bankruptcy system cannot fully internalize the consequences of its bias. It is an unreliable partner in a broader legal and policy project of deterring corporate misconduct.

Although for-profit companies are the most common type of fake person to file for bankruptcy, the system also offers legal help to artificial public persons: cities and other municipalities. Places like Jefferson County, Alabama, and the city of Central Falls in Rhode Island have gone through bankruptcy. If the government is a debtor, an additional array of legal obligations might arise. For example, public debtors may be accused of violating the civil rights of residents. How does bankruptcy affect those responsibilities? Chapter 4 takes a look.

4

Civil Rights in a Bankrupt City

In September 2013, Representative John Conyers Jr., chair of the House Judiciary Committee, convened an event at the Fellowship Church in Detroit. The event's topic was major news: the city of Detroit had just filed for bankruptcy. I arrived early to the venue, and watched the audience grow from a trickle to a flood to a standing-room-only situation, with hundreds in attendance. Most of the panelists—elected officials such as former Detroit mayor Coleman Young's son, Coleman Young II, by then a politician in his own right, and clergy and local union leaders—came to state their opposition to a federal bankruptcy case filed on behalf of the city of Detroit that July.[1]

A few months earlier, I would have had little to say about municipal bankruptcies. Because they almost never happened, few professors studied them. But when Detroit became the largest-ever city to file for bankruptcy, I dove headfirst into

the case and into Chapter 9 of the Bankruptcy Code, the federal law that lets municipalities use the bankruptcy system.
Although New York City had a close brush with bankruptcy
in the 1970s, no big city had ever entered Chapter 9 until
Detroit took the plunge. The judge presiding over the Detroit
bankruptcy made audio recordings of the hearings publicly
available, and I listened to each one in as close to real time as
possible. In between each hearing, the court docket filled up
quickly with new filings by the city, workers, retirees, members of the public, bondholders, insurance companies, and
more. Every day, I reviewed the docket entries to stay up to
speed. I wrote about what I learned on a blog about credit and
bankruptcy called *Credit Slips*. Congressional staffers read
blogs. That probably prompted the invitation to fly to Detroit
and participate in this event moderated by Detroit-born public
intellectual Michael Eric Dyson.

The immediate controversy over Detroit's bankruptcy filing
was not about whether Detroit was in a solid financial state. It
was not. Forty percent of the city's streetlights had gone dark.
Ambulances took too long to arrive. The fire department had
no working alarm bell and had to use an empty soda can atop
an ancient fax machine as an alert system.[2]

But the bankruptcy felt undemocratic because it was.
Along with other majority-Black Michigan cities, Detroit was
under emergency management, authorized by a statute that

the NAACP and others were challenging as unconstitutional. Governor Rick Snyder had selected Kevyn Orr, one of the nation's relatively few African American restructuring lawyers at an international law firm, to lead Detroit through its financial crisis. The largely African American population of Detroit (more than 80 percent of Detroit's residents identified as Black) worried that their city's bankruptcy was illegitimate. The bankruptcy was seen as tantamount to aiding and abetting state efforts to strip Black people of their rights.

What I remember from that day is the collective sense of unease about how this takeover, combined with the bankruptcy, would affect residents' interactions with the city. Which basic civic functions would go forward, and which would not? I did my best to predict some effects, although much remained unknown.

I do not recall fielding questions about the consequences of the bankruptcy for residents who had experienced police brutality or other civil rights violations. Perhaps the audience assumed that a process directed toward Detroit's *fiscal* problems would not interfere and I must have assumed the same. Our assumption turned out to be wrong, but as the person who was supposed to understand bankruptcy, I should have known better.

Although there is much to say about many elements of the Detroit bankruptcy, this chapter is about the impact of a city's bankruptcy on the civil rights of its residents, particularly its Black and brown residents. The operation of municipal bankruptcy signals greater value for the private property rights of financial institutions and other moneyed interests than it does for the constitutional rights that are supposed to protect people from state violence. Cities that have gone bankrupt in federal court tend to have among the highest rates of death at the hands of the police, and a much higher percentage of nonwhite residents than reflected by their police forces (although diversifying a police force does not itself resolve police brutality problems).[3]

This chapter inevitably continues the theme of the relief that bankruptcy law gives to fake people as debtors relative to human debtors. Cities and other government entities get corporate personhood. According to the Bankruptcy Code, entities such as cities, counties, water and sewer districts, and public hospitals may be bankruptcy filers if the state endorses the filing. Chapter 9 bankruptcy allows municipalities to restructure debts, operating similarly to Chapter 11, which governs reorganization for private enterprises. That means that municipalities get many of the privileges bankruptcy law gives to fake people, relative to real people, including broad latitude to cancel legal obligations, including those incurred by bad, violent, and even unconstitutional behavior.

Today's scope of municipal bankruptcy would be unimaginable to the architects of the original narrow municipal bankruptcy law in the 1930s.

A Brief History

Congress first adopted a municipal bankruptcy law as temporary emergency legislation in 1934, and then again in 1937 after the Supreme Court found the initial version of the law unconstitutional. The right to use the bankruptcy system was for a limited purpose: to restructure unpayable bond debt. The law was narrowly drawn. A majority of bondholders could bind dissenters to accept restructuring of the repayment terms. The city's plan had to have majority support before the city would file a bankruptcy petition rather than using the filing itself as leverage to force a deal.

Municipal bankruptcy became a permanent part of bankruptcy law in 1946 as a limited intervention into a city's relationship with its bondholders. There was little actual bankruptcy law in the early cases and the cases were overseen by federal judges with no specialization in bankruptcy, rather than by the expert "referees" who were precursors to today's bankruptcy judges.

Fear of a New York City financial collapse in the 1970s raised questions about whether this law could be sufficiently responsive to the distress of a big city. New York City struggled to pay its bills because of both local and national conditions, and President Gerald Ford famously declined to lend the city a hand. New York City's problems arguably went beyond its bond-based borrowing. Thus, with a major overhaul in the works of all types of bankruptcy (ultimately the 1978 Bankruptcy Code), Congress fast-tracked the expansion of municipal bankruptcy reform to make New York City a possible candidate for debt relief. Congress even considered, but ultimately rejected, a special bankruptcy chapter for cities with a population of more than 1 million people. New York City never did use the new law; it got by with renegotiated deals with its lenders and workers and with some federal help. But the scene was set for some other municipality to make aggressive use of the federal bankruptcy power.

The resulting overhaul looked more like Chapter 11 for businesses than like the original municipal bankruptcy approach. Not only did the new law abandon the requirement of securing majority creditor support in advance but it also gave the municipal debtor many of the extraordinary tools that private businesses are granted in Chapter 11. Indeed, because a municipality is a unit of a state, and state sovereignty must be respected, municipal debtors would have more control over the process than the law afforded private businesses. The expansion made it possible for a city to threaten to rewrite obligations to all sorts of parties, including retirees who had earned pensions and health care coverage and small businesses that had performed services for or supplied goods to the city.

Just as Congress was expanding municipal bankruptcy law, in an entirely separate legal development the U.S. Supreme Court decided a case in 1978 that set the stage for civil rights lawsuits against cities. *Monell v. Department of Social Services of the City of New York* established that municipalities were "persons" and thus could be sued and held liable under section 1983 of the Civil Rights Act of 1871. This statute, also known as the Ku Klux Klan Act, states that plaintiffs may sue "every person, who under color of" law deprived them of their constitutional rights. That cities were liable as "persons" should not have been a shocking legal development; corporations, including those established for public works, had long been liable for wrongdoing under common law tort theories.[4]

Monell's authorization of civil rights liability for cities had important implications for tackling structural conditions for unconstitutional behavior. It is important to name and hold liable the cities themselves, the court argued, lest an unduly individualized bad apple model of misconduct fester. Indeed, in the 1980 case of *Owen v. City of Independence*, the Supreme Court proclaimed, "A municipality has no 'discretion' to violate the Federal Constitution; its dictates are absolute and imperative." Yet *Monell* did not impose liability on cities merely because someone in their midst had committed a violation. The city's own actions had to be responsible. The harmed party had to show that the municipality's policy or custom caused the deprivation of constitutional rights.[5]

The text of the court's *Monell* decision, like many of the Supreme Court's discussions of this topic, indicates that the justices already accounted for cities' financial limitations when developing their rulings. At least one member of the court thought the court should do more to protect municipalities' budgets. Justice Lewis Powell, who spent his career championing the constitutional rights of for-profit corporations before President Richard Nixon nominated him for the Supreme Court, lamented in a dissenting opinion that "many local governments lack the resources to withstand substantial anticipated liability."[6]

I do not know whether Justice Powell ever predicted that cities would use bankruptcy to address liability for civil rights violations. But some cities have done just that.

Canceling Civil Rights Liabilities?

How can a seemingly narrow financial law like bankruptcy undo the mandates of the Constitution to protect life and liberty? In part because the American legal system prefers money damages as remedies for most wrongdoing. Most private lawsuits for civil rights violations are compensable with money and do not require a change in behavior (known in legal circles as *injunctive relief*). Beyond receiving coverage of medical bills and other direct costs, people hurt by the police might prefer a dramatic rethinking of community safety and an abandonment of the slavery roots of policing over receiving a check in their mailbox. But the law imposes many barriers to nonmonetary remedies. Instead, injured people are told to ask for money, and that money damages, in the words of the U.S. Supreme Court, will help vindicate "cherished constitutional guarantees" and serve "as a deterrent against future constitutional deprivations."[7]

Once a remedy for any harm takes the form of money, that remedy is a debt under the definitions in the Bankruptcy Code and the injured party becomes an unsecured creditor. Following the lead of the legal system generally, bankruptcy law equates a police brutality remedy with an overdue utility bill or an invoice for office supplies.

Cities face liability for police misconduct when their residents sue the municipality or individual actors in it. Victims can sue a city because of the *Monell* case. Debts for lawsuits filed against individual public officials, including police officers, may also end up in city coffers. Cases directly against police officers are harder to win in part because of *qualified immunity*, the controversial doctrine that protects police officers from liability if their conduct did not violate clearly established statutory or constitutional rights. But when a court does rule in favor of a plaintiff and against an individual police officer, the judgment technically can be executed against only the losing party—the individual police officer.

State law sometimes requires municipalities to indemnify their employees for at least some of these obligations. Other municipalities agree to do so by contract, such as collective bargaining agreements with police unions (these arrangements create another way the police officers may be creditors of the city). Professor Joanna Schwartz, a leading expert on police misconduct liability, has found that because of indemnity, a police officer has a greater chance of being struck by lightning than of paying the judgment out of pocket. The city typically pays, if anyone does, even if there is no law or contract requiring that result.[8]

None of this means that civil rights judgments are a driver of municipal financial distress. Schwartz has found that payments for constitutional violations are typically less than 1 percent of local budgets. Like Detroit, most cities that have filed for bankruptcy are wrestling with many types of financial problems, such as fulfilling pension and health care obligations to employees and retirees and the inability to pay municipal bonds on their stated terms. Canceling civil rights liabilities has become an incidental "benefit," one bankrupt cities explicitly write into their restructuring plans. Municipalities seek to shed liability for alleged mistreatment of their residents because bankruptcy presents that opportunity, even if doing so is unnecessary to return the city to solvency.[9]

The treatment of a discrimination claim in the bankruptcy of Orange County, California, offers an early glimpse of a municipality doing just that. The relatively flush Orange County got itself into hot water in the 1990s with fancy financial products gone awry. Prior to the bankruptcy filing, in June 1994, one of the county's employees, Carole O'Loghlin, had contacted the Equal Employment Opportunity Commission about disability discrimination. The EEOC did not issue a "right to sue" letter until May 1997, after Orange County had emerged from bankruptcy in 1996. When O'Loghlin sued, Orange County claimed its bankruptcy had already canceled the legal obligation. Another three years later, in 2000, an appellate court explained that bankruptcy gives the broadest possible sweep to the obligations subject to restructuring in Chapter 9 bankruptcy. To the extent that O'Loghlin's lawsuit involved county conduct from before confirmation of its plan, that liability no longer was enforceable.[10]

I do know of one instance in which a municipality filed for bankruptcy in direct response to a civil rights violation. Desert Hot Springs filed for bankruptcy in 2001 after being found in violation of the Fair Housing Act, a federal law designed to address long-standing racism in housing. Desert Hot Springs had blocked the development of a low-income mobile home park, apparently based on a fear of low-income Black and Mexican children wandering the town. The city believed its residents had other "spending priorities" and thus looked to bankruptcy to help manage its obligation to pay the judgment. Municipal bankruptcy cases are supposed to be dismissed if they are not filed in good faith. The bankruptcy court nonetheless found the city eligible for bankruptcy, and appellate courts dodged the issue.[11]

Detroit as a Big Test Case

The city of Detroit's bankruptcy would bring together financial problems and civil rights violations on an unprecedented scale. Detroit has been particularly prone to police violence against Black residents. By the time the city of Detroit went under emergency management and officially went bankrupt in 2013, its police department had been operating under a consent decree with the U.S. Department of Justice for a decade, following an investigation of excessive force and unconstitutional conditions of confinement in holding cells. In recent years, Detroit has taken second place among midwestern cities in terms of what it owes to victims of police brutality, behind Chicago and ahead of Indianapolis.[12]

Like Chapter 11 for businesses, Chapter 9 is supposed to give creditors a voice in creating and approving a municipality's restructuring plan, but residents who allege mistreatment do not readily get a seat at the negotiating table. In Detroit's bankruptcy, key stakeholders included financial creditors who remain very much a part of modern municipal bankruptcies: those who held or insured bonds, along with investors holding the right to collect on debts with opaque labels such as certificates of participation and interest rate swaps. While some holders had been long-term partners of the city, others bought these financial investments recently at a deep discount, set to profit no matter what happened in the restructuring.

Workers and retirees were also very much part of the negotiations. Knowing that its treatment of public workers would be under a spotlight because of its intention to cut pensions and health care, the city of Detroit offered to pay the expenses of a committee to advocate for retirees that could negotiate with the city. This committee of Detroit retirees hired one of the world's largest law firms and other professionals to represent them, with the city footing the bill.

Representing a subset of current workers, the police force also was well represented in negotiations. Police unions have access to experienced lawyers who can help them negotiate how the city's bankruptcy will affect them. The extraordinary debt cancellation that bankruptcy offers to cities can turn police brutality into a bargaining chip. Cities might offer to give police insulation against responsibility for misconduct as a concession for cutting officers' compensation or benefit packages. Relative to rich suburban locales, violent crime rates in financially distressed cities tend to be higher—but police officers tend to receive lower pay. Whether in or out of bankruptcy, cities convey the message that they need more police resources to respond to violent crime, even as researchers find that bigger police budgets do not have a direct impact on variables like homicide clearance rates.[13]

The national media often framed Detroit's bankruptcy as a battle between workers and Wall Street. That made it too easy to overlook other claimants who had alleged, and sometimes prevailed, in lawsuits claiming use of excessive force by the police or other violations of civil rights. In the Detroit bankruptcy, claimants with constitutional or even more basic tort claims—like being hit by a city bus—requested the same kind of representation and access to behind-the-scenes deliberation as retirees and the police union had. Detroit declined and opposed these claimants from having organized representation in the bankruptcy.[14]

Changing Your Rights from the Outset

As negotiations began about Detroit's treatment of creditors and what it would take for the city to emerge from bankruptcy, the case's immediate impact was unclear. Residents like those who attended the event at Fellowship Church understandably could not make sense of how bankruptcy would affect their rights and obligations and those of the city. Just as filing for personal bankruptcy stops credit card companies from calling Sylvia to collect debts, as we saw in chapter 1, municipal bankruptcy halts a lot of legal activity. What does that mean when a major city, rather than a single individual, is the debtor? The protection is even broader in municipal bankruptcy than in other kinds of cases. It even extends to many government officers. But there have been so few cases interpreting the law that even experts aren't always sure where to draw the lines.

Bankruptcy should not stop efforts to halt ongoing illegal or unconstitutional practices, but the procedures for going forward are not well developed. When residents filed a lawsuit alleging that Detroit violated their constitutional rights when it terminated residential water service, the appellate court not only upheld dismissal of their suit but noted that plaintiffs in other cases would need to undertake a more elaborate procedure to challenge the constitutionality of city activities during a bankruptcy. That is likely correct as a legal matter, but it increases the amount of information civil rights lawyers need to know to try to protect their clients or to determine whether it is feasible to bring the claim at all.[15]

Before Detroit filed for bankruptcy, the American Civil Liberties Union had challenged the city's practice of allowing police to remove children from homes without sufficient process; the suit sought procedural changes, not money. Upon learning of the city's bankruptcy, the presiding federal district court judge halted the suit.[16]

Detroit's bankruptcy also stalled the remedial phase of a class action lawsuit addressing the city's practice of lengthy detainments in inhumane conditions without probable cause. Johnathan Brown was the named plaintiff. Before the bankruptcy, a district court certified two classes and held Detroit liable for constitutional violations. The bankruptcy filing paused further developments for eighteen months, and the city's restructuring plan made it impossible to provide relief for class members.[17]

In an employment matter involving allegations that Detroit had engaged in sex and pregnancy discrimination, the arbitrator assigned to the matter asked Detroit to opine whether that matter could go forward notwithstanding the bankruptcy filing. The arbitrator got no response from the city for *over a year*. Only when the active phase of its bankruptcy was almost over did the bankruptcy court confirm that this arbitration could continue.[18]

One also might argue that some ongoing litigation for prior offenses in other courts should continue to determine liability. But when a civil rights claimant asked the court for permission to pursue her wrongful death lawsuit when a police officer killed her daughter (also a police officer and the killer's wife), the bankruptcy court used the request as an opportunity to push Detroit to develop a case management plan for all types of tort claims. Detroit chose to direct these matters to private arbitration, potentially removing claimants' access to jury trials as well as capping their remedies.[19]

Civil rights claimants argued that their claims could not be canceled in this bankruptcy. Although the definition of claim is broad, the Bankruptcy Code does not require that a city seek to erase its civil rights obligations or any other particular liability. The law recognizes the possibility of canceling some debts and not others. The Bankruptcy Code expressly states that the city does not cancel a debt that is "excepted from discharge by the plan or order confirming the plan." It is possible to satisfy the other Chapter 9 plan requirements while honoring constitutional obligations.[20]

Detroit's own bankruptcy provides proof of this point because the city was not allowed to cancel claims arising from loss of property under the Takings Clause of the Fifth

Amendment. The Solicitor General of the United States and
the bankruptcy court agreed that such claims were insulated
from Detroit's restructuring. This special treatment for property claims was not Detroit's first choice, but the city revised
its plan to comply with the court ruling.

Shouldn't civil rights claims, which also have a constitutional foundation, get the same protection as property rights
claims? Neither the Solicitor General of the United States nor
the bankruptcy court believed that excessive force claims
against residents' bodies warranted as much protection from
adjustment in bankruptcy as property. They attributed the distinction to language in the Fifth Amendment. While I question
that distinction, I make a more limited point here: If Takings
Clause claims can be carved out of a municipal bankruptcy,
civil rights claims can too.[21]

The bankruptcy court did not give Detroit the full insulation
it sought from responsibility for civil rights violations. Detroit
had intended to use its bankruptcy to relieve individual police
officers of their personal liability for excessive force allegations
as well as to relieve the city of its own direct responsibility. As
chapter 6 of this book will explore in the context of businesses
and nonprofits, it is controversial to use the bankruptcy case
of an enterprise to cancel the debt of a separate person. In the
case of Detroit, bankruptcy court did not rule out the possibility that a city could relieve officers of responsibility but found

that Detroit did not adequately demonstrate that protecting its police officers was essential to the city's reorganization. Lawyers no doubt took careful notes on this ruling for future cases.[22]

Detroit's restructuring plan got over the finish line with sufficient creditor support because of a deal that Detroit-based journalists called the Grand Bargain. A now-famous napkin doodle capturing the deal lives in the Detroit Institute of Arts, after an invitation-only installation party. It is a sketch made by the powerful case mediator Chief Judge Gerald Rosen of his two main priorities for resolving the bankruptcy: making sure the city's art museum holdings were not sold to pay creditors and protecting the pensions of public workers. This judge, via his role as mediator, even initiated a fundraising campaign to bring his Grand Bargain doodle to life, soliciting "donations" from foundations, the State of Michigan, and corporations. Prioritizing the art and pensions implicitly entailed deprioritizing other things, like ensuring accountability for police misconduct.[23]

Although the Grand Bargain limited the cuts to pensions for public workers and retirees, it did put retiree health care on the chopping block, offering instead modest stipends to help buy replacement health insurance. To incentivize retirees to support that deal, Rosen "wanted a coordinated media blitz." It worked. "You can't eat principles," said Shirley Lightsey, president of the Detroit Retired City Employees Association. The slogan was so potent it ended up on a campaign-style button. The one time I met Lightsey in person, in a swanky conference room near the top of the Sears Tower (now the Willis Tower) at a municipal bankruptcy event populated mostly by white men, Lightsey remained somber, frustrated by the bankruptcy plan she helped bring to fruition.[24]

Retiree support of Detroit's plan altered the leverage of other creditors. Like dominoes, each well-organized and well-lawyered financial creditor group made its own deals. One financial creditor, then another and then another. Lacking any leverage, civil rights and personal injury claimants got the weakest treatment. No justification has been offered other than the standard: this is bankruptcy, obligations get canceled, reorganization helps everyone. The lengthy court decision issued to confirm Detroit's restructuring plan contains only a sentence about improving the city's relationship with neighborhoods. It does not mention police brutality or misconduct.

Compensation to Civil Rights Claimants?

Detroit's restructuring plan promised civil rights claimants some compensation for canceled legal obligations, but recovery was neither quick nor simple. For purposes of voting on the plan, people alleging civil rights violations were in Class 14, along with myriad other unsecured creditors. Those other claimants had many different incentives for supporting or rejecting the plan and would not be affected by this bankruptcy equally. Officially, Class 14 rejected the plan by a small margin. That meant the city would have to make additional legal showings to get the plan approved through a process bankruptcy lawyers call *cramdown*. The presiding judge found that Detroit succeeded in making those showings, clearing the way for plan approval.

Class 14 claimants would receive "notes" (the right to collect payment) rather than cash, with a thirty-year maturity date. In 2014, Detroit predicted the notes would be worth 10–13 percent of the claims' face value. A claimant owed $100,000 would get notes worth $10,000–$13,000. By late 2019, the claimants in this class had not received anything. And the value of the notes was down to somewhere in the 4–7 percent range. Recovery on a $100,000 judgment claim could be worth as little as $4,000.[25]

It gets worse. In 2019, Detroit told the court, seemingly for the first time, that Class 14 claimants, including civil rights claimants, could not get compensated unless they had brokerage accounts. According to the Federal Reserve, 11 percent of Black families in America do not even have an ordinary bank account, let alone a brokerage account. Detroit went about collecting the brokerage account information at perhaps the worst possible time: asking people to mail the information during the COVID-19 pandemic shutdown. If Detroit didn't get injured parties' corrected information by June 24, 2020, these claimants would get no recovery. Not 13 percent, not 7 percent, not 4 percent. Zero.[26]

The Bigger Picture

The story of the treatment of civil rights claimants is only one example of how the city's bankruptcy intersects with race inequality. For example, Black residents are overtaxed relative to white residents, and in Detroit in particular, Black neighborhoods were ten times more likely to be subject to tax foreclosure than were white neighborhoods. Homeowners were overcharged approximately $600 million in a six-year period, with over forty thousand homes charged at least twice what they should have been. Struggling to make outsized payments to hang on to their homes depleted residents' ability to manage repairs, maintenance, and other ongoing expenses. Detroit sold delinquent tax debt to Wayne County, which tacked on high interest rates and profited from pursuing foreclosure. Professor Bernadette Atuahene calls these practices hallmarks of "predatory cities," defined as "urban areas where public officials systematically take property from residents and transfer it to public coffers, intentionally or unintentionally violating domestic laws or basic human rights."[27]

Detroit's tax foreclosure problems escaped broader public attention for a while. In the meantime, a small subset of over-charged Detroit homeowners received relief through a special program and remained in their homes. Detroit expressed no intent to return the wrongfully collected money.

Why not? You know the answer: the city's bankruptcy.

According to city representatives, the bankruptcy tied their hands. The city was on a strict budget. City representatives also argued reimbursement would be unfair to residents who paid their (inflated) tax bills.

Too Late Now

Because of the breadth of the bankruptcy law's definition of claim, Detroit's bankruptcy affected not only civil rights law-suits that already had been filed but also those filed years later. Davontae Sanford was charged with murdering four people when he was fourteen years of age. Sanford was "blind in one eye, functionally illiterate, and had a learning disability." San-ford didn't commit the crime, but he spent eight years in prison before the charges were dismissed after an investigation into police misconduct. Once Sanford was released, he sued Detroit in 2017 for wrongful conviction and confinement arising from police misconduct and malicious prosecution. The court imme- diately dismissed the suit against Detroit. Although Sanford was imprisoned throughout the entire bankruptcy, the court concluded that his civil rights suit against Detroit should have been in Sanford's "fair contemplation," and he should have done more to protect his rights. Had Sanford filed a claim in the bankruptcy, the claim would have been in Class 14 that you just read about. He would have needed a brokerage account to have a shot to recover 4–7 percent.[28]

Civil rights lawyers have figured out that there's no point in naming Detroit for civil rights allegations that arose in 2014 or earlier. Justly Johnson was exonerated in 2019 after spending twenty years in jail for a murder he did not commit. He sued two Detroit police officers for $50 million stemming from the 1999 event, but not the city.[29]

Johnson could sue the officers because Detroit fell short of showing that protecting police officers through its bankruptcy was necessary for reorganization. The city of San Bernardino will be more successful in this regard.

San Bernardino

Javier Banuelos suffered brain damage from a police incident in 2011. Paul Triplett was beaten at a traffic stop and put in a coma for three days. Terry Wayne Jackson, who had severe mental illness, was tased and wrestled to the ground in a park, leading to his death. San Bernardino County (which includes but is not limited to the city) has among the highest rate of police shootings of all California counties. I note these events because in 2012, the city of San Bernardino filed for Chapter 9 and these people or their families became creditors in a bankruptcy. When San Bernardino sought confirmation of its restructuring plan, about 40 percent of its pending lawsuits listed a police officer or a law enforcement agency as a party.[30]

San Bernardino's bankruptcy was not strictly bound by court decisions in Detroit, but that larger midwestern case proved influential. Like Detroit, San Bernardino had reached settlements with some groups of creditors when it asked the court to approve its restructuring plan. For example, bondholders would receive 40 percent of the face amount of their debt. By contrast, police brutality claimants would be in Class 13, which was promised recovery of 1 percent of their claims. To repeat: 1 percent. Some plaintiffs *might* be able to collect more from an insurance policy, although policy exclusions complicated that possibility. To assess the claims, the plan also moved civil rights disputes into arbitration and out of courts. Like Detroit's restructuring plan, San Bernardino's voting classes mixed police brutality claimants with a potpourri of others for voting purposes, including trade creditors. The civil rights claimants were significantly outvoted.[31]

San Bernardino's plan aimed to cancel not only the city's direct responsibilities for civil rights violations, but the legal obligations of individual police officers arising from misconduct. Learning from Detroit, San Bernardino's lawyer made sure to argue, emphatically, that this protection of police was necessary to the city's reorganization. At least seventeen civil rights claimants filed written objections to the city's proposed treatment of their claims.[32]

If San Bernardino had been a for-profit business in Chapter 11, it would not have been able to protect third parties over the objections of claimants. The U.S. Court of Appeals for the Ninth Circuit, which covers California, has made that clear. I had assumed the same would be true for municipal bankruptcy, but the Ninth Circuit ruled otherwise in a case well timed for San Bernardino. In 2016, the Ninth Circuit heard an appeal involving the bankruptcy of another city with police misconduct problems, the city of Vallejo. In a jury trial, a plaintiff harmed by the Vallejo police obtained a judgment for $50,000 and attorneys' fees of nearly $315,000. Everyone understood that the Chapter 9 had canceled Vallejo's liability for these obligations but disputed whether the Vallejo bankruptcy wiped out the liability of those individual police officers too. The Ninth Circuit held that Vallejo did not write its restructuring plan in a way that would protect police officers, but it did not rule out the possibility of shedding officers' direct liability in other cases because its Chapter 11 holdings did not apply to Chapter 9. The message was loud and clear: if San Bernardino wrote its plan properly, it could protect not only itself, but its police officers too.[33]

And it did. The Ninth Circuit's ruminations made it less of a surprise when the bankruptcy court approved San Bernardino's plan—first orally, and then in a published written decision to supplement the oral ruling—that included protection of individual police officers. Among many other things, the court found that the city had the obligation to indemnify its officers under state law, and, given its dire financial condition, could pay no more than 1 percent to compensate civil rights claimants.[34]

Enforcing the civil rights law of residents had become an unaffordable luxury for the city of San Bernardino.

Unintended Consequences or Predictable Effect?

Municipal bankruptcy started as a narrow mechanism to rewrite the terms of municipal bonds over some voluntary investors' objections. When Congress expanded the law so that a city like New York might find it useful, lawmakers almost certainly did not contemplate that a city would try to reduce or erase liability for unconstitutional conduct.

The U.S. Constitution is supposed to protect individuals from being harmed by state actors. Arguably that's one of its most important jobs. The equal protection clause of the Fourteenth Amendment, ratified after the Civil War, was supposed to protect Black people against discrimination. But the Chapter 9 experiences of Detroit, San Bernardino, and other cities tell a story about which rights get robust defense in federal courts and which are deemed dispensable.

Using bankruptcy to cancel responsibility for police misconduct can be seen as a by-product of a sophisticated restructuring practice coupled with insufficient guidance from appellate courts and Congress. Trained in the turnaround of private enterprise and often representing companies or voluntary lenders, professionals bring a hefty tool kit for using the extraordinary powers of the bankruptcy system when they turn their attention to cities. Bankruptcy lawyers are adept with arguments for why everyone is better off if debt relief for a corporate, nonprofit, or city debtor is as broad as possible. Their view of "everyone" may not be the same as mine or yours.

Ohio State University professor Treva Lindsey talks about policing as part of a criminal punishment system in which property matters more than the lives of Black people. That's why some Americans seem more upset about a convenience store window being shattered during a protest than about Black people being killed by the police, the event that prompted the uprising. Municipal bankruptcy reinforces that disparity, granting more protection for claims that the government has taken property than for claims that the government has unconstitutionally harmed or killed Black and brown people. As financially distressed cities struggle to find concessions to offer the police, they will use greater protection from civil rights responsibility as a bargaining chip if they are allowed to do so.[35]

One sometimes hears the argument that enforcing civil rights obligations hurts communities of color because they will endure the resulting financial burden. There indeed can be a circularity of city responsibilities to its residents. The concerns might be amplified when a city borrows more money to pay victims, as Professor Destin Jenkins, a historian of capitalism and democracy, explains:

> Black Chicagoans have been conscripted into a nasty compact. As taxpayers, they fund a police department that makes their lives more dangerous. And as tax and fee payers, many of those harmed by police brutality effectively pay for their own reparations, with bond financiers taking the cream off the top in the form of underwriting fees.[36]

But until bigger structural changes arrive, using bankruptcy to bluntly cancel responsibility for police violence, without alternative remedies in place, is unconscionable.

One root of this problem, as noted earlier, is the American legal system's single-minded approach to remedying harms. It treats big public health and inequality problems as financial liabilities, on par with an obligation to pay a credit card bill. But within the existing framework, if judgments and settlements are unenforceable, with only cents on the dollar potentially collectable, the legal system will deter civil rights lawyers from taking viable cases even more than it already does. Accountability for and deterrence of police violence drops even further. It is already an uphill battle to represent a civil rights plaintiff against a government actor. If the risk of bankruptcy further reduces the likelihood that the lawyers will get even their expenses covered, they can't afford to take the cases.[37]

Municipal bankruptcies remain rare—for now. But what happened in San Bernardino and Detroit should not be construed as exceptional. For example, when the city of Chester, near Philadelphia, filed a municipal bankruptcy with a range of serious financial problems, civil rights lawyers saw firsthand that bankruptcy is not just about bondholders. They had to reckon with how the case would affect their efforts to vindicate the civil rights of residents put in choke holds.[38]

The relative infrequency of municipal bankruptcy means

that the creativity of restructuring professionals remains concentrated in Chapter 11 business bankruptcy. Some professionals represent the companies themselves. Some represent big financial institutions or other enterprises who have loaned money and can profit greatly from the bankruptcy system if they exercise their leverage just right. Or their clients might be parties interested in buying a distressed company at a discount, ideally without any responsibility for a company's prior wrongdoings, whether they be employment discrimination and sexual harassment, environmental contamination, or contributors to gun violence. With expert guidance at a high price point, these parties have figured out how to dismantle the package deal of benefits and obligations embedded in Chapter 11 and how to extract the perks for themselves. In so doing, they will redirect the fruits of Chapter 11 from its intended beneficiaries, such as workers, suppliers, and customers, and its intended objectives, such as stabilization of viable businesses, to parties with power and resources and boosting their profits. The next chapter shows how far these practices have moved Chapter 11 from its reason to exist in the first place.

5

My Money, My Rules

On December 14, 2012, Adam Lanza killed twenty children and six adults at Sandy Hook Elementary School and then killed himself—all in a matter of minutes with a semiautomatic rifle made for military combat. Nine grieving families sued gun and ammunition maker Remington Outdoor Company for its role in their loved ones' deaths. Remington, alleged the families, had made and marketed a military weapon, meant to maximize physical harm on a battlefield, to individuals with no legitimate uses for such a weapon and a likelihood of using it recklessly. In pursuing wrongful death claims, coupled with punitive damage requests, representatives of the families told the press their goals were not remunerative: they wanted information to come to light about the marketing of deadly weapons, and to prevent future harms.[1]

The families' lawsuit hit many roadblocks. Remington tried

to shift the lawsuit to federal court. Remington made extensive and excessive demands in the state court for the attendance records and report cards of the dead children. Remington took its request to shut down this lawsuit all the way up to the U.S. Supreme Court.[2]

Having overcome these hurdles, the Sandy Hook families were preparing for trial when Remington filed a Chapter 11 bankruptcy in Alabama in 2020. That filing wasn't Remington's first bankruptcy. The company had filed for Chapter 11 in Delaware just a few years earlier. The first case flushed over $600 million of Remington's debt. This time, though, Remington had a different agenda: to sell itself, and fast.

The Bankruptcy Code offers remedies for companies that cannot reorganize. Sales can be handled by Chapter 7 trustees. To use Chapter 11 to sell an entire company, Congress envisioned a multistep process. The company would negotiate with representatives of all creditor constituencies, followed by creditor voting on the company's proposed plan. Assuming sufficient creditor support, the court would evaluate whether the plan satisfies a long list of statutory requirements. These steps allow creditors to share in deciding what happens to the company as well as how to allocate the company's value among creditors. These two paths, Chapter 7 trustee or Chapter 11 plan, require a sharing of governance and control.

Like many other companies before and after it, Remington

preferred that its bankruptcy follow a different script than what Congress wrote, one that undercuts the right to a voice and a vote of the parties whose rights the case will profoundly change. In that script, a company with no prospect of reorganization wants to stay in control of its bankruptcy (no trustee) and sell itself quickly without the Chapter 11 plan process and voting. Buyers demand assurances that they will not be responsible for the seller's wrongdoing, whether to injured third parties or workers or anyone else. That script, which cuts corners on the Chapter 11 process that Congress created, expedites the most consequential decisions, often to the benefit of the company's influential lenders and potential buyers.

Remington and its buyers and lenders got the quick sale they wanted, with the protections they requested, and that happens all the time in big bankruptcy cases. Even the government watchdog accepted the logic in the Remington case: "This has to be a fast sale because of their lenders . . . and . . . potential purchasers which we understand have also requested a fast process." The upshot for the Sandy Hook families was this: even if they prevailed in the long-sought trial, the company under new ownership would be insulated from any responsibility, no matter how profitable it became. Although the principal objectives were nonmonetary, a trial of this nature would not come cheap. The families settled with Remington's insurers.[3]

This chapter is about how companies, banks, private equity

firms, and other powerful parties use Chapter 11 as a forum for games of chicken that have implications far beyond the world of loans and debt. Congress enacted a Bankruptcy Code that provides an integrated package of benefits and obligations. Deviations from this package allow powerful parties to extract and divert the benefits of Chapter 11 for themselves.

The Chapter 11 Package

Chapter 11 is much newer than the general concept of bankruptcy. Congress started experimenting in the 1930s with allowing companies to reorganize, building on federal court practices that used equitable powers. Lawyers considered the 1930s version of corporate restructuring law difficult and inflexible, particularly for big companies with publicly traded stock and debt.

Business reorganization got a big renewal in 1978 by the creation of Chapter 11 in the Bankruptcy Code. Chapter 11 provides companies with a process to restructure debts with the support of most but not all creditors, without ceding control to a government trustee. Chapter 11 bankruptcy was designed as a collaborative effort between a company and its many constituencies to chart the future. Companies could use Chapter 11 to shed debt and rewrite contracts but those powers came with trade-offs, including allowing creditors of all kinds to vote on the most consequential things the company filed for bankruptcy to do and requiring satisfaction of a long list of statutory requirements. The company must provide extensive disclosures about the consequences of a restructuring before creditors vote on a plan. An official committee appointed by the government watchdog gets a seat at the negotiating table on behalf of unsecured creditors (claimants without collateral backing the debtor's obligations to them). The Chapter 11 package also included powers to investigate wrongdoing and pursue integrity-promoting lawsuits to find out where things went awry. The threat and reality of these checks and balances were designed to make the system operate fairly for everyone.

This package also reflects a policy unabashedly in favor of reorganizing distressed companies. Among other rationales, keeping viable companies alive is said to foster competition in a robust marketplace and to preserve jobs. Those rationales, however sound, help justify features of Chapter 11 that boost the odds a company in financial trouble will recover. For example, lenders that offer new financing to a financially distressed company can get more legal protection for new loans unavailable in private transactions. The bankrupt company also gets to make unilateral decisions (subject to court review) about contracts of many kinds. As this chapter explores, these federal boosters are hard to square with cases featuring quick sales of the company.

Bundling the checks and balances of Chapter 11 was necessary to reflect competing policy issues that inevitably go
into a project like the Bankruptcy Code. Bankruptcy law's
definition of claim goes well beyond what the average person
considers a debt. It encompasses legal obligations that go far
beyond borrowing money. A broad definition of claim makes
even an ordinary Chapter 11, in which a company uses Chapter 11 to reorganize, impactful for real people far and wide.
Consequently, bankruptcy has the capacity to sweep in liabilities arising from diverse legal doctrines far beyond contract
law, including tort, statutory, regulatory, and constitutional
law. If powerful parties can dislodge the perks of bankruptcy
law from the checks and balances, the people affected by these
cases lose important protections.

The package deal also is meant to promote fair distribution of financial resources to claimants. The very existence of
Chapter 11 increases the value of distressed companies. Ideally, the package deal restrains aggressive creditors with extra
leverage from taking more than their fair share.

Another reason the boosters especially don't make sense outside of Chapter 11 as a package comes from federalism—the
importance of state and local control in a democratic society
absent pressing national policies. States provide most commercial and corporate law as well as consumer protection, offering a laboratory to try out different approaches. The federal

government is not supposed to override those laws without a good reason relating to national policy. Chapter 11 bankruptcies featuring a quick sale of the company raise special risks of overriding state law and expanding the reach of national law and courts.

Their Money, Their Rules

If the Chapter 11 package is so important, how have parties managed to unbundle it with regularity? Reason number one is money. The same law that created the integrated package also requires Chapter 11 debtors to finance the process.

Use of Chapter 11 generally is not publicly funded. However much debt they have already incurred, companies often need to borrow more to use Chapter 11 and to continue to operate. Called *debtor-in-possession financing*, or DIP financing for short, the Bankruptcy Code authorizes financial and legal incentives for lenders to extend credit to a troubled company. These benefits include higher priority repayment rights and using more assets of the bankruptcy estate as collateral for the new loan. When a court approves a DIP loan, the contract is backed by an enforceable federal court order—a government intervention that private credit markets value greatly.

This federal policy intervention was meant to attract market actors into participating in the project of reorganizing distressed but viable companies, to ensure that overindebtedness and a temporary financial setback did not kill a company with a feasible future and a realistic chance of reorganizing. And Congress succeeded in creating an environment in which DIP loans are profitable and low risk. Over and over, studies have shown that these federal credit enhancements work not only to attract lenders but also to reward them handsomely.[4]

Although the ultimate point of getting DIP lending was to benefit all stakeholders of a bankrupt company, that does not happen automatically. DIP lending is more expensive than one would expect, given all the protections and the low default rates. A company's existing lender often can insist on charging very high prices to make a new loan, reallocating value to itself and away from other creditors. New high-cost debt may keep the company going for another day, but may not increase the odds a company will reorganize. If a lender with leverage over the company's future is not required to look reasonable in its demands, it also has more leverage to dismantle the package deal.

Concerns about the cost of DIP loans flare up especially during times of crisis, such as the global financial crisis of 2007–8 or the stay-at-home phase of the COVID-19 pandemic, but so does the pressure on courts to approve these loans. Creditors balked at the terms of the DIP loan to Chesapeake Energy Corp., an energy fracking company that filed for Chapter 11 in June 2020. The Houston bankruptcy court acknowledged that the lenders were being greedy and approved the loan over the objections of other creditors, who worried that they would pay the price for that greed. When the nutrition supplement company GNC asked a court to approve a costly DIP loan from existing lenders, the government watchdog and creditors decried the loan terms as "unnecessary and disproportionate relief" and "improper." The court approved it anyway, lest the company implode altogether.[5]

Bankruptcy professionals note changes in credit markets and lending to explain the leverage of lenders and they have a point. When Congress enacted the Bankruptcy Code in 1978, companies' financing arrangements did not encumber as many of their assets with security interests. A company with a seemingly viable future was an attractive borrower to new lenders, particularly with the boosted protections offered by bankruptcy law. Lenders would compete to extend credit to the company on competitive and profitable terms. Today, that company probably pledged its most valuable assets— manufacturing equipment and inventory, accounts receivable and intellectual property, and more—as collateral to its existing lenders long before the bankruptcy filing. Under state law and bankruptcy law, the company's lenders have rights against those assets that take precedence over the rights of other creditors, and can threaten to block other DIP loan offers.

With the power associated with having security interests in all those assets coming into the bankruptcy, lenders not only charge higher financial prices for the new loans but also try to rewrite bankruptcy law. A lender is interested in stripping parts of the Chapter 11 package deal that pose risks to the lender's status and power. The loan agreement includes a long list of events that terminate the lender's obligation to extend more money and/or require repayment of existing amounts immediately. If that happens in the middle of a bankruptcy, game over for the company.

What parts of bankruptcy law might the lender want to disable? A lender has incentives to write the DIP loan agreement to limit acts that could hurt its own rights to collect and profit in the case. For example, a thorough investigation might reveal that the lender made mistakes that make the loan terms unenforceable. When that happens, a lender expecting to be paid 100 percent of what it is owed, and then some, might be entitled to just pennies on the dollar. Lenders thus have incentives to curtail the period of investigation and to limit which parties can conduct it.

Another way DIP lenders rewrite bankruptcy law is by insisting that the debtor sell itself quickly, without creditor voting, without satisfying the requirements of a Chapter 11 plan, and without trustee oversight. Controlling the Chapter 11 timeline and insisting on a sale outside of a plan is attractive to the lender for several reasons. First, the faster the case moves, the faster the lender gets paid. Second, that quick process reduces the amount of time available to scrutinize the lender's pre-bankruptcy dealings with the debtor for any potential illegality. The lender may not need to ensure the company is sold for top dollar. Perhaps it can get repaid in full even if the company is sold to a third party at a discount. All in all, the lender has an incentive to depress the operation of checks, balances, and due process that protect other parties.

Let's apply these dynamics to the hypothetical pottery company discussed in chapter 3. During the company's profitable periods, a syndicate of banks provided loans to the company. Now that the pottery company is in financial trouble, those banks are willing to consider making a DIP loan. Before many of the company's creditors (suppliers, employees) are even aware that the company is considering bankruptcy, the company and the bank agree on the terms. The company's Chapter 11 petition is accompanied by a request for the court to approve a DIP loan as quickly as possible. The company's lawyers and the banks' lawyers (again, with a lot of power over what happens because of rights under the banks' existing loans) join forces to report that this crucial deal was reached after rigorous bargaining. Lawyers will warn that if the court denies approval of the loan, the business will shut down, fire its employees, be unable to repay small business suppliers.

The DIP loan agreement the debtor and banks present to the court, threatening the worst of all worlds otherwise, not only spells out financial terms—interest rate, repayment schedule, other fees—but also functionally unbundles the Chapter 11 package deal. If anyone requests the appointment of a trustee or initiates other integrity-promoting elements of Chapter 11, the loan will be immediately due and payable. And the DIP loan imposes a timeline on the Chapter 11 process that is not found in the law itself. The pottery company must be sold in, say, 120 days, or else.

Everything Must Go (On Our Terms)

The big thing DIP lenders demand in many cases, as suggested earlier, has been captured by this *Wall Street Journal* quote: "More companies that wind up in bankruptcy court are facing a stark demand from their banks: Sell yourself now." [6]

There is no bankruptcy system without some asset sales. Recall Fyre Festival and Bikram Yoga discussed in chapter 3. To recover and distribute money for and to creditors, trustees' duties included gathering and selling the debtors' property. Let's say a business is closing and has one tangible asset, such as a machine, and twenty creditors. The creditors do not want the machine broken into twenty pieces. They want the asset sold and to receive their share in money.

The Bankruptcy Code thus has a provision that authorizes sales of assets: section 363. This provision does not talk about selling entire operating companies, which is an inherently more complicated affair than selling discrete assets. The drafters of the Bankruptcy Code envisioned sales of company happening through a Chapter 11 plan approval process, with creditor voting.

As the *Wall Street Journal* quote tells you, business bankruptcy practice went in a different direction from what Congress intended, delinking operating company sales from the plan process. Many courts, including appellate courts that set precedent, have tolerated these practices if the company can articulate a good business reason. That good business reason invites sale advocates to articulate a parade of horribles if the company is not sold on this timeline and in this way: value will be destroyed, jobs lost.

Although it may not be intuitive to the public, buying a company in a Chapter 11 bankruptcy has significant benefits for the purchaser. In addition to the hope of a discounted price and a fast-track acquisition, ordinary mergers and acquisitions do not come with a federal court order blessing their terms. A bankruptcy sale delivers just that. If the court has approved the sale and the transaction has closed, an appellate court cannot unwind the sale if it later finds it flawed. Congress enacted that rule with simpler asset sales in mind, but it applies to sales of companies too. Objecting claimants can ask the court to halt the sale while they seek further court review, but as applied to sales of an entire business, doing so is prohibitively expensive for most stakeholders.

Quick sales of companies can cause various kinds of harm to parties that the package deal of Chapter 11 was meant to protect. Some harms are to legal rights. Creditors should have had the opportunity to vote on the sale, for example. The quick sale can cause financial harm, although the magnitude can be difficult to measure. People may receive a smaller recovery from the bankruptcy—either because the sale did not maximize value or because the privately negotiated sale procedures distorted the distribution of the sale proceeds. Remember the range of people who can be considered creditors in bankruptcy: workers, retirees, suppliers of goods and services, tort claimants, and many others with insufficient knowledge and leverage for protecting their interests in these fast-moving transactions, sometimes with limited or no access to legal representation.

Advocates of quick going concern sales have been effective gaslighters: Would you rather be hypertechnical about bankruptcy law requirements, or would you rather save jobs? Of course, there are no guarantees that the quick sale will save jobs. Recall the Weinstein Company, the entertainment firm discussed in chapter 3. It already was low on employees by the time it went bankrupt with the objective of selling itself quickly to a private equity firm. The company said the sale would save jobs. But the buyer made no binding commitment to keep the remaining employees. Indeed, seemingly at the buyer's request, the Weinstein Company laid off more employees before the sale was finalized. One of the buyers of Remington, the gun and ammunition company, promised to rehire two hundred workers, but the *Wall Street Journal* reported that it fired them in the interim, such that the workers lost their health benefits during the COVID-19 pandemic.[7]

No one can guarantee the future, but it can be risky to justify departures from the rule of law with puffery. A buyer looking for a good deal may not be able to keep the business operational and the people employed. Let's return to an ice cream–focused example, also from chapter 3. Ample Hills Creamery filed for bankruptcy on March 15, 2020. Stay-at-home orders for the COVID-19 pandemic were issued shortly after that. During the uncertainty and shutdowns this crisis fostered, the bankruptcy court approved the only viable option on the table: quick sale of the company to an Oregon gas tank manufacturer. The price? One million dollars—a fraction of the amount lenders had assumed the business was worth. Most creditors, beyond bank lenders and lawyers, would receive nothing.

At least the delicious ice cream and jobs were saved, right? Not entirely.

By 2022, the business fell behind on rent, and eviction was imminent. Ample Hills ended up in a New York State law debt collection procedure called *receivership*. Unbundled bankruptcies and their deviations from the rule of law as written by Congress are, themselves, a gamble.

Business bankruptcy lawyers sometimes acknowledge the shortcomings of the alternative system they have built. The American Bankruptcy Institute put together a commission to study Chapter 11. More than 250 restructuring professionals participated in the deliberations. The final report, published in 2014, was critical of quick sales of operating companies without the checks and balances associated with Chapter 11 plans. Too much rushing, too little information.[8]

Did participants in that reform discussion demand a quick sale on behalf of their clients in their next case? Surely they did.

Consequences of Quick Sales for Corporate Accountability

Buying a company starts with a voluntary transaction. The purchaser expects to pick and choose what assets to buy, as well as to limit what liabilities it takes on. If the buyer wants a federal court to bless the transaction in a bankruptcy case, the sale is not fully private; its terms must comply with the law. But what laws apply?

The provision of the Bankruptcy Code that governs sales, section 363, does not say as much as one would expect about this topic, perhaps because it was not designed with the sale of operating companies in mind. Subsection (f) of this provision identifies circumstances under which a buyer can take the assets free and clear of *interests* held by other people in those assets. As used in bankruptcy, the term interest typically means property interest, such as a mortgage on a building. If a court approves the sale of a building, the buyer can acquire the building free of the mortgage on it. The mortgage attaches to the proceeds of the sale of the building, protecting the lender.

Buyers of businesses have advocated for an expansive interpretation of the term interest because they want assurance they are not assuming obligations they have not specifically elected. They want to buy the company *free and clear.* Buyers say they pay more with assurance of being unencumbered from those obligations. But is stripping those obligations lawful in this setting, and are they paying enough for that privilege?

Although a buyer does not automatically become responsible for a seller's liabilities merely by acquiring its assets outside of bankruptcy, the doctrine of *successor liability* under state and federal law determines when a buyer should be on the hook. Successor liability doctrine is supposed to encourage compliance with laws that protect people from harm, whether or not the doctrine maximizes value. One should not be able to circumvent the rules simply by selling a company from one owner to another in a bankruptcy case, especially given that the Bankruptcy Code does not explicitly say that it overrides successor liability.

Some precedential rulings of appellate courts have increased the appeal of quick sales in bankruptcy because they have upheld the insulation of the buyer. They stretch the meaning of *interest* in ways unrecognizable elsewhere in bankruptcy law. Those rulings attract buyers to pursue a quick sale in Chapter 11, potentially undercompensating claimants for the protections they have lost in the process.

Prior to TWA's bankruptcy filing in 2001, flight attendants had settled pregnancy discrimination claims by agreeing to receive travel vouchers with no expiration date. Unfortunately for the workers, TWA itself was a frequent flier in the bankruptcy system. The goal of TWA's *third* bankruptcy, in 2001, was to sell itself quickly to the then-heartier American Airlines. American Airlines wanted to take on *some* of TWA's obligations but threatened to walk away from the deal if it had to honor the vouchers for TWA's flight attendants as compensation for the settlement.

The federal government opposed the sale on these terms. The Bankruptcy Code did not say such sales would override federal antidiscrimination laws. The federal government was also ready to call American Airlines' bluff. Would it really walk away if it had to honor the vouchers? Given the modest value of the vouchers relative to the sale price of the company, the government contended, those travel vouchers would "represent, at most, not even the tail, but the flea wagging the dog." [9]

The TWA dispute reached the U.S. Court of Appeals for the Third Circuit, which blessed the sale. Its written decision did not really engage with the government's arguments about the absence of authority in the Bankruptcy Code to support overriding discrimination law. The court took the bluff seriously— better to let the airlines merge and to dishonor the remedy for discrimination than to risk American Airlines walking away or insisting on paying a lower sale price. The Third Circuit cited job saving and future employee benefits as a rationale for approving these sale terms. [10]

The Weinstein Company filed for bankruptcy in Delaware, which falls within the Third Circuit. The case was preceded by evidence of long-standing sex discrimination and harassment of employees, as well as allegations of assault of other women. The order approving the sale of the company to Lantern Capital, a private equity firm, disavowed the buyer's responsibility for employment discrimination or other tortious behavior. The protection covers rape, gender violence, false imprisonment, discrimination, predatory conduct, negligent infliction of emotional distress, and failure to remedy or prevent these conditions. The sale order included factual findings relevant to successor liability determinations under other law, but those findings had never been formally presented or adjudicated. Lantern Capital's website proclaims its commitment to diversity and "radical candor," but website talk is cheap. Lantern promised to implement human resources policies, consult with diversity and inclusion experts, and hold antiharassment training, as pretty much any well-advised business would do, if only to strengthen the legal defense to accusations that arise in the future.[11]

The Third Circuit is not alone in holding that bankruptcy sales can protect buyers from obligations that other federal or state law might impose on successors. Leckie Smokeless Coal Company was one of several coal companies that sold itself quickly in Chapter 11 to a buyer that did not want to honor the retired coal miners' pension and health care benefits. Those benefits were not gifts or even only contract obligations. They were mandated by the federal Coal Act. Coal mining is, after all, a hazardous profession. The Fourth Circuit Court of Appeals said the buyer could buy the companies in bankruptcy free and clear of responsibility for the Coal Act obligations.[12]

To be sure, companies can use Chapter 11 to undermine major federal environmental, employment, and health care laws without insisting on a quick sale. Researchers have found coal companies used bankruptcy to cancel nearly $2 billion in environmental liabilities and more than $3 billion in retiree benefits. Those researchers also posited that reorganizing those companies contributed to the overproduction of coal.[13]

Or consider Exide Technologies, a 2020 Chapter 11 filer. This company wasn't the best of neighbors. According to the state of California, Exide "spewed lead and other powerful neurotoxins throughout six Southeast Los Angeles communities for years, including onto schools, parks, and thousands of homes in working-class, primarily Latino neighborhoods." The federal government directed Exide to perform remediation work. When Exide stopped that work in spring 2020, it had the COVID-19 pandemic to blame. In May 2020, Exide filed for bankruptcy across the country in Delaware, with the intent to sell itself. No one wanted to buy the closed plant in Southeast Los Angeles. Exide used its bankruptcy to abandon the site and to release itself from responsibility for remediating the continued contamination. The U.S. Department of Justice, under the Trump administration, supported the plan, shifting the burden to California to minimize harm to the people of Southeast Los Angeles. A local elected official saw this move as "just another reminder that if you're brown and poor, you're disposable." [14]

When Congress overhauled corporate bankruptcy law in 1978 on a bipartisan basis, drafters knew how to signal when the Bankruptcy Code was supposed to override other laws and policies. They exercised considerable restraint in that regard. Even for companies that go through a traditional reorganization, the bankruptcy system is not a zone of insulation from core democratic, constitutional, and legal commitments. To return where we started in this chapter, it makes even less sense to allow enterprises to create a new type of Chapter 11, one where companies sell themselves quickly at lenders' and buyers' demand, overriding other health and welfare policies without the governance processes or the benefits associated with reorganization.

Arranged Marriages

Another perk of bankruptcy meant to promote corporate reorganization involves contract rights. Contracts shape much of modern life, and bankruptcy cases are crawling with them: leases of equipment or storefront properties, joint ventures, licensing of intellectual property, promises to build things or to sell goods, and much more.

Rights under contracts are valuable assets to a company—sometimes more valuable than anything else the company owns. If someone wants to buy a security guard company in bankruptcy, that person may be particularly interested in acquiring the contractual rights the debtor holds. Perhaps it has a contract to work at the Super Bowl, an issue I remember from the Chicago bankruptcy court. Contracts are messy, though. If the company has been struggling, parties to contracts with the company may dispute whether their contracts are still in effect and the cost required to bring the contract into compliance if the debtor already has breached the contract.

The Bankruptcy Code provides a powerful right to debtor companies when it comes to making decisions about these contracts. For many kinds of contracts, the debtor can *assign* its contract rights to a third party. That means the third party steps into the debtor's shoes and is legally obliged to perform the contract. Although there are some exceptions to this rule, particularly involving contracts for personal services, the power to assign contracts effectively forces the third party into a pact with a stranger, even though doing so might be impermissible under state law.[15]

Why would Congress give a bankrupt company these strong rights that are unavailable to companies under ordinary law? To facilitate reorganization, to benefit the entire bankruptcy estate and all the company's stakeholders. For example, a discount department store chain may hope to stay in business, but to do so it needs to limit its number of stores going forward. By essentially selling storefront leases it won't use, the discount chain might generate more money to stay in business.

Transferring a contract to a third party might be in the best economic interest of a bankruptcy estate even if a debtor cannot reorganize. But that can be hard to assess when a company says it needs to sell itself immediately and give the buyer the right to pick and choose among the contracts itself.

The entertainment firm the Weinstein Company was a party to tens of thousands of contracts, many relating to intellectual property from films and television. Those contract rights were the bulk of the firm's value. The private equity buyer, Lantern Capital, was permitted to make a binding commitment to buy the company and *then*, having boxed everyone else out, decide which bundles of contracts it wanted and how much it was willing to pay for them. By contrast, other bidders were required to identify "with particularity" which among the many contracts the buyers would assume and how the bidder would cure any defaults on those contracts. The preference given to Lantern not only reduced the ability of others to submit competitive bids but it also made it impossible to determine whether the delegation of contract decision-making to Lantern was in the best interest of the Weinstein Company bankruptcy estate. Given that bankruptcy law gave Lantern no duty to maximize the welfare of the Weinstein Company bankruptcy estate, one expects it pursued its own interests in making contract decisions.[16]

Trucking to the Supreme Court

Chapter 11 cases featuring quick sales can be hard to review on appeal. Yet, a case that unexpectedly made it up to, and got reversed by, the U.S. Supreme Court shows how regressive the deals made in these cases can be.[17]

The business was a trucking company in New Jersey named Jevic. The company had its share of ups and downs, and the original owner left to start a competing business. A private equity firm named Sun Capital Partners borrowed money from the CIT Group to buy Jevic, and Jevic would be responsible to repay. In other words, Sun Capital didn't put its own money on the line. CIT made the loan (with lots of fees and interest), and the loans were secured by Jevic's assets. This transaction is known as a *leveraged buyout*. The leveraged buyout changed the risks of dealing with Jevic for other counterparties because the company was highly indebted and lacked the flexibility to adapt to changed circumstances.

Jevic could not pay the debts that Sun Capital and CIT had heaped on it, workout efforts failed, and in May 2008, Jevic told most of its employees to bid farewell to their jobs and health insurance. Had Jevic simply shut down, Sun Capital and CIT would have been vulnerable to lawsuits by Jevic's creditors and workers. Sun Capital and CIT needed a cleanup operation—more for themselves than for the deadish Jevic. The answer? Put Jevic into bankruptcy.[18]

Congress designed a particular type of bankruptcy case for a company in Jevic's situation (that is, dead). In a Chapter 7 case, the government watchdog, part of the U.S. Department of Justice, appoints a trustee to sell assets and pursue lawsuits as needed. Viable lawsuits against Sun Capital and CIT could have put as much as $100 million back into the pockets of Jevic's creditors, although bringing such lawsuits would be expensive (remember that the public does not fund such things). Sun Capital and CIT didn't want the government watchdog to appoint someone to poke around in their business, let alone to sue them.

As discussed in chapter 3, a Chapter 11 filing would permit Jevic's management to stay in charge even if the business had no chance of reorganization. And they could avoid the full-blown Chapter 11 process by saying they could only afford to sell the company on a fast track. They would use DIP loans and the sale process to extract the best parts of bankruptcy for themselves and limit the checks and balances.

CIT made a $60 million DIP loan to Jevic, with restricted use of the money. Could Jevic use the loan proceeds to file lawsuits to increase creditor returns? No! Could Jevic use the loan proceeds to award bonuses to executives Sun Capital put in place to run the (dead) company? Yes![19]

Because the case was a Chapter 11, the government watch-dog appointed a committee of creditors to participate more actively in the case. The committee quickly worked to get up to speed, including investigating prior transactions involving Sun Capital and CIT. In the meantime, Jevic was sold, with no creditor voting.[20]

The committee found enough evidence to file a lawsuit against CIT and Sun Capital based on the transactions that denuded the company. The lawsuits had sufficient merit to go forward, according to the presiding bankruptcy judge. But Sun Capital and CIT both planned to fight the suit at every turn and had the means to do so. Pursuing the lawsuit would there-fore be extra expensive, and the Jevic bankruptcy estate was hardly flush with cash.[21]

Eventually, in June 2012, Jevic, Sun Capital, CIT, and the creditors' committee announced a settlement. "Settlement" should mean that every affected party has agreed to the arrangement. But here, the parties to the settlement wanted to bind people who did *not* agree. The laid-off workers disagreed with the settlement because it provided them with nothing. Congress gave workers special status to be paid ahead of many other types of creditors in all types of bankruptcy cases; the right is supposed to be inviolable unless the workers consent to not being paid. Yet, the so-called settlement skipped over the workers and compensated lower-priority creditors instead.

This deal also purported to cut off their rights against third parties like Sun and CIT.[22]

Jevic explained that Sun Capital and CIT had offered a take-it-or-leave-it situation. If the court did not approve this deal, there would be no money to pay anyone—the lender, CIT, would have the right to take it all. When he approved the deal, the presiding bankruptcy judge observed that "the Code is not a suicide pact." Allowing for some money to be paid to some creditors seemed better than nothing.[23]

As a sign that no one predicted that this case was heading to the U.S. Supreme Court, as well as that bankruptcy judges have a lot of work on their plates, the presiding judge issued the ruling in open court and did not publish a formal written opinion. That's not unusual. What was unusual was that a trade association for corporate debt markets took an interest in this case. The trade association did not make a habit of defending workers. But if a so-called settlement could disregard the legal rights of workers, could it disregard the rights of lenders too? A prominent Washington, DC, law firm that represents that trade association agreed to represent Jevic's truckers pro bono (no fee), including trying to get the Supreme Court to take the case.

In 2017, nearly ten years after Jevic filed for bankruptcy, the Supreme Court held that the Jevic "settlement" violated the workers' legal rights and was invalid. Specifically, the Supreme

Court said the bankruptcy court did not have the power to enter an order rearranging the priority of claims set by the Bankruptcy Code unless affected parties consented to the rearrangement. This sounds like big news, but the impact may be limited. The decision outlawed *the exact maneuver* at issue in the case. The decision, authored by Justice Stephen Breyer, keeps the door open for other deviations if there is a credible argument that those deviations make all the creditors better off, even those who might complain.[24]

As such, Jevic is a speed bump but not a stop sign to unbundling the Chapter 11 package deal. And business bankruptcy lawyers are like Google Maps: when in a jam, they find another shortcut.

Congress built Chapter 11 with the hope that an overindebted company could stay in business if enough creditors signed on to the company's vision for restructuring its debts. Stakeholders were supposed to work together to sort things out and vote on the company's plan. If the company has no future, the government watchdog is supposed to appoint a trustee to step in. Using Chapter 11 for quick sales of companies turns this federal law into a platform for dealmaking among the most powerful parties, severing the law's perks (loans on preferential terms, overriding state law restrictions on contract decisions) from the reorganization objectives that justified them in the first place. Even though creditor payment is a central part of business bankruptcy law, too many people conflate the objective of maximizing value for the bankruptcy estate with showing that a bankruptcy case put *some* money back into *some* creditors' pockets.

The pressure cooker environment of a bankruptcy is not a great time for an on-the-spot evaluation of the efficiency or fairness of a proposal developed by self-interested parties. The rights and obligations in the integrated package were not intended to make Chapter 11 frictionless. They were supposed to be gateways to significant legal privileges.

If an enterprise wants to control all aspects of a transaction, it can do deals in a boardroom, enforced through contract law as needed. If investors want to change a national law, they know how to lobby Congress in the hope of swaying things their way. The dealmaking that powerful (and solvent!) parties seek in big Chapter 11 is the worst of both worlds. These parties want to coopt extraordinary bankruptcy powers for their private benefit, with potentially negative implications for other parties, and expect federal law and courts to back them up in doing so.

We will next turn to enterprises without overindebtedness on loans or other commercial obligations that use Chapter 11 to manage liability for various kinds of wrongdoing. Restructuring professionals are using bankruptcy as a legal Swiss Army knife. Inevitably, that expansion in usage takes the bankruptcy system into policy problems for which it has little training or preparation, such as the opioid crisis and longtime cover-ups of child sex abuse.

Chapter 11 cases driven by liability management affect an enormous number of people directly and indirectly. They alter the legal rights and remedies of ordinary individuals who made no intentional choice to be creditors. And, as we will see, these cases have been offering extraordinary legal protection to third parties who not only have refrained from filing for bankruptcy, but have some of the deepest pockets in the world.

6

From Overindebtedness to Liability Management

Close to midnight on a Sunday, OxyContin manufacturer Purdue Pharma filed its carefully planned Chapter 11 bankruptcy case in White Plains, New York. The company did not seek to restructure debt in a traditional sense because it did not have any. It owed nothing to lenders. It had a billion dollars in the bank. But profiting from the aggressive overprescription of high-dose opioids had run its course, and defending itself against lawsuits for its starring role in the opioid crisis was pricey. When Purdue Pharma brought its troubles to bankruptcy court on September 15, 2019, it sought a global resolution to all opioid-related civil litigation the company and its owners faced, including a firm cap on their liability.[1]

From the outset of its bankruptcy, Purdue Pharma's court

pleadings made Chapter 11 sound tailor-made for companies with no debt but flooded with accusations of hurting people. Yet, the drafters of Chapter 11 did not anticipate the bankruptcy system would be the forum for resolving a company's role in a public health crisis. Chapter 11 was designed for businesses burdened with commercial debts, to enable the company to rewrite repayment terms with the support of a majority of creditors. Under federal law, bankruptcy courts are not even authorized to hold trials on personal injury and wrongful death lawsuits.

On the other hand, the Bankruptcy Code opened the door to cases of this nature because it sweeps in many types of liabilities, including claims for personal injury, wrongful death, fraud, and unfair trade practices, all of which a case like Purdue Pharma implicates. Bankruptcy law considers all of them debts. It calls their holders creditors. Definitions of this breadth, coupled with letting companies stay in control of their Chapter 11 cases and not requiring insolvency as a condition of entry, increased the system's appeal to companies seeking to manage and limit liability for other legal problems far removed from borrowing too much money.

You know by now that bankruptcy's ultimate superpower is canceling obligations of the debtor. Can the bankruptcy filing of one person be used to cancel obligations of third parties that do not file for bankruptcy themselves? Doing so is essentially unthinkable in the kind of personal bankruptcy cases we studied earlier. Also recall the Chapter 11 of Ample Hills Creamery, after which its owners had to go through their own bankruptcy case. By contrast, the Purdue Pharma bankruptcy aimed to protect its wealthy owners, members of the Sackler family, from civil liability arising from their active leadership role in Purdue Pharma's profitable but disastrous expansion of the market for high-dosage opioids. Purdue Pharma framed this protection as part of an exchange. The Sacklers would give up ownership of the company and provide several billion dollars for opioid abatement and claimant compensation, among other details.[2]

To make this discussion more concrete, let's focus on Richard Sackler, a mastermind of flooding America with opioids for profit, portrayed by myriad actors on series like *Dopesick* and *Painkiller* and the show *Last Week Tonight with John Oliver.* If claimants are forced to terminate their rights against Richard Sackler, consider how his protection diverges from the treatment of individuals who seek bankruptcy relief that you learned about in chapter 1. Unlike Sylvia, Richard Sackler did not publicly disclose his disposable income and assets under penalty of perjury. He did not start handing over money to a trustee from the outset of the bankruptcy case, as Chapter 13 bankruptcy filers are expected to do. He expected relief long before completing the promised payments many years into the future. And the Purdue Pharma plan protected him even from civil liability for fraud and other wrongdoing.[3]

In or out of bankruptcy, I am free to make a deal with Richard Sackler that releases his alleged liability to me. But what if I do not consent to such a deal? Bankruptcy allows the majority of claimants to bind dissenters regarding the liability of Purdue Pharma, the debtor. Does majority rule apply to protecting Richard Sackler too?

On August 10, 2023, after decades of avoiding the question of third-party protections in Chapter 11, the Supreme Court halted implementation of the Purdue Pharma plan and agreed to examine the case. The request to intervene came from the Solicitor General of the United States, a high-ranking lawyer in the U.S. Department of Justice responsible for representing the United States before the Supreme Court. The Solicitor General agreed to do so at the request of the government watchdog for the bankruptcy system, the U.S. Trustee. Not to be outdone, Purdue Pharma and one wing of the Sackler family each would be represented in the Supreme Court by lawyers who served as Solicitors General of the United States during President George W. Bush's administration. Whatever positions these lawyers might have taken for the United States during that time, here they have signed on to argue for an expansive interpretation of federal bankruptcy law. Leading

up to the oral argument scheduled for December 4, 2023, the
Supreme Court docket filled with briefs of parties as well as
other people with opinions going every which way.[4]

To some people, Purdue Pharma's case is a baffling vehicle
for Supreme Court consideration of the legal issues at stake.
Families crushed by opioid addiction were unlikely to win lawsuits against Richard Sackler and others in his family, let alone
collect recovery from them. Theories under which Richard
Sackler is directly liable to individuals harmed by OxyContin
are not particularly well-tested (the bankruptcy had halted
the lawsuits, so we do not know how they would have come
out). Law firms would have to take big financial risks to pursue such lawsuits. States have more resources to pursue their
claims against the Sacklers, but all states dropped opposition
to the plan before the Supreme Court agreed to review this
case. Even if someone prevailed, enforcing judgments against
the Sacklers would face roadblocks. Family members set up
asset-protection trusts in places like the Bailiwick of Jersey in
the Channel Islands years before OxyContin came onto the
scene.

Given these circumstances, some people believe that extract-
ing a promise from the Sacklers to pay several billion dollars
in addition to nonfinancial concessions isn't a loophole for
the rich; it is, instead, a miracle. Two law firms representing

sixty thousand individuals harmed by OxyContin have told the Supreme Court that their clients support the Sackler-protecting plan, which has advantages for their clients over the civil justice system. Other families supporting the plan have filed a brief recounting the death of their children from overdoses from opioids prescribed for sickle cell anemia pain or an adolescent sports injury, and depletion of retirement funds on unsuccessful rehabilitation programs. Motivated to engage in substance abuse disorder advocacy, these families asked the Supreme Court to open the spigot to additional abatement resources by approving the Purdue Pharma plan.[5]

I respect claimants' ability to decide that supporting the Purdue Pharma plan, including its protection of the Sacklers, is right for them. They are entitled to make a contract to release Richard Sackler or anyone else from alleged responsibilities. The issue is how their assessments affect the rights of other grieving families against someone who is not bankrupt. Who gets to decide the fate of *your* legal rights, particularly when you have no seat at the negotiation table, and when you are not well acquainted with the people assigned to represent your interests there?

For example, Ellen Isaacs, whose son died of an opioid overdose, submitted a Supreme Court brief characterizing the Purdue Pharma plan as "special protection for billionaires" with unclean hands. At the very least, her brief contends, anyone who has profited from the Sacklers' acts should not get to keep their ill-gotten gains. Others opposed to the plan's protection of the Sacklers without their consent have held demonstrations and spoken to whoever will listen for years. Ed Bisch, a grieving father, has characterized the Purdue Pharma bankruptcy as a sweetheart deal for the Sacklers, although more often he simply calls it a scam.[6]

This dispute also is about the scope of coercive federal power. State law is the source of many allegations of Sackler wrongdoing. Should federal bankruptcy law have the capacity to terminate your legal rights against Richard Sackler when neither of you is bankrupt?

Since the outset of its bankruptcy, Purdue Pharma has told courts, and the world, that "bankruptcy is the only way to resolve the [opioid crisis] litigation rationally." What about the courts with actual responsibility, and the proper jurisdiction, to handle allegations against Purdue Pharma and the Sacklers? According to Purdue Pharma, "Case-by-case mass tort litigation of the type the Defendant Debtors currently face in the civil tort system is neither an efficient, nor an equitable, way to resolve their alleged liability." The presiding judge overseeing this bankruptcy seemed to agree, later calling the Purdue Pharma bankruptcy "a case about who should pay money, based upon claims, and whether that money is best used in a collective settlement, a collective proceeding, which is the very nature of bankruptcy." Phrased this way, bankruptcy sounds like a viable option to resolve all kinds of legal disputes that involve large numbers of people.[7]

Johnson & Johnson would like to be a beneficiary of that vision of Chapter 11. Having marketed talc-based products for decades as safe, Johnson & Johnson has been sued by tens of thousands of women with ovarian cancer and a smaller number of mesothelioma patients. Expecting more suits to come in the future, Johnson & Johnson created a special subsidiary, LTL Management LLC, to house the talc liabilities, hoping to use the Chapter 11 case of LTL to cap the entire corporate family's liability for talc-related cancer suits forever. Testifying under oath before the Senate Judiciary Committee, a top Johnson & Johnson executive said the company's circumstances demonstrated "a compelling need for uniform access to the unique tools afforded by bankruptcy." It essentially asked Congress to authorize use of Chapter 11 for profitable companies like Johnson & Johnson to limit liability for present and future product harm.[8]

Overriding the entire civil justice system is a lot to read into the Constitution's skinny little Bankruptcy Clause. It seems an especially big ask to protect deep-pocketed people, fake and real, that are not themselves bankruptcy filers and without the consent of all affected claimholders. How did it come to be that a system designed for corporate restructuring attracted enterprises and related parties seeking a very different type of intervention?

An asbestos company got the ball rolling in 1982.

The Magic Mineral

The heat resistance of asbestos made it seem ideal for insulation and other industrial products. Roof shingles, automobile parts, floor tiles, ironing board covers, soundproofing and insulation—asbestos was everywhere. Workers who made or used these products had heavy exposure to asbestos, day in and day out, for decades in factories or insulation installation sites or shipyards.[9]

Asbestos could lead to devastating disease, but establishing causation between a diagnosis and a particular asbestos source was anything but simple. Someone diagnosed with mesothelioma may have been exposed to asbestos from multiple sources, especially because the timeline from exposure to disease can extend for decades. Other illnesses caused by asbestos exposure could have come from, say, tobacco. And some asbestos-related diagnoses create minimal or no impairment.[10]

When people started suing asbestos manufacturers and suppliers in significant volume, courts relaxed legal rules to make these suits easier to bring and win. Alleged cover-ups and failure to warn people of the dangers of asbestos opened the door to punitive damages—large sums that companies' insurance policies would not cover. As companies settled with injured people to avoid bearing responsibility for those damages, lawsuits kept coming.[11]

Asbestos manufacturer and Fortune 500 company Johns Manville Corporation made history when it filed one of the first asbestos-focused Chapter 11 petitions in 1982 aiming to halt the lawsuits temporarily, and then forever. Manville contended that it would not be able to manage the waves of asbestos claims for decades to come, and its insurance companies hotly contested their own responsibility to pay. Chapter 11 was supposed to help save viable businesses and jobs, the company argued, so why not us? Notwithstanding objections that Manville was too well off for bankruptcy, it got to stay in Chapter 11.

The end game for the Manville bankruptcy was not merely to resolve existing claims of people already sick from asbestos, but to change the rights of people who discover they are sick from asbestos tomorrow, next month, next year, and for many decades to come. In other words, Manville tested the boundaries of the law in two big ways: a solvent company using bankruptcy for tort liability management, and altering the legal rights of people who could not participate in the bankruptcy case because they are not yet aware that asbestos harmed them.[12]

Prior to 1978, retrofitting bankruptcy law in these ways would have been impossible. The Bankruptcy Code changed the landscape because it broadened the type of liabilities that a bankruptcy could affect, including allegations of harm that had not yet resulted in a lawsuit, let alone in a judgment. The 1978 law also made it less onerous for a company to take the plunge into Chapter 11 in the first place. As discussed in earlier chapters, management did not have to hand over company control to an independent trustee appointed by the government. The company also did not have to prove, or even contend, it was insolvent.

Resolving the Manville bankruptcy was never going to be easy. Chapter 11 was new, and the application to large numbers of tort claims even newer. At the end of the day, though, the company's Chapter 11 plan created a new legal entity, structured as a trust, to be funded by stock in the reorganized company, proceeds from the company's insurance policies, and other assets. Around 95 percent of asbestos claimants who voted at all expressed support for the plan that promised to compensate claimants 100 percent of the value of their claims. The company paid a *future claims representative* to negotiate on behalf of unknown people who would become sick from asbestos in the future. Going forward, anyone hoping to collect from Manville on an asbestos-related claim would be directed to the trust (through a *channeling injunction*) rather than to the reorganized company or its insurers, a remedy the U.S. Court of Appeals for the Second Circuit upheld. Today, tomorrow, next month, next year, for decades to come. The goal of this case, and many to follow, was to relieve a reorganized company of responsibility for asbestos injuries in perpetuity.[13]

Take a moment to absorb the implications. Imagine you develop a severe illness from asbestos exposure. You learn that the company that made and marketed the product emerged from bankruptcy five years ago. You are now a *future claimant.* You are blocked from negotiating with the reorganized company or other protected parties directly and directed to seek recovery from a trust set up to compensate claimants under the protocols set by the approved Chapter 11 plan. You probably are not allowed to test your claim against the trust in the civil justice system, but even if you are permitted to have a day in certain courts, the terms of the approved plan limited the scope of recovery.

Manville was destined to invite the filing of more mass tort bankruptcy cases—asbestos and otherwise. Chapter 11 is a repeat-play business. If someone successfully pushes the envelope in a big case today, get ready for someone else to try it again tomorrow. *Manville* also prompted other asbestos bankruptcies because its payouts ended up so low, 100 percent prediction notwithstanding, that injured people sought to collect from other potential sources of asbestos exposure. Those companies, in turn, filed for bankruptcy.[14]

The Manville bankruptcy especially encouraged more asbestos bankruptcies after Congress enshrined many of the case's details into the Bankruptcy Code in 1994. Lobbied to ensure skittish investors of the legality of *Manville*, Congress added section 524(g) to the Bankruptcy Code. Section 524(g) made it official: companies could file a bankruptcy that would alter the legal rights of people diagnosed with mesothelioma or lung cancer ten, twenty, or more years in the future. Joining the twenty-five or so asbestos bankruptcies that preceded enactment of section 524(g), more than a hundred additional asbestos-related bankruptcies followed. Although the trusts are outgrowths of federal bankruptcy cases, they are privately managed by companies that specialize in such activities.[15]

When the National Bankruptcy Review Commission studied mass tort cases in the 1990s, a majority of the members supported allowing companies to include future claimants in their bankruptcies under limited circumstances. Yet Congress needed to step in, said the commission's Yellow-Pages-like final report. The asbestos bankruptcy authority Congress had enacted, section 524(g), did not go far enough to protect people who get sick in the future.

Also, the commission warned that companies should not construe bankruptcy as available any time they viewed bankruptcy as preferable to the civil justice system. A plan could include future claims only if financial threats to the enterprise were sufficiently dire and if there was enough of a track record from science and litigation to estimate or predict recoveries for the injured parties.[16]

Congress did not adopt these proposals, leaving enterprises free to continue to propose to cap liability, including for future claimants, without additional statutory safeguards. Most cases seek the appointment of one future claims representative—often a lawyer, typically selected by the debtor enterprise—to negotiate on behalf of a lifetime of disparate unknown clients. That appointment can be quite lucrative for representatives and the professionals they hire. But is it enough to protect your due process rights down the road?

Many companies that file asbestos bankruptcies propose plans that do not comply with section 524(g)'s details, but some also depart from its spirit. For example, section 524(g) reflects an expectation that an entire operating company will subject itself to the burdens and benefits of Chapter 11 to address asbestos liabilities. Such a bankruptcy would affect all types of creditors, which would share the pain of the restructuring process. However, profitable companies seeking to benefit from the tools of section 524(g) have cleaved a company's asbestos liabilities from its operating assets and ordinary debts. State law calls this transaction a *divisive merger.* After the divisive merger, the company sends the entity housing the asbestos liabilities into Chapter 11. The bankruptcy halts the pursuit of legal rights only of injured individuals, while the company continues to operate and pay commercial creditors in full outside of bankruptcy, without court oversight or application of bankruptcy rules. Koch Industries followed this path in a bankruptcy filed in 2017, but the tactic gained broader notoriety when Johnson & Johnson tried it for its talc claims.

The risk of these cases to future claimants is especially high because of the difficulty of predicting the volume and severity of future claims. The original Manville trust, which predicted 100 percent payment of valid claims, quickly became insolvent and had to be restructured. In 2021, the promised percentage payout was at 5.1 percent. The UNR trust, created by another of the earliest asbestos bankruptcies, predicted 17.2 percent recovery to injured people at the outset, was down to 1.1 percent by 2009, and thereafter had to ask for court permission to wind down the trust. The trusts established by many later asbestos bankruptcies have delivered similarly volatile payouts for identical diagnoses over time.[17]

The track record of asbestos trusts was sufficiently

underwhelming that Congress, with support from both sides of the aisle, came close to moving asbestos lawsuits out of the court system altogether. For example, the Fairness in Asbestos Injury Resolution Act, as introduced in 2005, would have created a regime to be overseen by the U.S. Department of Labor. Members of Congress worried that "none of the existing [bankruptcy] trusts pay claims at their full value," that injured parties were receiving "only pennies on the dollar," and that injured parties endured long waits for compensation. The lawmakers worried that too much recovery was directed to those with modest or no impairment from asbestos exposure (as well as lawyer and administrative costs), leaving too little for the most severe diagnoses. Other lawmakers' opposition to the FAIR Act suggested that the legislation borrowed too much from asbestos bankruptcies rather than too little. Although I do not always agree with congressional critiques of bankruptcy, as chapter 1 illustrated, concerns about the fairness and effectiveness of asbestos bankruptcy had a legitimate foundation.[18]

Manville helped chart Chapter 11's career in tort liability management, not limited to asbestos. Yet, *Manville* was a more conservative use of Chapter 11 to shield third parties than were other mass tort cases that followed. *Manville* channeled claimants and claims away from insurance companies that put policy proceeds into the trust. At least at the time, insurance companies were not accused of independent wrong-doing; they had to pay out under an insurance policy and they did. By contrast, the Purdue Pharma bankruptcy sought to shield the Sacklers from allegations of their own independent wrongdoing related to Purdue Pharma opioids.

To bridge the gap, let's turn to a case involving a hazardous birth control product.

"A Human Tragedy of Overwhelming Proportions"

A.H. Robins Company, a Fortune 500 company known for household staples like Robitussin, ChapStick and flea-and-tick pet collars, filed a Chapter 11 petition in Richmond, Virginia, in 1985. In so doing, A.H. Robins was the first big-name enterprise to try bankruptcy to manage non-asbestos mass tort liability, in this instance stemming from its venture into birth control.[19]

A.H. Robins entered this field by buying the Dalkon Shield intrauterine device and marketing it to doctors of many kinds as well as directly to women. The marketing was effective—the Dalkon Shield was implanted in about 2.2 million women around the world—but the device was not. The Dalkon Shield not only fell short on pregnancy prevention, but it triggered a host of medical problems, including inflammatory pelvic disease, ectopic pregnancies, uncontrolled bleeding, septic and

late-term spontaneous abortion, hysterectomies, loss of fertil-
ity, and death. A.H. Robins deflected responsibility to doctors and patients, suggesting the harms to patients arose from
sexual promiscuity and bad hygiene. It wrote to doctors to recommend removal of the device only when the television news
show *60 Minutes* was about to air a damning report about it.[20]

Over time, lawyers found evidence that the company actively
concealed harms of the product, as did members of the Robins family and the Aetna insurance company. That generated
more litigation activity, including a class action and a big punitive damages judgment in a Kansas case. The company's bankruptcy shortly followed.[21]

A.H. Robins had common ground with Manville. Neither
would have been an obvious Chapter 11 candidate to the
drafters of the 1978 Bankruptcy Code. Their solvency sub-
jected them to allegations that their bankruptcies were inap-
propriate (in *A.H. Robins*, an unsuccessful request to dismiss
the bankruptcy case came from the National Women's Health
Network). The Chapter 11 cases of both companies resulted in
trusts from which injured parties could request compensation
going forward.[22]

But *A.H. Robins* differed from *Manville* in a key respect:
A.H. Robins's Chapter 11 plan, confirmed by a court in 1988,
gave the equivalent of a discharge to members of the Robins
family, Aetna, and others. That insulation did not depend on

claimants' consent, and it was granted notwithstanding credible allegations that these third parties had committed independent wrongs. The fine print of the A.H. Robins plan bans claimants from suing anyone for personal injuries caused by the Dalkon Shield, even doctors for medical malpractice. The Robins family contributed about $10 million to the fund to compensate injured women. But the family also received stock worth several hundred million dollars, tax free, when the A.H. Robins plan went into effect and the company was sold. These details are not evident from the decision of the U.S. Court of Appeals for the Fourth Circuit to uphold the plan's protection of third parties. The Fourth Circuit cited the Second Circuit's approval in *Manville*, even though the scope and the mechanism of protection in the A.H. Robins plan was quite distinct. Unlike *Manville*, which focused on protecting the proceeds of an insurance policy, *A.H. Robins* essentially canceled the liability of the Robins family and others for allegations of their own wrongdoing. The endorsement of the insulation of third parties in *A.H. Robins*, including wealthy owners accused of wrongdoing, would itself have a long tail.[23]

Securities Fraud?

Companies might find bankruptcy appealing to manage lawsuits and cap liability stemming from harms other than

personal injury. That became relevant in a bankruptcy arising from a securities fraud controversy. The efforts of banker
Michael Milken made Drexel Burnham Lambert one of the
most profitable investment firms in history, until it wasn't.
Securities fraud allegations and the collapse of the high-yield
bond market (sometimes called junk bonds), coupled with
pressure from the Securities and Exchange Commission and
the Federal Reserve Bank of New York, sent the firm into
Chapter 11. As in all bankruptcy filings, the company immediately was shielded from lawsuits. Due to other orders entered
by the court, non-debtors would also get a temporary shield,
putting further pressure on claimants to negotiate a deal.[24]

Courts called the result of those negotiations a settlement, in
part because it resolved a class action, but the term is a misno-
mer when its end game is to change the legal rights of people
who were not in the room for the dealmaking and who did not
consent to the deal. Drexel Burnham Lambert's Chapter 11
plan canceled personal liability for many key players, including Milken. Again, that liability shield changed the legal rights
of claimants who had not consented to release Milken and
others from their independent liability. Milken made financial
contributions to be used for creditor repayment, but like the
Robins family he retained considerable wealth, much of which
was in trusts held in his family's name. The district court that

approved the Drexel Burnham Lambert plan cited *A.H. Robins* as well as *Manville*.[25]

In reviewing the Drexel Burnham Lambert resolution, the U.S. Court of Appeals for the Second Circuit, which decades later will have to rule on *Purdue Pharma*, conveyed that third-party liability shields were no big deal, perhaps the cost of doing business when parties are negotiating disputes of such complexity. Devoting little more than a paragraph to the issue, the court cited *A.H. Robins* for the proposition that protecting third parties without claimant consent was okay if that protection played an important part in the debtor's reorganization plan. The court noted that parties would have been less likely to settle related disputes without getting this umbrella of protection. The concept of third-party protections being part and parcel of intersecting agreements, and of unlocking more value for claimants, will continue to grow.[26]

Hidden in the Fine Print

Although the circuit court decisions in *A.H. Robins* and *Drexel Burnham Lambert* may undervalue the significance of protecting non-debtors from unconsenting claimants, at least some constituencies in those cases discussed and agreed to those liability shields. The temptation to slip liability shields into the fine print of a plan without any negotiation looms large in a wide range of bankruptcies. I watched an example from the Continental Airlines bankruptcy play out when I served as a law clerk for the Honorable Marjorie O. Rendell on the Court of Appeals for the Third Circuit.

A Delaware bankruptcy court had confirmed Continental Airlines' Chapter 11 plan in 1993. The approved plan did more than adjust the relationship between Continental and its own creditors; it protected the company's directors and officers from their own independent liability in a shareholder class action. The protection was independent of claimholders' consent or any consideration in return. When claimholders asked a federal district court to review the bankruptcy court's ruling, that court did not rule for over five years. When the district court finally issued an unpublished opinion, it upheld the plan.

Dissatisfied with the outcome, the claimholders asked the Third Circuit to review the case. Pointing to the calendar, Continental Airlines complained that it was too late. Among all that transpired over the many years the appeal was stuck in the district court—new trends in clothes and music, world events—Continental's restructuring plan had gone into effect. Under a court-made doctrine called *equitable mootness*, courts can decline to review the merits of an appeal if it seems too late to implement relief (one cannot unscramble an egg, courts sometimes say). Continental urged the Third Circuit to apply that doctrine to this case and dismiss the appeal. The Third Circuit forged ahead on the merits, however, and found the liability shield unlawful.

As Judge Rendell described the situation on behalf of the unanimous panel of three judges in 2000, "Plaintiffs, who have never had their day in court, have been forced to forfeit their claims against non-debtors with no consideration in return." Noting that the Bankruptcy Code contains no explicit authorization for terminating claims against third parties involuntarily but that other courts sometimes permit such plan provisions, the Third Circuit found that the Continental Airlines plan's terms were "legally and factually insupportable." The decision established no hard and firm rule on liability shields and instead identified principles to guide bankruptcy courts. If it were ever okay to use a Chapter 11 to protect third parties without claimant consent, a party seeking to include the liability shield would have to work much harder to justify it.[27]

The Third Circuit ruling was not the kind of full-throated endorsement some lawyers might have preferred—the court invalidated this particular liability shield, after all—but the court also did not slam the door shut on the concept. Lawyers cite *Continental Airlines* less for the specific ruling and more for its ruminations about what might be possible. Counterintuitively, Continental Airlines helped make lawyers comfortable that they could ask courts within the Third Circuit to approve liability shields, so long as lawyers were prepared to apply the standards discussed in *Continental Airlines* to the facts of their cases.

This tour of cases and circuit law could have been longer, but it would have led to the same place: lawyers have been able to credibly tell clients that, in some courts, it can be lawful not only to cap liability for alleged wrongdoing in a Chapter 11 bankruptcy but to shield people who are not filing for bankruptcy themselves. It seems not to matter that the protected non-debtors are solvent given that the filers may be solvent themselves. Circuit court decisions such as *Continental Airlines* warn that these protections should be rare and extraordinary, if they are used at all. But such warnings are a mere speed bump to lawyers with high-profile cases they are eager to characterize as extraordinary.

The Billion-Dollar Pill

In the words of addiction recovery advocate and author Ryan Hampton, "Purdue Pharma singlehandedly created a new generation of people with substance abuse disorder and caused the deaths of countless Americans." Since the Food and Drug Administration approved OxyContin in 1995, waves of litigation and government interventions, including a federal plea agreement in 2007, and advocacy by opioid survivor families, did not stop Purdue Pharma's relentless pursuit, directed by members of the Sackler family, to flood communities with high-dosage and addictive opioids. Sell, sell, sell: that was the company's instruction to the sales force about Oxycontin. The Sacklers moved from rich to the super-rich stratosphere. Responses to concerns about addiction and pill distribution followed the A.H. Robins playbook: blame the users.[28]

In 2017, the federal court system consolidated 2,200 opioid crisis–related lawsuits for pretrial management in a procedure known as *multidistrict litigation* (MDL). The suits spanned about two dozen defendants, including Purdue Pharma. The judiciary assigned this bundle of work to the Honorable Dan Polster, a life-tenured district judge in Cleveland, Ohio. The consolidated lawsuits shared a common allegation about the manufacturers of opioids: that they "grossly misrepresented the risks of long-term use of those drugs for persons with chronic pain" and that misrepresentation contributed to the "current opioid epidemic." This MDL procedure did not capture all existing opioid-related court actions because MDLs have no power to include *state* court lawsuits. Yet, voluntary collaboration and coordination with state courts was available even if coercive legal force was not.

Although it was no secret that Judge Polster aspired to

settle these lawsuits, trial preparation generated important information that could facilitate resolution. *Bellwether trials* are cases selected for their ability to educate all parties on the strength of the evidence and arguments. Those discoveries led to facts supporting allegations of independent Sackler wrongdoing, leading plaintiffs to add the Sacklers as named defendants to their lawsuits, such as for unfair trade practices and violating consumer protection laws (the Purdue Pharma bankruptcy will halt these suits so they reached no outcome). In any event, settlements with other big corporate defendants came out of this activity—with dollar amounts for opioid abatement much larger than the amount promised in Purdue Pharma's bankruptcy or any other bankruptcy to date.[29]

Purdue Pharma's response to the litigation was complicated by a family feud that divided members of the Sackler family into an "A side" and a "B side," with different opinions on strategy. A further wrinkle was the possibility that Purdue Pharma would sue members of the Sackler family because, from 2008 through 2019, the Sackler family and entities they control took more than $10 billion in cash out of the company (some of which was to pay taxes on Purdue Pharma income), plus an additional $1.4 billion in other benefits and noncash assets."[30]

Notwithstanding these rifts, Purdue Pharma and the two

camps of Sacklers were united in the goal of putting legal responsibility for the opioid crisis behind them once and for all. Purdue Pharma anticipated less risk from future claims than in many previous mass tort bankruptcies, especially the asbestos cases, but otherwise drew on many of those cases' lessons. Purdue Pharma went into bankruptcy with a detailed vision of the objectives plus representations of support from at least twenty-four state attorneys general plus lawyers in leadership roles for claimants in the Ohio MDL. The ownership of Purdue Pharma would be transferred and a mechanism would be established to compensate claimants and for opioid abatement. The Sackler family would contribute funds over time that would be used for opioid abatement and some compensation for individuals and families. The Sacklers would receive protection not only from the claims Purdue Pharma had held against it for taking company money but also from civil opioid-related liability, whether or not holders of those claims consented. The Sacklers would retain substantial personal wealth, the origin of much of it being the overpromotion of opioids.[31]

The Sacklers' chance of comprehensive protection was partly a function of geography. Although bankruptcy law is national, choice of court shapes how cases unfold. Federal law gives big businesses far more latitude on where they can file for bankruptcy than it gives plaintiffs initiating ordinary civil lawsuits.

The most well-advised companies can pick their bankruptcy court, and Purdue Pharma and each wing of the Sackler family were nothing if not well-advised. After companies facing widespread lawsuits engage in a first level of forum shopping by opting out of the civil justice system and into bankruptcy, they inevitably do a second round to select the best bankruptcy venue.

In some parts of the country and courts, comprehensive protection of the Sacklers against nonconsenting claimants would have been hard if not impossible to achieve. Purdue Pharma also sought a particular judicial philosophy about the function and scope of bankruptcy. To prepare further for the case, therefore, Purdue Pharma moved its registered corporate agent to rented space in White Plains, New York. A small city to the north of Manhattan and part of the Southern District of New York, White Plains had just one bankruptcy judge. At the time Purdue Pharma was considering where to file for bankruptcy, it was possible to select White Plains knowing that the resident judge would preside absent a conflict.[32]

With only one judge to study, the company and its lawyers could plan their most effective arguments rather than consider a menu of contingencies. By filing in White Plains, Purdue Pharma had selected a judge whose actions reflected the belief that pushing for a comprehensive resolution to Purdue Pharma's role in the opioid crisis was part of the job of the court. For the situation in which Purdue Pharma found itself, that had to be a material consideration.

It is an understatement to say that a lot happened between the Chapter 11 filing on September 15, 2019, and the bankruptcy court's approval of Purdue Pharma's plan on September 17, 2021. Although I listened to nearly all of the hearings and monitored the docket throughout the case, most of the underlying work on big bankruptcies occurs behind the scenes, out of public view. In Purdue Pharma, representatives for various constituencies had to work through issues at an intricate level of detail. Given the enormity of the opioid crisis and the scope of its harm, anything Purdue Pharma and the Sacklers could offer, monetarily and otherwise, would be too little, too late. How to allocate the money among states, local governments, and devastated families? What about other companies (pharmacies, drug distributors) implicated in the crisis but holding claims of their own against Purdue Pharma? How much for all the lawyers? Dividing up the pie would be principally negotiated by representatives of these claimant groups rather than by Purdue Pharma and the Sacklers. These responsibilities included determining how to set up trusts to compensate claimants and how to structure opioid abatement obligations. Constituencies tried to come together on the details of an emergency relief fund for opioid claimants (they could not). Ultimately, individual claimants ended up with a much smaller share of recovery than the abatement funds allocated to governments. Lawyers doing bankruptcy, insurance, and personal injury work stood to collect more than injured individuals and families.[33]

Although the negotiations included representatives of a variety of constituencies, they had a restricted guest list. You had to be invited. The official creditors' committee was heavily involved and had a duty to look out for the interests of all unsecured creditors, a category that included but was not limited to individuals harmed by OxyContin. That committee could not bind individual claimants, however. It could commit only itself, such as promising to recommend the plan to claimants and to refrain from challenging arguments of the debtor or other plan supporters.

As negotiations progressed, but still more slowly than Purdue Pharma preferred, the company's lead lawyer wondered aloud if the public health protocols associated with COVID-19 had hindered their progress—not because of illness but because it shifted the levers of resolution: "With no ability to be dragooned and stared down by mediators and forced to stay until two in the morning, I believe we need some external help pressurizing this phase of the mediation so we can go on to the next phase." More settlements with states followed after the requested in-person marathon negotiations.[34]

Several early decisions of the court increased pressure on

constituencies to drop their strenuous objections. The filing of a bankruptcy halts most actions against a debtor and the debtor's property (the *automatic stay*), but the court expanded this protection in material respects. First, the court granted Purdue Pharma's request to halt all litigation against the Sacklers. To address the concern that litigation might have generated more information through the trial preparation process, the court required that the Sacklers provide information, albeit only to parties that signed nondisclosure agreements.[35]

Second, the court agreed to stop all government activities against the company even if those activities qualified for an exception to the automatic stay for public health and welfare activities. This exception exists because businesses are not supposed to use bankruptcy to evade regulatory oversight. Businesses are permitted to present evidence that government activity does not fit the exception because the action is more about money than protecting the public. (Contrast this procedure with the treatment of government penalties in individual bankruptcy cases discussed earlier, where even parking tickets or fines for an overgrown lawn are given special treatment and cannot be canceled.)

Noting the inefficiency of the typical process because Purdue Pharma and the Sacklers were being investigated by so many, Purdue Pharma did not present evidence and arguments about the nature of government activity. It asked the court to *block it all*, except for actions by the Trump administration Justice Department. In exchange, Purdue Pharma offered to be monitored by a high-profile public figure and to refrain from marketing opioids. In other words, Purdue Pharma got to develop a private substitute for the law that Congress wrote. Even if the debtor and co-defendants make voluntary concessions to alleviate concerns about ongoing harm, those actions do not make the granting of extra injunctions any less significant an exercise of federal court power. As is often the case, Purdue Pharma presented its requests as pragmatic resolutions and the consequences of denial of its requires dire. If it did not get the full umbrella of protection it sought, Purdue Pharma warned, the company—"and their prospects of successful reorganization—will suffer crushing and irreparable injury." [36]

In effect from the fall of 2019 through 2023 via many extensions, these court orders prevented both governments and individuals from exercising legal rights against the company and the Sacklers. In so doing, those orders increased the odds that the Purdue Pharma bankruptcy strategy would be effective. After all, objectors had no idea if and when they would be able to continue pursuing Purdue Pharma and the Sackler family. The presiding judge made clear during court hearings and written orders that it expected parties to negotiate for a comprehensive resolution to these disputes and expressed frustration toward some parties when they expressed concerns about the process.

Pressure to drop objections also came from a settlement between Purdue Pharma and the U.S. Department of Justice during the late days of the Trump administration. As had occurred in 2007, Purdue Pharma admitted to wrongful conduct and no charges were brought against the Sacklers. The agreement stipulated that the United States held a $2 billion claim that would be entitled to the highest possible priority under bankruptcy law. If the bankruptcy court approved a plan structured like Purdue Pharma had proposed, however, the United States would stand down and allow more of the money to be used for opioid abatement. The agreement suggests a threat: failure to confirm the Purdue Pharma plan would dramatically reduce the resources available for opioid abatement.[37]

To announce approval of the plan, on September 17, 2021, in White Plains, New York, the Honorable Robert Drain spoke for six hours straight. He published a written opinion thereafter to explain his ruling in a case he posited might be the most complex Chapter 11 in history. The opinion expressed frustration and disappointment that the Sacklers did not contribute more money, but Purdue Pharma met its burden to prove that the plan met the legal standards. Claimants were well represented in negotiations, Judge Drain found, and their representatives drove hard bargains. The plan would generate several billion dollars for opioid abatement over time and compensation for other claimants, plus a public repository of data (which the Department of Justice settlement required in any event).[38]

The Sacklers' ability to dodge liability and shield wealth from any coercive collection process seemed to play a big role in the court's analysis. Even if claimants were permitted to chase the Sacklers around the world, Judge Drain worried they would recover less than the plan provided. If the court denied approval of the plan, opioid abatement funds could disappear.[39]

The written decision also emphasizes the high level of creditor support for the plan, measured by settlements and voting. By the time the debtor presented the plan for confirmation, the number of states opposed to the plan had been whittled down to nine, plus the District of Columbia. As for individual personal injury and wrongful claimants, over 58,000 of those who voted did so in favor of the plan, while slightly over two thousand people voted to reject the plan. That comes out to an over 95 percent acceptance rate among those who voted (bankruptcy law does not count the tens of thousands of individuals who held claims and did not vote). The ruling does not dwell on people who voted against the plan without filing detailed objections or the large number of claimants of all types that did not cast a vote either way but nonetheless would be bound.[40]

Although the bankruptcy court's decision cited and applied the expected case law, the Honorable Colleen McMahon of the district court found a problem when she was asked to review the decision on appeal: nothing in the Bankruptcy Code authorizes such comprehensive protection of the Sacklers (or the Robins or Milken families, for that matter). Scouring the statute and appellate decisions and coming up empty, the district court reversed the ruling of the bankruptcy court and held the plan's protection of the Sacklers from their independent liability was unlawful with respect to people who did not consent to release them. Unless Purdue Pharma and other supporters could persuade the Second Circuit to say otherwise, Purdue Pharma could not implement this plan.[41]

Judge McMahon's significant ruling sparked another round of confidential negotiations between the objecting states and the plan supporters. By March 2022, all of the remaining states and the District of Columbia settled with Purdue Pharma and the Sackler family. The Sacklers increased their financial contribution to opioid abatement, although they also extended the payout period to eighteen years. Members of the Sackler family also agreed to attend a virtual court hearing at which twenty-six individuals and families spoke.[42]

The U.S. Court of Appeals for the Second Circuit heard oral argument shortly thereafter, but did not issue a ruling for over a year. When the Second Circuit finally ruled, it held the plan's liability shield for the Sacklers was lawful. Although Chapter 11 plans could not always or automatically include liability shields, the Second Circuit explained, courts had the authority to approve such terms in appropriate circumstances so long as a life-tenured judge like a district court signed off on the plan too.

How did the Second Circuit answer Judge McMahon's question about legal authority? The opinion cited two provisions of the Bankruptcy Code. The first provision, section 105, says that "the court may issue any order, process, or judgment that is necessary or appropriate to carry out the provisions of this title." To answer the question of what provision is being carried out, the court cited a sentence in Chapter 11, section 1123(b)(6). Here is what it says: "A plan may . . . include any other appropriate provision not inconsistent with the applicable provisions of this title." [43]

One of the three judges on the Second Circuit panel, Judge Richard Wesley, wrote a separate decision to say he found these two generic provisions utterly inadequate to justify giving the Sacklers the extraordinary relief the Purdue Pharma plan afforded them. He also recognized how that relief differed from the *Manville* channeling injunction the Second Circuit approved once upon a time. But, said Judge Wesley, the ship sailed on this issue years ago. Remember Michael Milken? With scant discussion, the Second Circuit had approved the resolution of a class action and the bankruptcy of investment bank Drexel Burnham Lambert that released Milken and his colleagues of liability without unanimous consent of claimholders. That decision put the Second Circuit on the record allowing liability shields of this nature, and Judge Wesley felt bound to follow it. Noting the law was different in other circuits, Judge Wesley ended his concurring opinion by suggesting the need for a U.S. Supreme Court or congressional intervention.[44]

Judge Wesley's wish came true: the Supreme Court put the Purdue Pharma plan on hold until it could decide on its lawfulness. As glimpses at the outset of this chapter suggest, responses to the Supreme Court's intervention were decidedly mixed. Under the plan, $1.3 billion was to be disbursed immediately once the plan took effect, with the rest following over time. The plan cannot go into effect because the Supreme Court put the case on hold. That stopped the flow of Sackler money into opioid abatement as well as individual recoveries. Individual claimants and providers of abatement services had been ready to put that money to use. Others directly affected by the case cheered the Supreme Court intervention, whether or not they could have put the money to use. It is not for me to say what all claimants should prefer. The question for the Supreme Court, and for the legal system, is whether a settlement among some claimants with the Sacklers can bind everyone else through the vehicle of Purdue Pharma's federal bankruptcy case.

Liability Management for Child Sex Abuse

The U.S. Conference of Catholic Bishops was among the organizations with a sufficiently strong view about the Purdue Pharma bankruptcy to submit a brief to the U.S. Supreme Court. The bishops implored the Supreme Court to bless the Purdue Pharma bankruptcy, including its protection of the Sacklers. Why? So that dioceses could continue using Chapter 11 in response to allegations of child sex abuse. The organization referred to child sex abuse cases as "mission-crippling litigation."[45]

As manufacturers of asbestos, faulty birth control, and high-dose opioids have made bankruptcy a centerpiece of their liability management strategies, so too have nonprofit and religious institutions with long histories of child sex abuse. Bankruptcy law permits nonprofits, including religious organizations, to file for Chapter 11 bankruptcy. Unlike public municipalities, nonprofits and religious organizations do not have their own chapter of the Bankruptcy Code even though they differ from commercial enterprises in material respects.

Nonprofits receive tax-preferred treatment and must hold and honor goals of helping the public. They rely on donations as well as credit. They have no owners or shareholders.

Most religious organizations that have filed for bankruptcy have done so for the traditional reason: overindebtedness. They have unaffordable mortgage payments on real estate they are struggling to keep. They rent out subsets of their property to third parties that remain vacant for too long. They are reckoning with leadership that has resulted in the decline of revenues.[46]

Since 2004, more than thirty Catholic dioceses have used bankruptcy for an entirely different rationale: to manage and cap liability for decades of child sex abuse. Absent some intervention, that number is likely to grow as bankruptcy becomes a stock response to state legislatures' efforts to give the proverbial day in court to adult survivors of child sex abuse. The Archdiocese of Boston is thought to be the first to publicly consider bankruptcy after a now-famous *Boston Globe* investigation, although it never filed. As the Supreme Court brief of the Catholic bishops indicates, they use these cases not only to protect the entity that files but related parties that might also share responsibility and insurance policies.

Following the path of the dioceses, USA Gymnastics filed Chapter 11 in Indianapolis on December 5, 2018. A not-for-profit entity lacking the religious complexities and constitutional arguments of a diocese, USA Gymnastics is the governing body for gymnastics in America. Over 350 gymnasts had sued USA Gymnastics arising from sexual abuse, largely for failures of the organization in connection to Larry Nassar, who served as a volunteer physician for the organization and is in prison for life.

After four years of the USA Gymnastics bankruptcy halting pursuit of other remedies, the organization's confirmed plan provided $380 million in a compensation fund, mostly provided by insurance policies, and a renewed commitment to athlete protection. But it also permanently shielded the non-bankrupt U.S. Olympic Committee, among others, for its own liability relating to these abuses, and the plan blocks punitive damages against all protected parties. As lawyer, former gymnast, and abuse survivor Tasha Schwikert Moser testified to Congress leading up to that outcome, "I thought it was unfair and unconstitutional. I thought it was unfair because, without my consent, a bankruptcy court could take away my claims against an organization that has not declared bankruptcy . . . without a jury trial, without my consent, and without the right to opt out of a bankruptcy plan." She said that bankruptcy "has felt like a giant black hole of truth and accountability against non-bankrupt entities in many ways." [47]

The Boy Scouts of America took to a whole new level the combination of child sex abuse, bankruptcy, and third-party protection. "Never before," said the Boy Scouts, "has a congressionally chartered non-profit corporation with a nationwide mission affecting millions of Americans sought the protection of a bankruptcy court." The cost of trying to resolve these matters through the bankruptcy system, in legal and financial fees alone, would be "staggering." The Boy Scouts would shell out at least $250 million to lawyers and financial advisors for bankruptcy- and insurance-related work leading up to court approval of the plan, before accounting for attorneys' cut of survivors' eventual recoveries.[48]

Whereas USA Gymnastics and some dioceses have used their bankruptcies and the resulting pause on litigation as leverage in negotiations with several hundred claimants in each case, the Boy Scouts of America bankruptcy would change the rights of a much larger number of child sex abuse survivors. Eighty-two thousand people filed paperwork alleging abuse in scouting. Although the Boy Scouts initially reported that most allegations were at least thirty years old, a significant proportion of survivors, around 18,000, reported incidents in the decade prior to the bankruptcy filing. Because some people were likely not ready to come forward about child sex abuse, that figure almost certainly is an undercount.[49]

The Boy Scouts of America is headquartered in Irving, Texas, but the nonprofit chose Delaware for its Chapter 11. The enterprise did so by creating a new nonprofit corporation in

Delaware and opening a bank account there in 2019. That tiny subsidiary, with zero debt and under $10,000 in assets, filed for Chapter 11 on February 18, 2020. As federal law permits, the national organization followed its new subsidiary into that venue. No parties asked to move the case.

At the first bankruptcy court hearing two days later, the Boy Scouts of America conveyed that scouting had a bright future if only the organization could put child sexual abuse liability behind it. The Boy Scouts wanted closure not only for its national organization that filed for bankruptcy, but also for its local councils and chartered organizations that were not in bankruptcy. The national organization was not on the front lines, so to speak, of scouting activities, or the source of most of its assets, or even the primary defendant in all of the lawsuits. The Boy Scouts delegated employee and volunteer training and oversight to several hundred local councils, each of which held variable amounts of assets. Local councils would be seeking protection from the main Boy Scouts case. This objective almost certainly played a role in filing for bankruptcy in Delaware rather than Texas.[50]

Local councils recruited over forty thousand organizations that chartered troops, such as national guard and military regiments, schools, synagogues, the Lions Club and Kiwanis Club, police and fire departments, community centers, and lots and lots of churches. Chartered organizations in turn recruited and vetted troop leaders and volunteers. Local councils and chartered organizations may have more culpability for their abuse and insufficient institutional responses than the national organization has, and the grounds for their potential liability might be different.[51]

Lengthy negotiations and financial contributions from third parties notwithstanding, the Boy Scouts of America initially was unable to attract sufficient numbers of survivors to support its plan. The official committee of survivors, appointed by the government watchdog, had recommended that claimants reject the plan. The committee warned that survivors might recover less than 10 percent of their claims. The committee also pointed out that contributions from local councils, chartered organizations, and insurance companies were too small relative to the legal protection those entities would receive.[52]

The survivors' committee eventually settled with the Boy Scouts of America after negotiating for stronger youth protection and to strengthen the independence of the parties that would run the trust that handled survivors' recoveries. The committee thus moved from objector to plan supporter. The Boy Scouts also were able to reach an agreement with several insurance companies to secure their contributions to the compensation fund. During this time, the Boy Scouts offered a new assertion: under this plan, survivors would recover 100 percent of their claims. To get there, its expert witness revised downward his estimate of the value of abuse claims. In the second round of voting, support by survivors grew to exceed 85 percent of those casting any vote.[53]

On July 29, 2022, applying the evidence presented in a twenty-two-day trial, the bankruptcy court approved the Boy Scouts of America bankruptcy plan, albeit with some changes required. The courts' approval included most of the requested liability shields for a long list of the local councils and a somewhat more complicated set of protections for chartered organizations (the plan had not proposed to protect individual abuse perpetrators). The court also described in detail and accepted the only evidence presented at the trial on the aggregate value of abuse claims, evidence that was central to the prediction of payment in full to survivors.[54]

When the district court in Delaware reviewed the bankruptcy court's ruling, it upheld the bankruptcy court's detailed decision in all respects, including the liability shields. That ruling cleared the way for the Boy Scouts of America plan to go into effect on April 19, 2023. The trust created by the Boy Scouts bankruptcy is predicted to be in operation for decades.[55]

In their plea to the U.S. Supreme Court to uphold the Purdue Pharma bankruptcy, members of the Sackler family, represented by former Solicitor General Paul Clement, sought to assure the high court that using Chapter 11 to tackle a company's role in the opioid crisis was fully in the legal main-stream. The brief referred to bankruptcy as "a tool that bank-ruptcy courts have historically employed to efficiently and fairly resolve mass tort litigation that would otherwise destroy value for debtors and creditors alike." A group of governments supporting the plan went further, stating that "almost every mass tort crisis of the last 30 years—Dalkon Shield, breast implants, Boy Scouts, Dioceses cases, to name a few—has been resolved through bankruptcy plans." The accuracy of this "almost every" assertion depends on your definition of a crisis; at least for now, most mass tort matters are processed outside of bankruptcy, including the bulk of opioid crisis liti-gation. Yet, to the extent that "too many lawsuits" becomes a sufficient basis for Chapter 11 eligibility, enterprises accused of wrongdoing can use the threat of bankruptcy as leverage in negotiations in all mass tort contexts.[56]

Even if bankruptcy has not yet captured the market for mass tort resolutions, what has transpired since the 1980s is remarkable. A system designed for reorganizing businesses seeking to change the terms of their loans and other contracts is now routinely characterized as a natural forum to resolve lawsuits stemming from hazardous products and failed organi-zational responses to child sex abuse. Lawyers who specialize in bankruptcy have marketed the system's power tools—the automatic stay, the ability to change people's rights without consent, cancellation of legal obligations—to enterprises with the thorniest of legal problems that are not fundamentally about money.

Assertions of the suitability, and indeed greatness, of bankruptcy for mass tort problems rarely are accompanied with details about the actual treatment of injured people during bankruptcy cases and in their dealings with the private trusts that these bankruptcy cases establish. Supporters of mass tort bankruptcies might cite aggregate dollar amounts contributed to trusts but not how that money was spent or how long it took for people to recover. A benign explanation would be that bankruptcy experts focus on the "mass" in mass torts. A more cynical explanation might be that the details are uninspiring—both in terms of the money and the overall experiences of injured people and survivors of child sex abuse who find themselves creditors in bankruptcy cases. Some things that go awry might have transpired in other dispute resolution systems, but bankruptcy dramatically changed the consequences. Chapter 7 takes up these issues.

7

Beyond the Victory Lap

Although it owed billions of dollars to lenders like the typical big company in Chapter 11, the Irish pharmaceutical company and generic opioid manufacturer Mallinckrodt PLC had a lot in common with OxyContin maker Purdue Pharma. Mallinckrodt was a defendant in several thousand lawsuits relating to the opioid crisis. When Mallinckrodt filed for Chapter 11 in Delaware on October 12, 2020, it had lined up substantial backing for a restructuring plan. Negotiations ensued, constituencies entered settlements, and the great majority of opioid claimants who cast a vote on the plan supported it.

The bankruptcy court approved the plan creating a trust to compensate opioid claimants in February 2022. The plan bound and offered compensation not only to people already holding opioid claims but to people who would experience harm in the future based on earlier opioid use. In addition to permanently altering Mallinckrodt's obligations, the company's plan included liability shields of a "vast" number of third parties—the bankruptcy court's term, not mine—without the consent of all claimants. Overriding objections, the court held the liability shields were integral to the success of Mallinckrodt's plan, among other requisite findings. The court noted the urgency of distributing money to people suffering from opioid addiction using "a well-funded trust" as soon as possible; time was of the essence. Mallinckrodt had committed to fund the trust with $1.725 billion. Implementation of the plan started in June 2022.[1]

Just a year later, still owing the opioid trust $1.2 billion, Mallinckrodt was in financial trouble, its hedge fund lenders circling. There was talk of a second Chapter 11 filing. Might the opioid claimants be willing to take just $200 or $300 million more and call it a day?[2]

The looming default notwithstanding, Mallinckrodt paid several millions of dollars in bonuses to executives, just like it did on the eve of its first bankruptcy. Meanwhile, Mallinckrodt's shareholders filed a class action lawsuit, alleging the company made false and misleading statements about its financial health.[3]

On August 28, 2023, Mallinckrodt filed a second Chapter 11 bankruptcy, reporting a deal with its lenders and with the trust responsible for compensating opioid claimants.

Forget the $1.2 billion. The trust would accept cash payment of $250 million as the company's final contribution. The trust's lawyer described this result as "gruesome" even as he announced the deal was done. Opioid claimants had no claims or votes in this second case because the first bankruptcy canceled obligations to them. Ordinary commercial claims would get 100 percent of what the company owed them.[4]

Unlike Manville (the early asbestos case) or the Boy Scouts of America, Mallinckrodt had not predicted claimants would receive full payment. Mallinckrodt made and broke a blunter promise: to fund the trust to a certain money level.

It is an understatement to say bankruptcy cases prompted by hazardous products and child sex abuse are about more than money. But if bankruptcy lawyers are going to sell the system's ability to deliver value to injured people, let us kick the tires. To do so, one needs to look beyond approval of the plan itself. What happens next?

A Promise Is a Promise and Money Is Money, but a Promise to Pay Is Not Money

Mallinckrodt illustrates a basic truth that far transcends bankruptcy or any kind of law: people promise to do things and predict results that do not come true. One hopes that big enterprises that have paid top dollar for legal and financial advice have a better chance of predicting the near future fairly well, but those experts also get things wrong all the time. Again, these are background facts about the everyday world. Bankruptcy does not change them. Bankruptcy does, however, alter the consequences when the promises ring hollow.

When a court approves a Chapter 11 reorganization plan, it must make a finding that the plan is unlikely to be followed by liquidation or the need for subsequent reorganization. A feasibility finding is an element in all repayment plan chapters of the Bankruptcy Code. To satisfy the requirement in big Chapter 11 cases, a company typically presents evidence about its projected future financial circumstances. The depth of the feasibility inquiry at a plan confirmation hearing depends on whether anyone objects on this ground and presents competing evidence for the court to evaluate. Otherwise, the court may construe silence as support for the debtor's predictions, or at least willingness to take the risks associated with this plan. That's especially true in a big case where competing constituencies and committees have hired financial advisors of their own, albeit often at the expense of the bankruptcy estate.

The feasibility of the Mallinckrodt plan was only mildly contested at the plan confirmation hearing. One party (not an opioid claimant) pursued a narrow objection, and the court overruled it. The court accepted the testimony of the company's chief restructuring officer, mostly uncontested, that things were likely going to be fine.[5]

Eighteen months later, things were not fine.

Unfulfilled predictions are not uncommon in any kind of bankruptcy, but the stakes diverge depending on the type of case. The Bankruptcy Code requires that approval of every Chapter 13 plan for individuals is accompanied by a finding that the debtor will be able to make all of the payments. Debt relief for individual Chapter 13 filers is deferred until plan completion, rather than granted at plan confirmation. If a case falters and gets dismissed, creditors resume their legal relationship with the debtor as before, including collection and enforcement.

By contrast, Congress front-loaded debt relief for Mallinckrodt and other fake people in Chapter 11. Plan confirmation terminated the original legal rights of unsecured creditors, including opioid claimants. The company's admission that it cannot honor its promises to fund the trust to compensate opioid claimants does not make claimants' legal rights spring back to life unless a plan expressly provides such a remedy. And once lawyers and financial professionals receive top dollar for their services, they are unlikely to offer a refund.

Lawyers tout Chapter 11's comprehensive finality for mass tort problems. They suggest finality translates into enhanced claimant compensation, an association that sounds theoretically promising even if it lacks systematic empirical support. Yet, Chapter 11's finality operates in one direction. One needs granular information to assess whether these cases resolve mass tort liability as rationally and equitably as bankruptcy lawyers routinely assert. Mass tort bankruptcies and the resulting trusts are not as transparent as they could and should be and that makes it harder for non-insiders to figure it all out. Even if an enterprise predicts payment in full, it typically makes no guarantees. Unless a plan establishes otherwise, claimants have no right to go back to the debtor or another third party if the trust cannot pay a claim to the predicted level, and third parties do not have the obligation to put in more money.[6]

Some claimants may be untroubled by one-way finality because they never would have pursued a remedy in the civil justice system. Perhaps their injuries are mild. Maybe they don't have strong proof that the debtor harmed them. In that situation, the potential for any recovery from the company's bankruptcy is a low-cost lottery ticket. Severely injured parties may have carefully developed lawsuits that were ready to be tried in the civil justice system, with strong evidence of the defendants' culpability. People in this camp have much more at stake when their attempt to reassert control over their lives gets superseded by instructions to resolve their legal disputes in a Chapter 11 in a distant federal bankruptcy court.

As we will see throughout this chapter, debtor enterprises often have an incentive to treat claimants all along the spectrum of severity as interchangeable for purposes of negotiations and voting. Debtors also have an incentive to find and make deals with lawyers who can recruit and represent people with little to lose by supporting a deal that caps liability through bankruptcy.

Chapter 11 plans can and do fail to deliver what they promise for many reasons. Professor Lynn LoPucki's database of large publicly held companies that filed Chapter 11 between 1982 and 2022 tracked whether companies refiled within five years after emerging from the first case. Of the 696 large public companies that filed for Chapter 11 between 1982 and 2016, 117 had refiled. In each case, companies had presented evidence that they were not likely to need further restructuring.[7]

Public company bankruptcies that identify a mass tort or related problem have a lower rate of refiling in five years, not controlling for other variables. But in cases that channel injured people to trusts after a bankruptcy, the key issue typically is the viability of the trust, separate from survival of the reorganized company. Although Manville, the early asbestos bankruptcy filer, was solvent when it filed for Chapter 11, the trust it created to compensate injured people quickly went broke. Manville did not file a second Chapter 11 petition. Its trust got restructured in federal court and claimants received much-reduced compensation relative to the company's rosy projections. Highly variable payouts have been common among asbestos trusts, with percentage payouts dipping into the single digits. This inequality of compensation among similar claimants not only falls short on promises—it undercuts the main justification of letting enterprises use the extraordinary tools of bankruptcy for mass tort problems in the first place.[8]

All Chapter 11 mass tort bankruptcy debtors must allege their plans are feasible, but only some predict they will pay claimants in full. Promising the trust will be able to pay in full can help persuade claimants to support a plan, and likely increases a court's comfort in approving it, especially if the plan contains liability shields that terminate claimants' rights against third parties and binds future claimants.

When the Boy Scouts of America offered expert testimony at its plan confirmation hearing that survivors would be paid in full, no party offered an alternative expert or other type of evidence. Silence stemmed from a deal among plan supporters, not from agreement on the prediction. An expert hired by the survivors' committee had predicted the total value of abuse claims to be *ten times* greater than the figure the Boy Scouts' expert presented at the confirmation hearing. Once the committee had become a supporter of the plan, which had incorporated enhanced youth protection protocols and other nonmonetary objectives, the committee agreed not to challenge the predicted recovery. If the committee did so, survivors could lose the hard-fought improvements.[9]

It is not shocking that abuse claim estimates were so far apart. When someone borrows money from a bank, evidence relevant to the value of the obligation comes from the contract. When tens of thousands of people allege injuries that have not been adjudicated, the value is uncertain, especially if the track record of prior resolutions has been limited. An industry of experts is available for hire to predict the aggregate value of tort claims, present and future, against an enterprise. As the history of asbestos bankruptcies suggests, their predictions can miss the mark greatly when all is said and done. The complexity and error rate of valuing all future liability raises the stakes of using bankruptcy to permanently cap the responsibilities of a debtor and third parties.

In virtual town hall meetings, the retired judge overseeing the Boy Scouts of America trust as its trustee was candid with survivors: there was no guarantee they would receive full payment, or any particular percentage. And to avoid the fate of earlier asbestos trusts, the initial payments on survivors' allowed claims would likely be modest, however severe the abuse and consequences. As the trustee explained, the trust staff had not yet learned how many survivors would have allowable claims, the severity of abuse, and how the required aggravating and mitigating factors would apply. On the flip side, the trust's access to assets would come over time, not all at once. Contrast the trustee's straight talk with a nearly contemporaneous assertion by Boy Scouts of America to the U.S. Supreme Court to support Purdue Pharma's case and the legality of liability shields: "Notably, [Boy Scouts of America]'s plan will compensate *in full* all allowed claims of its abuse-survivor creditors." No qualifications offered.[10]

Implementation of the Boy Scouts of America trust helps identify other ways any enterprise's predictions might fall short in real life, at least from the perspective of claimants. For example, the Boy Scouts plan offered survivors an optional individualized review process. That process was intended to most closely replicate a trial, albeit within a private dispute resolution system created by parties in the bankruptcy. To engage this process, however, a survivor must make an up-front payment of $10,000 and then another payment of $10,000 to see the process through. Individualized review offers the potential for the highest monetary rewards. But if a survivor pursues this process and loses, he recovers nothing, and gets no refund. In addition, the extra compensation for individualized review participants comes from a fund that remained empty as of the fall of 2023. Some claimants may not be able to afford to take on these risks.

It should be considered extraordinary to use the bankruptcy

system to block child sex abuse survivors' use of the civil justice system for several years, and then require survivors to pay
$20,000 for a private resolution process to substitute for pub-
lic trials. The story gets further complicated, however, because
the Boy Scouts of America was late in providing the documen-
tary evidence necessary for survivors to prove their abuse and
harm, or even to decide whether to pursue and pay for the
individual review option in the first place. The court granted
the trustee's request to extend the deadline for opting into the
independent review option, albeit for less time than some lawyers said was necessary.[11]

A different set of challenges surrounded an election to take
an expedited payment of $3,500 as full compensation for child
sex abuse. That election was embedded in the ballot for voting on the Boy Scouts of America plan, a document exceeding
twenty pages that did not even fit in the return envelope. To
get compensation, survivors who had made the election had
to submit a form to the trust electronically by a set deadline.
Survivors represented by lawyers were not permitted to submit
the document themselves; their lawyers had to do it. Just a few
days before the deadline, the trust reported that more than
half of all survivors who had selected expedited payment on
their ballots had not submitted the required form. Apparently,
survivors had contacted the trust saying they had not been able
to get in touch with their lawyers and asking how to get their

lawyers to return their calls. The trustee extended the deadline, and a day before that extension on the deadline was set
to expire, the trust was still missing forms from 31 percent of
survivors who had checked the box on the ballot.[12]

Embedding the expedited payment option in a complicated
ballot introduces another possible route for perceived under-
compensation and claimant dissatisfaction with the process.
In the fall of 2023, about five hundred survivors asked the Boy
Scouts of America trust to change their ballot selection. For
example, a survivor of severe sexual abuse had voted *against*
the Boy Scouts bankruptcy plan but also checked the expedited payment box, limiting recovery to $3,500. He reported
under oath to the court that he did not mean to limit his recovery. Numerous other survivors wrote to the court expressing
confusion about their ballot elections (including one who had
been represented by two law firms) and asking not to be bound
to the $3,500 limitation.[13]

Even without logistical or interpretive difficulties, expedited
payment options complicate an assessment of whether injured
people have been compensated fully. For example, the A.H.
Robins bankruptcy offered injured Dalkon Shield users a flat
payment of $725. They were promised faster payment but
would forfeit the opportunity for a greater recovery in a more
elaborate claim review process. A few years into the trust operation, 64 percent of women who filed timely claims against

the A.H. Robins trust elected the expedited payment. Most were not represented by lawyers. Many may have been influenced by correspondence suggesting that the trust did not have enough money to compensate women at higher levels. Given the hazards of the Dalkon Shield, one might wonder whether $725 really was payment in full for many of the women who went with that option.

The sufficiency of payment is also affected by multiple layers of professional fees. In A.H. Robins, for example, personal injury lawyers for some women claimed entitlement to as much as 50 to 60 percent of their recoveries. One woman who wrote a book after advocating for herself and others injured by the Dalkon Shield characterized the handling of the bankruptcy as a revictimization. These details—the pressure to select the limited payment option, the huge bite of professional fees, and assertions of revictimization—tend not to be mentioned when lawyers cite A.H. Robins as a mass tort bankruptcy success story. The official committee for unsecured creditors in the Purdue Pharma bankruptcy lauded A.H. Robins in its brief to the U.S. Supreme Court, with no mention of the detailed concerns many women have put forward in the intervening years.[14]

Another element complicating the evaluation of payment in full is the preclusion of punitive damages. Punitive damages have constituted some of the largest components of recoveries in the civil justice system. Debates about punitive damages could fill many books, but the point here is more basic: claimants with serious injuries and egregious stories to tell may not perceive their recovery from the bankruptcy system as payment in full. The preclusion of punitive damages also attracts solvent companies, such as Johnson & Johnson, to the bankruptcy court's doors.[15]

Sometimes timing is especially important to mitigate harm. In A.H. Robins, the presiding district judge granted a request for the company to establish an emergency treatment fund while the case was still ongoing. Two years had passed since the bankruptcy had brought things to a halt, and the clock was ticking on the necessary medical interventions. Women were aging out of eligibility for treatment. The fund would contain about $15 million, requests would be medically screened, and the money would go directly to compensate health care providers for their services. Supporters of the fund explained that spending the money now on medical interventions would reduce the size and number of requests for compensation later. They also pointed out that, absent the bankruptcy, A.H. Robins would have funded treatment.

Shareholders of the company did not want that money walking out the door, no matter the damage inflicted by their company's product. They took the issue to the U.S. Court of Appeals for the Fourth Circuit. Siding with the shareholders, the Fourth Circuit prohibited the emergency fund because the court could not find a specific authorization in the Bankruptcy Code to pay certain creditors early. (As you now know from chapter 6, the Fourth Circuit will later uphold a liability shield for the Robins family without a specific authorization in the Bankruptcy Code.) Women lost the chance to repair serious harm to their bodies while there was still time to do so. The possibility of collecting more money from the trust later was hardly a consolation.[16]

Unmassing Mass Torts

An enterprise hoping to cap mass tort liability in bankruptcy has reason to care more about its aggregate obligation than allocation. As suggested in chapter 6, members of Congress have expressed concern that too many asbestos bankruptcy trust resources have been allocated to people with no active impairment, shortchanging those who are seriously ill from mesothelioma and lung cancer. Mass tort bankruptcy norms encourage a search for weak claims to include in the process. That affects not only recovery but also leverage in the negotiations about whether the company should be able to cap liability through bankruptcy and what the details should look like.

When lawyers talk about mass tort cases, they tend to emphasize the undifferentiated mass. That approach overlooks the variation among individuals, with a spectrum of injuries and circumstances. Even among those with similar injuries, claimants may have stronger or weaker proof of the link between their harm and the debtor enterprise. State law may make it easier or harder to win a case and determine whether it is too late to bring a lawsuit at all. This spectrum does get addressed as a compensation issue after a plan is confirmed. But these distinctions matter during the bankruptcy case, when key decisions are made.

When the system treats tort claimants as an indistinguishable mass, some of Chapter 11's most protective features become less effective for injured people, particularly those with the most to lose by moving their legal disputes into bankruptcy. One big example involves voting on the proposed plan and the negotiations that lead up to that consequential event. Voting is essential to Chapter 11, not only because it gives creditors a voice but because bankruptcy allows the majority to bind others to changes in legal rights if other requirements are met. Understanding the voting rules, in theory and in practice, is therefore key.

In Chapter 11, voting happens by class. The debtor is the only one that can propose a plan, at least at first, so the debtor leads the process of grouping claims into classes and has a fair amount of discretion in doing so. The claims need to be substantially similar to be grouped together, a standard the

Bankruptcy Code does not define and leaves to courts, but at the very least, the claims in a class must have similar legal priority (the debtor cannot build a class that combines secured and unsecured claims, for example). Legally similar claims can be separately classified if the debtor can articulate a good reason for doing so. Although refined classifications give a more distinct voice in the process to subsets of injured parties, a big enterprise in Chapter 11 often has no incentive to structure the plan that way.

Bankruptcy law creates a high standard for a class to be deemed to have accepted a plan. The test first counts the number of claims that voted in favor of the plan relative to those that voted against it. The plan needs to secure at least half in favor of the plan among those who vote. The asbestos bankruptcy provision, section 524(g), increases the threshold of supportive claims to 75 percent, and other types of mass tort bankruptcies tend to use that threshold as a benchmark. Again, the tally is among claimants that cast a vote, disregarding claimants who do not cast a vote or whose votes are disregarded for some reason.

A majority in number is not supposed to be sufficient, however. The second part of Chapter 11's conjunctive voting test considers each claim's dollar value. Two-thirds of the total dollar amount among voting members of the class must support the plan. In other words, if the debtor owes one creditor $200 and another creditor $2,000, the latter claimant's position on the plan carries more weight.

Mass tort bankruptcies distort the effects of the voting rules because they typically assign a value of $1 to all tort claims and put them all in one class, regardless of severity of harm or any other differentiating factors. Creditors with more serious harm and stronger proof lose the leverage that commercial creditors get from these voting rules. The one dollar, one vote norm tends to apply even to claimants who obtained a judgment or reached a settlement prior to the bankruptcy.

The Boy Scouts of America illustrates these norms. "You've heard me tell my story," said John Humphrey, in a publicly available virtual town hall for survivors of sex abuse. "You know that I was pervasively abused for over 200 times in a two-year period, and that my abuser had complete and total control over my life for a long, long time." His claim was valued at $1 for voting. The Boy Scouts of America definition of abuse claims in the case was deliberately broad. Someone groped by a fellow scout would be in the same class as John Humphrey, with his claim also valued at $1 for voting purposes.[17]

The vast scope of the Boy Scouts of America bankruptcy allows for even more gradations. The abuse occurred in different decades, with different direct perpetrators, in different parts of the country and as far away as Guam. Depending on the timing, the organization might have a lot of insurance to cover the incident or none at all. Depending on the location, the applicable local council may have deep pockets or shallow ones. The location also determines if the claim was time-barred by the statute of limitations. Some survivors had been working on their lawsuits for a long time and were days away from picking a jury for trial when the bankruptcy brought everything to a halt. Others never would have brought a lawsuit at all. It is an understatement to say abuse claims involve a remarkable diversity of circumstances.

The Boy Scouts of America trust will use many of these factors to determine compensation for survivors according to a matrix negotiated during the bankruptcy ranging from $3,500 for the expedited claims to $2.7 million for survivors who prove they endured the most pervasive abuse. It makes sense to differentiate these claims for compensation, of course, but that is separate from having a distinct voice in the process that decides whether the bankruptcy system should permanently alter legal rights at all and what the terms should be.

Bankruptcy lawyers may believe that tort claimants care less about process than they do about money, an issue I will address in more detail a few pages from now. That mindset may be reinforced by working with creditors that are lenders or commercial parties that extended credit voluntarily to the debtor. Those creditors made contracts with the debtor in which money played a central role. But commercial creditors expect their higher-value claims to carry more weight in negotiations and voting. If one dollar, one vote is really preferable way to manage voting in Chapter 11, then perhaps it should apply to commercial claims too.

Pragmatism is a big driver of the one dollar, one vote norm. Many claimants have not tested their case in the civil justice system or settled before the bankruptcy halted such activities. Estimating individual claims for voting purposes, say lawyers, takes too long and costs too much. In the Boy Scouts of America bankruptcy, among others, there was at least enough information to classify the claims by alleged type of abuse.

When women injured by the Dalkon Shield challenged the one dollar, one vote method in the *A.H. Robins* case, the Fourth Circuit was skeptical that it had much impact, calling the approach harmless error at best. Drawing on reasoning from the Second Circuit in *Manville*, the original asbestos bankruptcy, the Fourth Circuit offered an after-the-fact arithmetical analysis. The vote tally was overwhelmingly in favor of the plan. Even if all the "no" votes had bigger dollar values, the class still would have accepted the plan. That reasoning does not reflect how the norms shape behavior and negotiations during the bankruptcy and whether a claimant votes at all. The classification and valuation of claims affected how much leverage claimants with bigger claims had to shape the process, which is how Chapter 11 was intended to operate.[18]

Again, one should assume that an enterprise seeks the lowest possible aggregate financial obligation when it seeks to cap liability for wrongdoing with respect to all claimants, present and future, in a bankruptcy. The enterprise has reason to be indifferent to how claimants (and lawyers) divide the money. In some cases, the inclusion of weaker claims and giving them equal weight helps enterprises get less well-funded plans over the 75 percent voting threshold and through the bankruptcy process. Claims might be legally weak for any number of reasons, including minimal injury, lack of proof connecting the injury to the enterprise, and being time-barred because the harm happened too long ago. If you follow mass tort bankruptcies, notice when enterprises are working with law firms that, seemingly out of thin air, generate large numbers of new claimants. The plaintiffs' lawyers will receive a significant proportion of their clients' recoveries and the bankruptcy is, again, more like a low-cost lottery ticket for clients with unvetted claims who might not have otherwise pursued recovery at all. Once an enterprise decides to manage and cap tort liability through bankruptcy, large volumes of weaker claims with less substantiation are its friend rather than its adversary. In short, the voting process in mass tort bankruptcies strengthens the hand of the debtor enterprise and co-defendants seeking to cap liability and change legal rights for all tort claimants.

Alternative Justice Vibes

As they enter bankruptcy to cap liability for alleged wrong-doing relating to a dangerous product or child sex abuse, some enterprises disparage the civil justice system and juries. According to some prominent companies and lawyers, trial avoidance for the debtor and related parties is one of bank-ruptcy's incidental benefits.

If the inner workings of the civil justice system in state courts need fixing, they should be fixed. But bankruptcy is not the complaint department or ombudsperson for the legal system. Filing a bankruptcy to permanently alter the rights of hundreds, thousands, or hundreds of thousands of people is an extraordinary exercise of federal power. Particularly when the enterprise has no real debt problems, such cases are at best tenuously connected to the bankruptcy clause of the U.S. Constitution.

Like we saw in chapter 6, companies and their lawyers insist the ends justify the means. Let's revisit the lawsuits against Johnson & Johnson relating to its talc-based products. Some research links use of their products to ovarian cancer and mesothelioma. The fact that talc may contribute to these types of cancer does not mean all plaintiffs suffering from these serious diseases will or should win lawsuits against the company. One would expect some to win and some to lose, particularly because the law is not the same from state to state.

Drawing on the longtime strategy of organizations like the U.S. Chamber of Commerce, the company wants to shift your focus away from the cosmetic talc industry and toward the cosmetic talc *litigation* industry—that is, toward plaintiffs' lawyers. When Johnson & Johnson put a subsidiary created to hold talc liabilities, into bankruptcy, the subsidiary filed a 130-page document that cast Johnson & Johnson as a victim of plaintiffs' lawyers and efforts to taint potential state court juries. These are the contents of a pleading in a federal *bankruptcy* court. It characterized the civil justice system as a "constant and overwhelming threat" to American companies. This document also was used to complain about the U.S. Supreme Court, which declined to review a state court ruling on punitive damages after two justices recused themselves.[19]

Even if all these things were true, they are irrelevant to whether Johnson & Johnson is entitled to use the extraordinary power of the bankruptcy system to protect its entire corporate enterprise from talc-related liability in perpetuity. Because its subsidiary, LTL, was not in financial distress, the Court of Appeals for the Third Circuit ordered the bankruptcy court to dismiss this case. Unwilling to let jury trials resume, LTL refiled a second Chapter 11 petition the very same day its first case was dismissed. In the two cases combined, both truncated by dismissal for lack of good faith, lawyers and financial advisors had billed tens of millions of dollars, over $40 million for LTL's lead counsel alone. In the fall of 2023, Johnson & Johnson announced on an investor call its intent to try a third bankruptcy.[20]

Another large and profitable company, 3M, tried to turn bankruptcy into the complaint department about federal multidistrict litigation, the process Congress established for consolidating litigation preparation for similar lawsuits. In 2022, 3M's Aearo Technologies subsidiary filed Chapter 11 in Indiana hoping to cap the corporate family's liability for a huge number of claims involving hearing loss among members of the military using 3M earplugs. Most claims already were consolidated in an ongoing MDL in Florida, which was well underway. According to 3M and Aearo, however, it needed to move the action to Indiana bankruptcy court because the MDL system was "broken beyond repair." Finding the debtor to be financially healthy with no impending solvency issues, the Indiana bankruptcy court dismissed Aearo's bankruptcy, a ruling that 3M and Aearo went on to challenge on appeal.[21]

When nonprofit and religious organizations use bankruptcy to halt child sex abuse litigation seeking accountability, they often admit that they are acting in direct response to state legislatures' efforts to offer a path to justice for survivors in state court. A statute of limitations is a defense to a lawsuit: the claim is too old, the events too long ago. Organizations like Child USA say that blocking child sex abuse suits merely due to the passage of time is unjustified, especially given research on how long it takes for survivors to be able to come forward. Following that line of advocacy, and over the avid objections and lobbying of organizations facing accusations of sex abuse cover-ups, states have heeded the call to change the law, either temporarily or permanently. The recent spike in diocese and other bankruptcies filed only to deal with sex abuse lawsuits correlates with a wave of new state law changes. The oldest Catholic archdiocese in America, in Baltimore Maryland, filed a Chapter 11 case two days *before* Maryland's Child Victims Act became effective. An attorney general investigation in Maryland had discovered abuse of at least six hundred children over many decades, protected by cover-ups by church officials.[22]

States have the capacity to do more than invite people to file lawsuits; they can try to prepare their courts to handle legal matters steeped in trauma. For example, the New York Child

Victims Act aimed to make the civil justice system more accom-
modating to the complexities of childhood sex abuse. Judges
and other court staff involved in these cases were required to
be trained in subjects relating to sexual assault and abuse of
minors. The cases would be assigned to a dedicated division of
the court, and put on a special timeline designed with this kind
of case in mind. The federal bankruptcy courts currently have
no such features.[23]

How you assess the use of bankruptcy by a religious organization or nonprofit to manage child sex abuse allegations
intersects with your perception of litigation more generally.
Using bankruptcy in response to state law access-to-justice initiative may seem fine if you believe the civil justice system is
an inefficient and unreliable way to identify a dollar amount
for compensation, and if you assume that money is the point.
From this perspective, bankruptcy may look like a mechanism
to facilitate recovery after state law reforms encourage people
to come forward.

It is hard to evaluate this position when information about
actual compensation rates does not freely flow. For example, in
supporting the Purdue Pharma bankruptcy plan, the Catholic
bishops told the Supreme Court that diocesan bankruptcies
aim for equitable compensation, making it appropriate to cut
off all survivor rights against non-debtor parties that have contributed to a trust for survivors. But the bishops cited no data

on whether survivors received what they expected or how long survivors had to wait.[24]

To civil procedure experts like Professor Alexandra Lahav, litigation is about much more than fixing a dollar amount on a legal problem. She has identified democratic values associated with the litigation process such as enforcement of legal rights, information disclosure, and participation in self-government. Likewise, Professor Gillian Hadfield studied people who were injured or lost loved ones on September 11, 2001. In deciding whether to accept an offer from a compensation fund or to pursue litigation, financial recovery was far from the only consideration. In favoring litigation, survivors of 9/11 cared about getting access to information that was otherwise unavailable to them at that time, accountability, and what Hadfield refers to as "responsive policy change—making sure that lessons were learned and heeded in the future, emphasizing that states have more than money in mind when they change the law to "open the doors of justice" to survivors of child sex abuse.[25]

To those who find this research persuasive, an enterprise's use of bankruptcy in response to a state's access-to-justice initiative for survivors looks more like an override of the will of democratically elected state governments. The use of bankruptcy, at least in its present form, risks being seen as a way to silence requests for accountability.

Can You See and Hear Me?

Debates about business bankruptcy tend to focus on financial resolutions. Real people involved in a case, as well as the public, tend to evaluate the fairness of a legal system on other criteria. The bankruptcy system's basic premises—letting support by the majority of claimants change the legal rights of everyone, significant fees charged by lawyers and financial advisors—may have justifications, but they may also generate distrust. These are issues in all bankruptcy cases, but particularly in Chapter 11 cases involving large numbers of claimants who never thought of themselves as creditors until the bankruptcy system signals that's what, and all, they are.

It is true that all confirmed mass tort bankruptcy plans are accompanied by records showing that a majority (and likely a supermajority) of claimants who voted did so in favor of the plan. Supporters of mass tort bankruptcy would like to take that as more of a sign of claimant confidence in the process than it likely is. A high volume of individual claimants in some of the larger mass tort cases are not voting at all, a dynamic that raises the question of whether there should be some minimum threshold of turnout in order to bind everyone. We have reviewed how the lumping of all tort claims together encourages the recruiting of less carefully vetted or weaker claims. But also, voting in favor of a plan, or even signing onto a brief

asking the Supreme Court to uphold a plan, is a noisy signal of belief in the legitimacy of the process. Among other
things, claimants have been warned of a parade of horribles
if the bankruptcy does not result in a plan, and they may see
no other reasonable alternative. If they are following the case
closely, they see millions of dollars going out the door to lawyers and financial professionals while they wait. Doug Kennedy, Boy Scouts of America abuse survivor, has told the press
that "Bankruptcy is not justice. Bankruptcy is business." Perhaps the vote is a plea for closure of some sort, not necessarily
enthusiasm or confidence. It is even possible that some claimants misunderstand the process and believe that they won't be
able to participate in recovery if they vote against the plan. I
can hardly fault the claimants for any misinterpretation. When
I read voting materials in these cases, I often struggle to understand them.[26]

Procedural justice is the study of how individuals perceive the
fairness of systems of authority, distinct from outcomes. Individuals value decision-making processes that they believe to be
fair. When it comes to the legal system, procedures, more than
outcomes, may be the largest contributor to dissatisfaction.
Respect for each party—something that is difficult to demonstrate in cases with tens of thousands of claimants—is one
of the procedural elements, as is the opportunity to tell one's
side of the story. The other pillars to procedural justice include

having a voice, the perceived trustworthiness of the institution and its decisionmakers, and the institution's neutrality. Neutrality can be implicated not only if the decisionmaker seems to be favoring a particular party, but if the decisionmaker favors a particular outcome. Repeatedly encouraging people to settle in a bankruptcy so that a plan can be confirmed will not necessarily be perceived as neutral.

Studies of procedural justice in bankruptcy are limited so far, but we can extrapolate from analyses of other systems. Early in her career, Professor Elizabeth Burch identified elements that make multidistrict litigation procedures in federal court seem less fair. Those elements, which almost certainly carry over into bankruptcy, include reduced attention to individuals, privatized governance, and extensive nonpublic activity. In a system that leans heavily on private actors to negotiate in confidence on behalf of large groups of people, procedural justice responsibilities fall on those lawyers and leaders as well as on public officials.[27]

A case that could have benefited from the teachings of procedural justice was A.H. Robins. Even Professor Georgene Vairo, who had a role in overseeing the A.H. Robins trust, wrote later that "many Dalkon Shield claimants felt victimized by the legal process and by lawyers both before and during the bankruptcy process." This observation was consistent with the writings of women involved as claimants and others who studied it. Although some critiques related to the methods of compensation, concerns about treatment during the bankruptcy and in the trust far transcended monetary issues. And yet bankruptcy lawyers continue to cite A.H. Robins as a positive example of the system's potential.[28]

If survivors of child sex abuse and people harmed by hazardous products listen to or watch court hearings in big bankruptcy cases, they might be struck by how lawyers center themselves and their peers. Lawyers talk about the years of their lives they personally devoted to a case, the sacrifices they made as they coaxed complicated and sensitive public policy problems into something resembling a bankruptcy. Lawyers report the late nights and weekends they worked, the Super Bowl game they didn't get to watch, the Valentine's day dinners their wives did not get (these are real examples). The claimants also can do the math, realizing that a lawyer speaking about his labor will make more money that week on the bankruptcy that blocked their jury trials than the claimants are likely to recover when all is said and done.

Part of the challenge is that a mass tort bankruptcy contains two significant but sequential procedures rather than one. Bankruptcy lawyers know that the trust distribution process will offer individualized attention to claimants and their alleged harms and stories. That is very important and appreciated if and when it works. But by that time, claimants have had a year, or two years, and sometimes longer, to form perceptions about a bankruptcy system they did not ask to be part of, and about the lawyers who look as if they are calling the shots.

When I think about elite lawyers and injured people and social class, I remember attending a panel at a conference early in my career titled "The Trouble with Tribbles." I had not seen the *Star Trek* episode that inspired the title but have since learned that Tribbles are small furry aliens that replicate quickly and can overwhelm a room and thus become an annoyance. The panel was composed of lawyers who represented consumer lenders and companies. In this context, Tribbles referred to people who had complained about being harmed or the lawsuits they filed, or both. I remember wondering whether I would reach a point where I would find the analogy amusing, as the panel apparently did. My younger self interpreted the discussion as a sign that the accomplished panelists did not see the complainants as equal in dignity to their own clients or to their well-pedigreed lawyer colleagues. I hope no lawyers working on mass tort bankruptcies conceptualize injured people as Tribbles, but these lawyers may benefit from thinking about how the stereotypes (or schemas, as psychologists say) they hold about survivors of child sex abuse or people seriously injured by hazardous pharmaceuticals may affect how they talk about and treat the people whose legal rights are up for grabs in mass tort bankruptcy cases.

Recognizing that bankruptcy is not just about money also implicates the range of potential remedies. In the Boy Scouts of America bankruptcy, the official survivor committee worked to ensure that the plan included operational changes, including an upgraded youth protection plan for scouting going forward. USA Gymnastics also committed to implement comprehensive changes. The field of restorative justice is full of ideas and processes geared toward meaningful remedies for harm. The commitments of that field include direct participation of both offenders and injured people, discussion of the offending behavior and its effects, collaboration on how to repair the harm, and acceptance of responsibility. Studies also suggest the importance of apologies—not only intrinsically, but instrumentally, in increasing the odds of a genuine settlement among all affected parties.[29]

Mass tort bankruptcy filers and defenders of this use of the system claim that the burden of a jumble of lawsuits on their enterprise justifies using bankruptcy's full arsenal of special tools. Those tools were organized around a different set of problems grounded in the system's authorization by the Constitution's bankruptcy power. The Chapter 11 filers walk a tightrope: they claim to face unprecedented and unique challenges, but also try to cast the requested relief as mainstream, no big deal. In search of finality, which is supposed to maximize economic value, mass tort bankruptcy plans tend to cap financial responsibilities no matter how awry the predictions go, no matter how successful the enterprise is in the future, such that they could help injured people more. Although some exceptions exist, these cases are less likely to reckon with restorative justice, let alone the trauma of the claimants, because bankruptcy was designed around debt and money. The consequences are not internalized by those with the most power over the big decisions.

Injured people find themselves strangers in a strange land when enterprises move their disputes into the bankruptcy system. Independent of the effects on the people in each case, routing public health and sex abuse cover-up lawsuits into the bankruptcy system imposes costs on the big concepts that shape our democracy. The practices of Chapter 11 bankruptcy undercut federalism, because they override state law and state courts well beyond achieving basic debt cancellation. The practices undercut separation of powers, as lawyers ask judges to bless new regimes within a bankruptcy case that cannot be found in the Bankruptcy Code that Congress enacted. The practices undercut due process as cases change the legal rights of people all over the country and sometimes around the world, with relatively minimal notice, and for future claimants, none.

My lawyer friends often view bankruptcy through a pragmatic lens. Sometimes you need the leverage of bankruptcy, a little shove, to get the job done. Isn't that a better way forward?

I have come to believe that compromise is less of a neutral virtue than it is often perceived to be. What English professor Rachel Greenwald Smith has argued outside of the legal world is arguably true within it:

> But when compromise is understood as an end rather than a means, it promises to be more than that: compromise is supposed to solve problems and maintain stability such that no one needs to feel substantial loss. Of course what this means in practice is the maintenance of hierarchies, the preservation of power. Because people do lose in all compromises; it's just a matter of who feels it.[30]

CONCLUSION

Having worked through tough material, you deserve an ice cream break. Let us revisit Ample Hills Creamery, which went bankrupt in 2020, as did the company's owners, Brian and Jackie. The gas tank manufacturer that acquired Ample Hills for a low price in the company's Chapter 11 could not make a go of it. In 2022, eviction notices rather than flavor lists graced the stores' front doors.

The year 2023 brought a remarkable turn of events: investors re-bought the remnants of Ample Hills Creamery and brought Brian and Jackie back into the business. On the summer solstice, June 21, 2023, they reopened the original location, on Vanderbilt Avenue in Prospects Heights, Brooklyn. I was there—field research! The ice cream was delicious, the spirit joyous, the customers happy. The bankruptcy system offered no special treatment to Brian and Jackie. But it put them in a position for a second chance.

In all likelihood, the bankruptcy system is going to be in demand in coming years. Filings were historically low during the worst of the COVID-19 pandemic. The tide is shifting. In 2023, credit card debt exceeded $1 trillion for the first time, with aggregate credit limits at $4.6 trillion. Consumer credit is generally understood to be an indicator, albeit with a time lag, of personal bankruptcy filing rates. Business Chapter 11 filings jumped considerably from mid-2022 to mid-2023. Big companies took on heaps of debt when the costs of corporate borrowing were low. If and when companies are unable to repay or refinance those obligations, Chapter 11 bankruptcy is where many will turn, whether or not they have any prospect of reorganization.[1]

Meanwhile, Chapter 11 continues to be a litigation stopper. Right-wing conspiracy theorist Alex Jones and his company Infowars filed Chapter 11 cases to halt further progression in litigation, after Jones and his company had put families' lives and livelihoods at risk by spreading lies that the 2012 Sandy Hook school shooting was a hoax. Corizon Health, in the business of providing health care services to prisons, put a liability-only subsidiary into Chapter 11 to halt hundreds of lawsuits for serious allegations of harmful and neglectful medical care as well as sex abuse. The International Longshore and Warehouse Union, carrying no debt, filed for bankruptcy to halt further developments in litigation over its own alleged unfair labor practices.[2]

Common themes of this book include how a system that

could promote equality of opportunity instead entrenches existing hierarchies and power structures, how bankruptcy is another example of a seemingly neutral law with a racially disparate impact, and how allowing powerful people to unbundle the law and write their own extensions of it can be regressive as well as undercut important democratic principles. This book is not a complete account of the bankruptcy system or the system's impact on equality and liberty. Many other stories could and should be told. But to the extent you are troubled by what you have read, you might ask how to translate these concerns into actionable responses.

The most basic function American bankruptcy law serves is to cancel contract-based debts of real people. The current personal bankruptcy system falls short. Economists Rich Hynes and Nathaniel Pattison have called for dramatically streamlined debt cancellation for families of modest means and limited assets. The system should not require over twenty complicated forms for a financially distressed person even to get started. Senator Elizabeth Warren and others have introduced legislation that would simplify personal bankruptcy and would reduce racial disparities as well as time spent on scrutiny of small-dollar personal choices. Ideas in this vein should be the focal point to take personal bankruptcy forward.[3]

When it comes to the bankruptcies of enterprises, modesty and minimalism are in order. A narrower interpretation of the federal bankruptcy power and adherence to the rule of law would better protect other legal and constitutional principles. Chapter 11 is a package deal, and unduly flexible interpretations of what can be done in the name of financial exigency may generate regressive outcomes. Lawyers for large enterprises and other parties with power often make instrumental public interest arguments designed to erode strict construction of the Bankruptcy Code in their favor. If a company files for bankruptcy to sell itself quickly to a private equity firm, it will emphasize job saving, even if the buyer has made no binding employment commitments. Consideration of public interests should be understood as *constraints* on party discretion in bankruptcy, not as grounds for departure from the rules. Chapter 11 is far from perfect, but as written balances a variety of considerations. Power tools are least dangerous when one abides by the instruction manual. Lenders and speculators should not be able to unbundle and rewrite Chapter 11 for their own benefit. If they want to lobby Congress to write a federal mergers and acquisition law with the standalone perks they seek, they should identify authority unrelated to bankruptcy.

Although these ideas dovetail with bedrock principles—federalism, separation of powers, and due process—better than current bankruptcy practice, they are unlikely to be successful without rethinking how the bankruptcy system is funded. Right now, private lenders have outsized influence on which parts of Chapter 11 are operational. Market-based funding of Chapter 11 is supposed to serve an important signaling function—if no one wants to put money into the reorganization, maybe the business should not continue. But the ability of the lender to cherry-pick the portions of the system it will permit to operate has serious consequences, especially as bankruptcy is used more expansively and to manage accusations of wrongdoing. If investigations can go forward only if a private lender wants to pay for them, if Robert Weinstein gets to stay in charge of the Weinstein Company because the lender insists on continuity until a quick sale of the company, the integrity of the system is at risk. If the public does not want to fund the system, Congress should narrow the entryway to Chapter 11 as well as restrict its uses.

As for enterprises without overindebtedness using Chapter 11 for litigation management, I have tried and failed to understand why these activities belong in bankruptcy. Bankruptcy courts are not the complaint department for the civil justice system or a forum to hash out the science of disease when defendants do not like how courts with authority and jurisdiction resolve those matters. Some more specific proposals would become unnecessary if there were broad acceptance of the *just debts* principle: cases filed to cut off litigation for accountability amount to an illegitimate use of the national bankruptcy power. Those who want to use federal law to limit injured parties' recourse to the civil justice system need to find authority other than bankruptcy to pursue this mission.

If you spend your professional life in the world of bankruptcy, it can be easy to forget how extraordinary it is as a legal matter to alter everyone's rights by majority rule. It is one thing to say that 80 percent of bondholders can bind a dissenting 20 percent to a new interest rate and payment schedule. It is something else entirely to force unconsenting injured people to forfeit legal rights arising from alleged misconduct. At the very least, when determining if the requisite majority of creditors has approved a plan, perhaps there should be a quorum requirement, a minimum voting turnout, to validate the results. If nine out of ten claimants support a plan, and another five hundred do not vote at all, is it legitimate to use the bankruptcy system to change the rights of everyone, especially if the claimants are not voluntary commercial creditors?

Chapter 11's one-way finality also should be reconsidered. Right now, Chapter 11 gives an immediate discharge of existing legal obligations to the debtor, and similar relief to additional parties. When the plan falls short of promises, the risk falls on the claimants. By contrast, an individual's debt relief in Chapter 13 is conditioned on plan completion. If Chapter 11 is going to continue to be a forum for mass tort resolution, perhaps the Chapter 11 discharge and the full effect of any third-party liability shields should be deferred until the enterprise has fulfilled more of its commitments under the plan.

Minimalism should apply to the reorganization of all types of enterprises, including cities. The original step to allow the majority of municipal bondholders to bind the minority was already significant. The statutory expansion and changes in practice have morphed municipal bankruptcy into something completely different. The result unduly undercuts constitutional and statutory protections of residents meant to protect them from bodily harm and discrimination at the hands of the state.

To improve its public reputation, the bankruptcy system should restore its commitment to transparency. A bankruptcy case changes people's rights from its first moment of existence, with expectations of even more consequential effects down the road. Public disclosure is part of the trade-off. Bankruptcy court hearings have become more accessible to the public because of technology, although the top echelons of the federal judiciary are less supportive of this development than one would hope. Yet, bankruptcy practice has gone too far in the direction of keeping secrets—requests to redact and seal documents, and using confidentiality agreements to restrict access, sometimes for lawyers' eyes only—while expecting relief from a public system. Bankruptcy becomes too private given the stakes of these cases. The fact that a bankruptcy will generate a historic depository of information in the future, only after significant legal rights have been irrevocably altered, is not as reassuring as lawyers may expect it to be.

Accessibility is not just a matter of information volume but of expression. Lawyers often refer to their cases as complex, somehow each more so than the last. When a lawyer repeatedly characterizes a case as complex, they may be obscuring who wins and loses from this exercise of federal bankruptcy power. Information also must be shared in a format suitable to address foundational questions. If lawyers want to say the private trusts created by bankruptcy cases work great to resolve large numbers of claims, the trusts should generate more data that can be readily shared and evaluated.

I will end with what might sound technical to a general audience but major to bankruptcy lawyers: narrowing what counts as a claim or debt under bankruptcy law. Many stories in this book would not exist if bankruptcy applied to *just debts* as commonly understood. Bankruptcy is best matched with contractual obligations, especially those from incurring credit or borrowing money. Inclusiveness makes sense if a business is truly closing its doors and liquidating. But for municipalities, businesses, and nonprofits that file reorganization cases, the breadth has compromised policy objectives distant from bankruptcy's intended domain.

Who Works Here?

Might the bankruptcy system have evolved differently had the people working and gaining prominence in the field reflected the range of backgrounds and communities of the people affected by their decisions? The ideas and solutions developed by a heterogeneous team might be more readily accepted by other people whose lives are changed, promoting legitimacy and trust. The system may be more trusted by the people whose lives are changed. Among other findings in psychology research, homogeneity breeds cognitive bias, confirmation bias, and group polarization, to adopt terms from another field with jargon. In other words, a diverse team is likely to produce better ideas. Producing better ideas is especially important if the boundaries of a system are being pushed.[4]

Private actors such as lawyers shape the dynamics of the bankruptcy system on a daily basis, arguably even more so than the courts and government watchdog. Personal bankruptcy lawyers advise financially distressed individuals whether they should file for Chapter 7 or Chapter 13, and as we have seen, the patterns generate racial disparities. In cases involving enterprises, whether for-profit, nonprofit, or a city, private lawyers play a central role in legitimizing problems as suitable for redress in bankruptcy. They are in the conference rooms hammering out the deals that they will publicly insist are essential to maximize economic value. As private lawyers distribute and redistribute bankruptcy's benefits and burdens, they redirect money and power. I have not found a recent and reliable statistical report on the demography of bankruptcy lawyers overall, but by all indications they tend not to be a particularly heterogeneous crew, particularly in the biggest cases.

Bankruptcy judges have been working to expand the pipeline of people who enter the profession and ultimately judgeships. In 2021, the Honorable Frank Bailey of the District of Massachusetts testified before the U.S. House Judiciary Committee: "My fear is that unless there are judges on the bankruptcy bench that reflect the populations in our districts, certain communities may not feel welcome in our courts." There is no shortage of work to do. As of 2018, among judges who reported demographic information, 79 percent of bankruptcy judges identified as white (a higher percentage than among life-tenured federal judges). Less than 4 percent identified as Black, 2 percent as Hispanic, and 2 percent as Asian American. Two-thirds of bankruptcy judges in 2018 were men.[5]

What about professors who specialize in bankruptcy? Before she became a U.S. senator, Elizabeth Warren cultivated an alternative crew of teachers and scholars drawn from diverse economic classes, racial and ethnic identities, and sexual orientations. They are transforming the study of consumer protection, among other fields, and are making a real-world difference. The demography of law professors focused on corporate and municipal distress has not expanded to the same extent.

Perhaps there has been a little bit of progress. In the 1990s, Professor Karen Gross was one of few women writing about business bankruptcy and one of even fewer applying feminism and communitarianism theories. At a conference at Washington University, in Saint Louis, men had advice for Professor Gross if she expected them to take her seriously: cast arguments in economic terms and avoid the term "feminist." Most of the men who spoke at that Washington University conference continue to be professors studying business bankruptcy. The same cannot be said for the small handful of women who participated.[6]

Even today, if you are a law student at an elite and highly ranked school, there's a decent chance your bankruptcy course won't talk much or at all about personal bankruptcy or smaller business bankruptcies, even though they are the majority of cases. Elizabeth Warren was an outlier in that regard. Her comprehensive approach, which I adopted for my own students, made that early morning class tougher, but it also prepared us to draw comparisons and make connections they would not have seen otherwise. Had I attended a different law school or dropped that early morning bankruptcy class, would this book even exist?

ACKNOWLEDGMENTS

Much gratitude to people who took the time to read and comment on parts or, in a few instances all, of this book when they had so much else to do: Abbye Atkinson, Ralph Brubaker, Babette Ceccotti, Mechele Dickerson, Vicki Eastus, Pamela Foohey, Sara Sternberg Greene, Ryan Hampton, Kirk Hartley, Ted Janger, Meredith Jury, Doug Kennedy, Katie Kosma, George Kuney, Robert Lawless, Donna Nixon, and Joanna Schwartz. This book found its ultimate publishing home thanks to Maxine Eichner and Amy Glickman. Thank you to Marc Favreau for edits and guidance, and also for believing in the project in the first place, and to Emily Albarillo and the team at The New Press for all the help along the way. I am most grateful to Beth Zasloff for comprehensive editing advice and to Kat Thomas for copyediting. Dorothy Brown, Matt Carlini, Carissa Byrne Hessick, Beth Macy, and Jennifer Taub generously shared publishing advice at crucial moments. This is also an important time to recognize the people thanked in the first footnote or endnote of each scholarly publication listed at the end of this acknowledgment section. Their input undoubtedly shaped what ended up in this book, as did the feedback from readers who prefer to remain anonymous. Mark Weidemaier was indispensable from start to finish, as well as before the start and after the finish.

Many former students who agreed to be research assistants during law school contributed to the research reflected in this book over many years, including Michael Maloney, Robert El-Jaohari, Tyler Talton, Michelle Walker, Britton Lewis, Safa Sajadi, Brett Neve, Gabrielle Gorman, Ricky Willi, Tyler O'Hara, Mary Ellen Goode, Joshua Showalter, Cordon Smart, Sarah Russell Cansler, Caleb Johnson, Amy Leitner, Charles Plambeck, and Grace Henley. Kelly Clarice Newcomb and Heather Alyn Newton went above and beyond to help me fact-check the manuscript in a compressed time period.

The University of North Carolina at Chapel Hill and its law school financially and intellectually supported this project, including through a senior faculty leave award. Nicole Downing and the Kathrine Everett Law Library came through many times with crucial library help.

My exposure to the dynamics of details of large business, nonprofit, and municipal cases deepened when bankruptcy courts offered public remote access to hearings in real time, and/or made digital recordings available on the court docket.

Here's hoping that the federal judiciary will maintain and build on this transparency-promoting step.

Unjust Debts was written anew but also builds on a subset of my scholarly research projects listed here.

"Sorting Bugs and Features of Mass Tort Bankruptcy," 101 *Texas Law Review* 1745 (2023).

"Unbundling Business Bankruptcy Law," 101 *North Carolina Law Review* 1703 (2023).

"Fake and Real People in Bankruptcy," 39 *Emory Bankruptcy Developments Journal* 497 (2023).

"Shocking Business Bankruptcy Law," 131 *Yale Law Journal Forum* 409 (2021).

"Bankruptcy Sales," *Research Handbook on Corporate Bankruptcy Law* (Barry Adler, ed. Edward Elgar Publishing 2020), with Edward J. Janger.

"Corporate Bankruptcy Hybridity," 166 *University of Pennsylvania Law Review* 1715 (2018).

"Tracing Equity: Realizing and Allocating Value in Chapter 11," 96 *Texas Law Review* 673 (2018), with Edward J. Janger.

"Presiding Over Municipal Bankruptcy: Then, Now, and Puerto Rico," 91 *American Bankruptcy Law Journal* 375 (2017).

"Federalism Form and Function in the Detroit Bankruptcy," 33 *Yale Journal on Regulation* 55 (2016).

"Who Pays for Police Misconduct in Bankrupt Cities?," UNC Legal Studies Research Paper No. 2796582 (2016) with Mary Ellen Goode.

"Superdelegation and Gatekeeping in Bankruptcy Courts," 87 *Temple Law Review* 875 (2015).

"What Should Judges Do in Chapter 11?," 2015 *University of Illinois Law Review* 571 (2015).

"Ice Cube Bonds: Allocating the Price of Process in Chapter 11 Bankruptcy," 123 *Yale Law Journal* 862 (2014), with Edward J. Janger.

"Bankruptcy Reform and the Financial Crisis," 13 *North Carolina Banking Institute Journal* 115 (2009).

"Fast, Cheap, and Creditor-Controlled: Is Corporate Reorganization Failing?," 54 *Buffalo Law Review* 401 (2006).

"The Bankruptcy Code at Twenty-Five and the Next Generation of Lawmaking," 78 *American Bankruptcy Law Journal* 221 (2004)

"Negotiating Bankruptcy Legislation Through the News Media," 41 *Houston Law Review* 1091 (2004).

"Collecting Debts from the Ill and Injured: The Rhetorical Significance, but Practical Irrelevance, of Culpability and Ability to Pay," 51 *American University Law Review* 229–71 (2001).

Appendix A

TYPES OF BANKRUPTCY

Type of bankruptcy	Intended for . . .
Chapter 7	
Relief for individuals, typically on a fast timeline. Also has a mechanism to liquidate business assets.	Individuals, businesses with no viable future
Chapter 9	
Allows municipalities to restructure legal obligations, operating most similarly to Chapter 11 in its current iteration.	Municipalities (cities, counties, water districts, public hospitals)

Type of bankruptcy	Intended for . . .
Chapter 11	
Provides the opportunity to restructure liabilities and make operational changes, typically keeping management in control.	Companies, nonprofits, individuals/sole business owners/operators
Chapter 12	
Special restructuring rules for family farmers and fisheries.	Small family farms and fisheries
Chapter 13	
Individual commits all disposable income to repayment plan.	Individuals with regular income and debts that are not too large
Chapter 15	
Coordinates procedure for transnational bankruptcies primarily being pursued outside the United States.	Companies with a cross-border legal presence

Appendix B

GLOSSARY

341 meeting: A debtor must show up at a certain date and
time to be questioned by a trustee and creditors. Judges are
neither invited nor welcome. The name of the meeting comes
from the section of the Bankruptcy Code that authorizes it.

363 sale: Selling property of the bankruptcy estate under
section 363 of the Bankruptcy Code. Sometimes this term is
shorthand for selling an entire company as a going concern
without creditor voting or the requirements associated with
a Chapter 11 plan.

9019: Rule of procedure that governs settlements in bankruptcy
but says nothing of substance. Case law fills in the blanks,
and the resulting standard is deferential to the parties as well
as to whoever brokered it—often another sitting or recently
retired federal judge or a private mediator appointed by the
court to move the case along. Court approval of a settlement
typically comes after considering whether the claim will be

successful, the likely expense, length, and degree of the complexity of the litigation, the potential difficulties of collecting on a judgment, and other factors relevant to a full and fair assessment of the wisdom of the proposed compromise. In other words, the standard is highly discretionary.

Absolute priority rule: If a proposed plan does not pay in full a class of claims that has no collateral, and that class of claims opposes the plan, then shareholder interests must be wiped out, signifying that the dissenting creditors are getting any remaining value in the reorganizing company.

Adequate protection: Money, property, or other value offered to a lender to protect against the risk that the creditor's collateral will decline in value while the bankruptcy case unfolds. If the debtor cannot provide the extra protection in the form of money or other property interests, the lender gets to take its collateral and the case may be over.

Ad hoc group: In Chapter 11 cases, creditors sometimes join together and advocate in concert, sharing a set of professionals. Their acting in concert must be disclosed to the public. Ad hoc groups often can get themselves a seat at the negotiating table and sometimes even get their professional fees paid out of the bankruptcy estate. Ad hoc groups were active in cases like Purdue Pharma and the Boy Scouts of America.

Automatic stay: Stops all collection and other legal activity against a debtor when a bankruptcy petition is filed.

Avoidance powers: Lawsuits to unwind completed transactions. Those transactions might be simple like a transfer of an asset or more complicated like a leveraged buyout. Examples include fraudulent transfers, voidable transfers, and preferential transfers.

Bankruptcy appellate panel: In some parts of the country, and particularly on the West Coast, U.S. Court of Appeals can select bankruptcy judges to sit on panels of three to hear appeals from bankruptcy courts. Parties in a dispute can request that the panel hears an appeal rather than a federal district judge (those assigned the full range of civil and criminal federal cases). Called BAP as shorthand.

Bankruptcy Clause: An original part of the U.S. Constitution. It empowers Congress to write uniform laws of bankruptcy. Not even a full sentence.

Bankruptcy Code: The federal statute, originally passed in 1978, governing the bankruptcy system. It is Title 11 of the U.S. Code, starting with section 101. Most of the dollar amounts in the Bankruptcy Code are indexed for inflation every three years. Some chapters of the Bankruptcy Code specify particular kinds of cases, while others contain rules applicable to many types of cases.

Bankruptcy court: A unit of the federal district court. Typically a designated bankruptcy judge fills the role, but the law is written such that district judges also can serve as the bankruptcy court. Bankruptcy courts are not necessarily distinct federal buildings. About a decade ago, I asked a research assistant to categorize the locations of bankruptcy courts because I could find no public source of that information. About 30 percent of bankruptcy courts were in buildings owned by the federal government but separate from the other courts. The Manhattan division of the Southern District of New York shares space with a division of the Smithsonian Museum, the Museum of the American Indian, quite a few subway stops south from the federal court complex. Other bankruptcy courts, like in Raleigh, North Carolina, share historic buildings with the U.S. Postal Service. Another 10 percent of bankruptcy courts were in rented private spaces, blending invisibly into the streetscape. The Wilmington, Delaware, bankruptcy court, a popular location for Chapter 11 filings, is in an office building with a Jimmy John's sandwich shop on the bottom floor, last I checked. The rest shared buildings with other federal courts, like in my first job in Chicago.

Bankruptcy estate: Protection for assets that arises the very moment a federal bankruptcy case is filed with a court. You will often hear people talk about property of the bankruptcy estate or that certain expenses are to be paid out of the bankruptcy estate.

Bankruptcy judge: Congress sets the number of bankruptcy judges and has authorized about 350 bankruptcy judges to sit in various locations around the country. These judgeships last fourteen years—unlike U.S. Supreme Court justices, they are not appointed to a judgeship for life, and they need not go through Senate confirmation. Congress created a different process whereby the U.S. Courts of Appeals, the highest level of federal court below the Supreme Court, select bankruptcy judges. Reflecting a hierarchy in the judiciary, bankruptcy judges get paid 92 percent of what federal district judges are paid. Bankruptcy judges nearing the end of their fourteen-year term and seeking to serve a second term must file an application with the circuit. That prompts the solicitation of the industry equivalent of Yelp reviews from lawyers. Alternatively, after finishing a term, a judge can serve on a year-by-year basis on "recall" to help with cases.

Bankruptcy judges handle more cases and spend more time in court than other federal court judges do. Bankruptcy judges are often the final word in a case on even controversial matters—presiding over courts of last resort in more ways than one. Congress has occasionally considered giving bankruptcy judges life tenure, prompting some life-tenured judges, most famously former chief justice of the United States Warren Burger, to lobby vigorously against the change.

Bankruptcy professional: Lawyers, investment bankers, financial experts, and others who regularly provide services to parties in a bankruptcy case. Some bankruptcy professionals are known under the moniker restructuring professionals, which signals the debtor is a bigger enterprise. Lawyers are often, although not always, segmented by type of client and size of case. To say that someone is a bankruptcy lawyer is only a starting point to understanding what they do and how they do it. Some lawyers bill $1,800 an hour. Others charge $1,800 for an entire case. Some lawyers in private practice are appointed by the government watchdog to serve as trustees in consumer and certain business cases. Especially on the far ends of the spectrum of lawyering, they have little in common with one another other than they go to the same court and cite the same Bankruptcy Code.

Bellwether trial: A procedure used when courts encounter cases with many similar allegations. They are used particularly in multidistrict litigation to help parties evaluate the strengths and weaknesses of many cases. They are not commonly used in modern mass tort bankruptcies, but they could be.

Chapter 7: Two very distinct purposes are embedded in this type of case. One purpose is for financially burdened consumers to get relatively swift debt relief. The other is to wind down the affairs of a doomed business. Either way, the government watchdog appoints a private party to serve as the trustee for the case.

Chapter 9: The type of bankruptcy used by Detroit, San Bernardino, and other cities and assorted municipalities like public hospitals and water districts and school districts. Municipality is defined broadly in bankruptcy law.

Chapter 11: What businesses file if they want to stay in control of their case. Nonprofits also can use Chapter 11. It is also available to individuals, including sole proprietors (business owners/operators) but is not the typical choice for the average financially distressed person.

Chapter 12: Available to help small family farmers and fisheries restructure their debts. This book does not tell stories from Chapter 12.

Chapter 13: Repayment plans for individuals with regular income. Often touted as a way to save a home or car, it is an expensive and uncertain way to do those things. If filers do not finish their plan, they generally do not get debt relief.

Chapter 15: When a company is international and is coordinating relief in more than one place. This book does not tell stories from Chapter 15.

Classes: Voting on restructuring plans in bankruptcy is tallied for separate groups of creditors, labeled classes. The claims in the classes must be substantially similar to justify their grouping in a class, but bankruptcy law gives the debtor the first opportunity to make that assessment. The law also gives the debtor flexibility to classify claims with similar legal priority and rights separately. The law then measures a class's acceptance of a plan in two ways under section 1126 of the Bankruptcy Code: (1) at least two-thirds in dollar amount and (2) more than half in number have voted in favor (the percentage is 75 percent for asbestos bankruptcies). Just like redistricting can shape outcomes in political elections, classification of claims can determine whether a bankruptcy plan has sufficient support to go forward.

Collateral: Property of the debtor in which a lender has contracted for rights, particularly in the event the debtor defaults on the loan. The car in a car loan. The house in a home mortgage.

Cramdown: Like a lot of jargon, this term does not appear in the Bankruptcy Code. Restructuring professionals use it to mean asking a court to confirm a plan over the objection of a dissenting class. In that instance, the plan must comply with the requirements Congress set forth in section 1129(b) of the Bankruptcy Code. Sometimes cramdown refers to reducing debt to the value of collateral.

Credit bid: This concept especially comes up in quick sales of operating companies, but the concept is more fundamental. I owe you $60,000, and my long-haul truck is collateral for this loan. You can offer to buy the truck for up to $60,000 without actually spending any new money: you buy the truck by canceling the debt. If a lender buys property through a credit bid, that means it generates no cash to pay other creditors. Because credit bidding can chill other potential buyers from competing to buy the property, parties affected by the sale should be on the lookout for anticompetitive behavior, and courts can disallow credit bidding for cause under section 363(k) of the Bankruptcy Code, although such disallowance is rare.

Creditors' committee: Congress says a sampling of creditors should have a seat at the negotiating table in larger Chapter 11 cases and in Chapter 9 municipal bankruptcy cases. The members get no compensation, but the bankruptcy estate must pay the committee's professionals. Committee creation is authorized by section 1102 of the Bankruptcy Code. The government watchdog selects the members of the committee. The committee has a duty to represent all creditors with unsecured claims (claims without collateral). In terms of member selection, Congress directs the government watchdog to favor creditors who are owed the largest dollar amounts by the debtor. The Bankruptcy Code authorizes the appointment of additional committees to represent specialized groups of claimants but that is relatively rare. Even more rarely will a committee be appointed to represent equity interests (shareholders), who have the lowest priority rights in the bankruptcy system.

In some cases, the committee picks up duties that the debtor does not want to execute, such as investigating prior wrongdoing. Congress did not explicitly authorize this *derivative standing*, but some courts permit it.

Critical vendors: After filing a Chapter 11, a company asks the court to authorize it to pay some creditors right away, on the theory that those creditors will stop doing business with the debtor otherwise and that will harm the prospects of reorganization.

DIP: Debtor-in-possession, meaning that a company that goes bankrupt can keep its own management in charge.

DIP financing/DIP loan: Congress created incentives for lenders to loan money to a company in bankruptcy so that the company has a better shot at reorganizing. Because the lender will get stronger rights and higher priority than existing creditors, the loan should not be approved unless there is a decent chance it will expand the value of the debtor enterprise. At the very least, the debtor requesting court approval of the loan is supposed to show the loan satisfies requirements set forth in section 364 of the Bankruptcy Code.

Discharge: Permanent bar to collecting a debt. A person is no longer personally liable for the obligation. Made possible because of the Bankruptcy Clause in the Constitution.

Disclosure statement: "Adequate information" must be provided to creditors so that they can make an informed decision before voting on a restructuring plan. The basic rules are provided in section 1125 of the Bankruptcy Code. In bigger cases, these documents can run into hundreds of pages and can be very confusing.

Equitable mootness: A court-made doctrine that appellate courts use to avoid ruling on the merits in big Chapter 11 cases if restructuring plans already have gone into effect.

Equitable subordination: An underused doctrine expressly authorized by section 510 of the Bankruptcy Code that gives courts the right to reorder the payment priority of creditors, whether secured or unsecured, when one engages in wrongdoing that harms the collection rights of others. The statute is short on detail, setting the standard to be only "under principles of equitable subordination." Congress intentionally left this standard to further court development.

Federalism: A principle to reserve power for states relative to the national government. Frequently undermined in practice in the bankruptcy world, although exalted in theory.

First-day motions/hearings: Lawyer Marshall Huebner once characterized these as follows: "First day hearings in large cases invariably involve dumping large amounts of paper on an already very busy court and chambers on very short notice." At their best, they help a company smoothly transition to operating under the restrictions of federal bankruptcy law with minimal disruption. At their worst, they redistribute money and power when the case has barely started and when most parties don't know what is happening.[1]

Fraudulent transfer (aka fraudulent conveyance, voidable transfer): Authorized under sections 544 and 548 of the Bankruptcy Code, a lawsuit to unwind a transaction either because the company actually intended to defraud its creditors or because the transaction stripped too much value from the company when it already was financially shaky. One of the causes of action that Jevic, the trucking company in chapter 5, had against the private equity firm and lender that stripped its value.

Funded debt: Extended by voluntary investors in an enterprise, typically used to refer to long-term (matures in more than a year) financial obligations of a company.

General unsecured claim: A party says the debtor owes a legal obligation, but the party has no collateral or special priority. In a liquidation, it will share pro rata any remaining value after secured creditors have been paid out of their collateral and after priority claimants have been fully compensated. *See also* unsecured claim.

Going concern sale: Selling a company while it is still operating, often pursued outside of a Chapter 11 plan and thus without creditor voting. Going concern is what a company is worth in the aggregate while the employees are still working and the machinery is still running.

Government watchdog: A term Congress used to refer to the U.S. Trustee Program, part of the U.S. Department of Justice, when it created it as a pilot program in the Bankruptcy Reform Act of 1978, the same law that created the Bankruptcy Code. The program was made permanent in 1986. In Alabama and North Carolina, an arm of the judiciary, bankruptcy administrators, play the role.

Although it composes a tiny fraction of the human resources of the Department of Justice, Congress gave this watchdog broad supervisory functions in all types of bankruptcy cases. The watchdog appoints and oversees private trustees, typically lawyers in private practice, who have statutory duties to administer individual cases of consumer debtors, and some business cases. The government watchdog had to build a system to oversee the financial education and credit counseling briefing requirements imposed on personal bankruptcy filers in 2005.

In addition to duties set by statute, the watchdog has the right to be heard in court on virtually everything that happens in bankruptcy cases and has the platform to develop its own priorities, albeit within the pressures and constraints of being part of the Department of Justice family. In addition to this executive office, the watchdog has regional units throughout the country. The program has a thousand employees around the country.

The watchdog grew out of a perceived ethical problem. Earlier in the twentieth century, life-tenured judges selected local lawyers to serve as "referees" in bankruptcies, and these lawyers were expected to do it all: oversee operations of a bankrupt business and then preside over disputes. The referee system blurred the lines between the court and the parties. It didn't help that the people involved were less than pristine in trying to reinforce boundaries. It conveyed the sense of being the umpire and playing third base at the same time. Would parties feel they had a fair day in court under these circumstances? So Congress divided the oversight in two, with bankruptcy judges as presiders and a government watchdog as managers of the administrative side.

Hedge fund: I will defer to journalist Sheelah Kolhatkar's definition. Originally these were investment funds that included actual hedging (betting some stocks would go up and others would go down). "Over time, the name hedge fund lost any connection to the careful strategy that had given such funds their name and came to stand, instead, for unregulated investment firms that essentially did whatever they wanted . . . the defining attribute of most hedge funds was the enormous amounts of money the people running them were taking in." She also notes, "The hedge fund moguls didn't lay railroads, build factories, or invent lifesaving medicines or technologies. They made their billions through speculation, by placing bets in the market that turned out to be right more often than wrong." [2]

Insolvency: The primary definition in section 101 of the Bankruptcy Code involves a comparison of debts and assets, where the debts exceed the value of assets. In some contexts, it can mean that a debtor is unwilling or unable to pay debts as they become due. A company does not need to be insolvent to file for bankruptcy.

Involuntary bankruptcy: Under section 303 of the Bankruptcy Code, three parties can file a bankruptcy petition in someone else's name if that party owes them enough money and other criteria are satisfied. An important creditors' remedy, but creditors risk being sanctioned if they put someone in bankruptcy who does not belong there.

Leveraged buyout: An investor buys a company with only a little bit of cash and finances the rest with debt secured by the assets of a company. The company owes way more money than it did just moments before.

Maximize economic value: An objective of bankruptcy law, although not exclusively so. Something that bankruptcy lawyers refer to, repeatedly, in big Chapter 11 cases when they want the court to approve something.

Multidistrict litigation (MDL): Congress provided this method of aggregating similar federal lawsuits for pretrial activities. A panel of judges decides whether to consolidate the cases and which judge should oversee them. Some companies have filed for bankruptcy stating a preference to use bankruptcy to consolidate their lawsuit problems rather than using the MDL, where suits against them have been sent.

Plan proponent: The parties negotiating and seeking to get approval for a restructuring plan. Often, but not always, includes the management of the bankrupt company.

Prepack/prepackaged plan: Creditors vote on a plan to restructure a company's debt under ordinary securities law before any bankruptcy filing, and then the company files for bankruptcy to seal the deal. The Bankruptcy Code honors prepackaged voting but not the extremely short stays in Chapter 11 that some companies seek.

"Primarily consumer debts": Personal, family, and household obligations, according to section 101 of the Bankruptcy Code. Cases involving these obligations face heightened scrutiny in American bankruptcy law, fueled in part by consumer credit industry advocacy.

Priority debt: Debts on a list that get special treatment in a bankruptcy. The main list is in section 507 of the Bankruptcy Code, with some cross references. In a case where assets are liquidated, someone holding a claim on the priority list has a right to recover their debt in full before general unsecured creditors are entitled to anything. In a repayment or restructuring plan, priority creditors are generally entitled to be paid in full. That includes the bills of lawyers and other professionals. A small amount of wages and benefits owed to employees from prior to the bankruptcy are entitled to priority. In individual debtor cases, fewer than three in ten owe priority debts. Tax obligations are particularly common. Child support and alimony are often discussed but are less common.[3]

Private equity: Funds created by firms to buy a controlling share in companies while using very little of the funds' partners' own money, with extensive debt borne by the company being acquired, typically with the goal of reselling within a few years. Because the fund loses little if the company fails but gets a big return on investment if it ends up hitting the jackpot, the moral hazard is significant. Eileen Appelbaum and Rosemary Batt wrote an important book on this topic.[4]

Professional fees: In Chapter 11 cases, lawyers, bankers, accountants, auctioneers, and advisors who wish to get paid out of the bankruptcy estate are entitled to priority repayment of their bills, although their bills are subject to court approval. At the time this book goes to press, fees for the most senior lawyers in the biggest business bankruptcies exceed $2,000 an hour. Fees for representing personal bankruptcy filers typically are case-based rather than hourly. Those fees jumped significantly when Congress made personal bankruptcy more complicated in 2005.[5]

Pro rata: When all general unsecured claims are entitled to the same percentage of recovery rather than the same dollar amounts. If there is $10,000 left in the pot to pay these creditors, and creditors' claims add up to $100,000, creditors get 10 percent of their claims.

Restructuring professional: A subset of bankruptcy professionals who work on larger business or municipal bankruptcies. Includes but is not limited to lawyers. For example, financial advisors or investment bankers may also be considered restructuring professionals.

Secured debt/secured credit: Borrowing money backed by collateral. To get the loan to buy the house, you convey a mortgage on the house. The lender has more leverage to encourage you to pay and has more remedies if you default. State law provides procedures that must be followed to ensure the lender has the full protections of a secured creditor, especially if the debtor files for bankruptcy. If the lender has made a mistake in those procedures, it might lose its security interest.

Stalking horse bidder: I make a binding offer to buy a company. If someone makes a better bid, I get a very big fee.

Lantern Capital was the stalking horse bidder in the Weinstein Company bankruptcy.

Successor liability: A doctrine, typically from state law but sometimes from federal law, that identifies circumstances under which a buyer is liable for certain obligations of a company it acquired. As discussed in chapter 5, buyers of bankrupt companies ask courts to enter orders finding that the buyer has no successor liability.

Trustees: Private parties appointed by the government watchdog. Obliged to oversee the bankruptcy estate. Chapter 7 trustees are paid a nominal amount for every case they oversee. They would get more if the debtors were flush with assets, but debtors in Chapter 7 typically are not. Chapter 13 trustees also get paid to administer payment plans, and they strongly influence whether a court confirms a Chapter 13 plan in the first place. The subchapter V trustee, for very small businesses in Chapter 11, is a relatively new invention.

One should distinguish the trustees for bankruptcy cases whose duties are defined by the Bankruptcy Code, from trustees who oversee the compensation of mass tort or sex abuse survivors after a Chapter 11 case. In the latter context, trustees follow the guidance of documents generated in the bankruptcy but the Bankruptcy Code does not govern those trusts or trustees directly.

United States Trustee Program: Official name for the bankruptcy system's watchdog other than in Alabama and North Carolina. Part of the U.S. Department of Justice.

Unsecured claim: Payable in money, not backed by collateral. Broader in substance and temporality than you ever imagined before reading this book.

Appendix C

BANKRUPTCY IN THE FEDERAL COURT SYSTEM

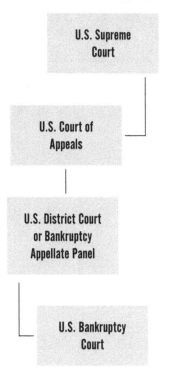

NOTES

Introduction

1. One in ten: Pamela Foohey, Robert M. Lawless, and Deborah Thorne, "Portraits of Bankruptcy Filers in the United States," *56 Ga. L. Rev.* 573 (2022). Calculations: Bob Lawless, "How Many People Have Filed Bankruptcy," *Credit Slips*, June 22, 2020, www.creditslips.org/credit slips/2020/06/how-many-people-have-filed-bankruptcy.html.

2. "We need new jargon" cartoon: D. Fletcher for CloudTweaks.Com.

1. Bankruptcy for Real People

1. Mary Eschelbach Hansen and Bradley A. Hansen, *Bankrupt in America: A History of Debtors, Their Creditors, and the Law in the Twentieth Century* 53, 153 (U. Chicago Press 2020).

2. Paul: *In re* Richardson, 09-51342 (Bankr. W.D. Ky.). More details: Melissa B. Jacoby, "Superdelegation and Gatekeeping in Bankruptcy Courts," 87 *Temple L. Rev.* 875, 877, 891–2 (2015).

3. *Bloomberg News*, "Filings Worry Greenspan," *Times-Picayune*, Mar. 20, 1997, at C6.

4. Jacob S. Hacker, *The Great Risk Shift: The New Economic Insecurity and the Decline of the American Dream* (Oxford U. Press Second Edition 2019).

5. Testimony of Robert E. Ginsberg, Vice-Chair National Bankruptcy Review Commission and Bankruptcy Judge, Northern District of Illinois, U.S. Senate Committee on the Judiciary, Subcommittee on Administrative Oversight and the Courts, Oct. 21, 1997.

6. Hillary Rodham Clinton, "Bankruptcy Shouldn't Let Parents off the Hook," *Wash. Times*, May 7, 1998, at A2. Pieces attracting attention of

women's groups: Elizabeth Warren, "Bankrupt? Pay Your Child Support First," *N.Y. Times*, Apr. 27, 1998, at A15; Christine Dugas, "Women Rank 1st in Bankruptcy Filings," *USA Today*, June 21, 1999, at 1A. Women's groups involvement: Melissa B. Jacoby, "Negotiating Bankruptcy Legislation Through the News Media," 41 *Hous. L. Rev.* 1091, 1139 n.233 (2004).

7. Amanda Terkel, "Joe Biden Reluctantly Backed Abortion Amendment in Bankruptcy Bill Fights," *Huffington Post*, Jan. 9, 2020 (reporting on earlier bankruptcy debates).

8. Jacoby, "Negotiating Bankruptcy Legislation," at 1105, 1140 n.236. *See generally* Tom Curry, "Abortion Collides with Bankruptcy in the Senate," msnbc.com, Mar. 8, 2005 (describing how abortion amendment got defeated, clearing way for passage of new bankruptcy law).

9. No cost to the public: Bankruptcy Administrative Improvement Act of 2020, S. 4996 §2(a)(1). No constitutional right to bankruptcy access: U.S. v. Kras, 409 U.S. 434 (1973).

10. Lois R. Lupica, "The Consumer Bankruptcy Fee Study: Final Report," 20 *Am. Bankr. Inst. L. Rev.* 17, 107 (2012). Between 2012 and 2022, less than 4 percent of personal bankruptcy cases were granted fee waivers, nearly all in Chapter 7 cases. FJC Integrated Petition Database data analysis supplied by Professor Robert M. Lawless (on file with author).

11. Pamela Foohey, Robert M. Lawless, and Deborah Thorne, "Driven to Bankruptcy," 55 *Wake Forest L. Rev.* 287, 288 (2020).

2. Race Disparities in Bankruptcy for Real People

1. Mary Eschelbach Hansen and Bradley A. Hansen, *Bankrupt in America: A History of Debtors, Their Creditors, and the Law in the Twentieth Century* 109–10 (U. Chicago Press 2020); Elizabeth Warren, "The Economics of Race: When Making It to the Middle Is Not Enough," 61 *Wash. and Lee L. Rev.* 1777, 1786, 1789 (2004).

2. The study: Jean Braucher, Dov Cohen, and Robert M. Lawless, "Race, Attorney Influence, and Bankruptcy Chapter Choice," 9 *J. Empirical Legal Stud.* 393, 411 (2012). *New York Times* coverage: Tara Siegel Bernard, "Blacks Face Bias in Bankruptcy, Study Suggests," *N.Y. Times*, Jan. 21, 2012, at A1. Event: Jean Braucher, Dov Cohen, and Robert M. Lawless, "Reflections on the Responses to 'Race, Attorney Influence, and Bankruptcy Chapter Choice,'" 20 *Am. Bankr. Inst. L. Rev.* 725 (2012).

3. Dov Cohen, Robert M. Lawless, and Faith Shin, "Opposite of Correct: Inverted Insider Perceptions of Race and Bankruptcy," 91 *Am.*

Bankr. L. J. 623, 624, 625, 637–38 (2017) ("Practicing attorneys fail to notice the 2:1 racial disparity in chapter choice between African Americans and whites. Moreover, they in fact believe that the 2:1 disparity runs in the *opposite* direction.") (emphasis in original).

4. Robert M. Lawless and Angela Littwin, "Local Legal Culture from R2D2 to Big Data," 96 *Tex. L. Rev.* 1353, 1373–74 (2018); Pamela Foohey, Robert Lawless, and Deborah Thorne, "Portraits of Consumer Bankruptcy Filers," 56 *Ga. L. Rev.* 573, 624 tbl. 6, 625 (2022).

5. Sara S. Greene, Parina Patel, and Katherine Porter, "Cracking the Code: An Empirical Analysis of Consumer Bankruptcy Outcomes," 101 *Minn. L. Rev.* 1031, 1086–87 (2017) ("More than amount of debt, prior bankruptcies, trying to save a home from foreclosure, or having a job . . . race matters.").

6. A. Mechele Dickerson, "Systemic Racism and Housing," 70 *Emory L. J.* 1535, 1538, 1575 (2021) (prior discriminatory policies, while now illegal, have entrenched racial homeownership and wealth gaps that cannot be dislodged without antiracist responses); Keeanga-Yamahtta Taylor, *Race for Profit: How Banks and the Real Estate Industry Undermined Homeownership* (U. North Carolina Press 2019).

7. Jacob William Faber, "Segregation and the Geography of Creditworthiness: Racial Inequality in a Recovered Mortgage Market," 28 *Housing Policy Debate* 215, 224, 231 (2018).

8. Greene, Patel, and Porter at 1086–87.

9. Abbye Atkinson, "Modifying Mortgage Discrimination in Consumer Bankruptcy," 57 *Ariz. L. Rev.* 1041, 1046 (2015) ("The anti-modification provision functions to further entrench racialized disparities in wealth.").

10. Data points on cars in this and prior paragraphs: Pamela Foohey, Robert M. Lawless, and Deborah Thorne, "Driven to Bankruptcy," 55 *Wake Forest L. Rev.* 287, 308, 323, 328 (2020).

11. Edward R. Morrison, Belisa Pang, and Antoine Uettwiller, "Race and Bankruptcy: Explaining Racial Disparities in Consumer Bankruptcy," 63 *J. L. & Econ.* 269 (2020) (Black debtors in Chicago were more likely to accumulate debt to the city from parking tickets and related problems, more likely to be targeted for enforcement, and more likely to file Chapter 13 cases). *See also* Melissa Sanchez and Elliot Ramos, "Chicago Hiked the Cost of Vehicle City Sticker Violations to Boost Revenue. But It's Driven More Low-Income Black Motorists Into Debt," ProPublica, July 26, 2018. www.propublica.org /article/chicago-vehicle-sticker-law-ticket-price-hike-black-drivers-debt.

12. City of Chicago v. Fulton, 141 S. Ct. 585 (2021).

13. A. Mechele Dickerson, "Race Matters in Bankruptcy," 61 *Wash. & Lee L. Rev.* 1725, 1736, 1763–65, 1772–75 (2004) ("Congress either consciously or unconsciously exhibited a bias in favor of a specific demographic profile.")

14. A. Mechele Dickerson, "Race Matters in Bankruptcy Reform," 71 *Mo. L. Rev.* 919, 960–61 (2006); Leslie A. Pappas, "Bankruptcy's Racial Disparities Poised to Add to Pandemic's Pain," *Bloomberg Law*, Aug. 31, 2020 (quoting Dickerson).

15. Kevin Krause, "She Has No Home, Car or Job After Bankruptcy, but Still Owes for Student Loans," *Dallas Morning News*, Feb. 2, 2018.

16. Thomas v. Department of Education (Matter of Thomas), 931 F.3d 449 (5th Cir. 2019).

17. Laura Sullivan, Tatjana Meschede, Thomas Shapiro, and Fernanda Escobar, "Stalling Dreams: How Student Debt Is Disrupting Life Chances and Widening the Racial Wealth Gap," Institute on Assets and Social Policy (Sept. 2019) (among student loan borrowers who started college in 1995–96, the typical Black borrower still owed 95 percent of the debt, while the typical white student owed 6 percent). *See also* Amy Traub, Laura Sullivan, Tatjana Meschede, and Thomas Shapiro, *The Asset Value of Whiteness: Understanding the Racial Wealth Gap* 6 (Demos 2017).

18. Abbye Atkinson, "Race, Educational Loans, and Bankruptcy," 16 *Mich. J. Race & L.* 1, 43 (2010).

19. Devon W. Carbado, *Unreasonable: Black Lives, Police Power, and the Fourth Amendment* 157 (The New Press 2022); Devon W. Carbado, "Blue-on-Black Violence: A Provisional Model of Some of the Causes," 104 *Geo. L. J.* 1479, 1487–88 (2016); U.S. Commission on Civil Rights, Targeted Fines and Fees Against Communities of Color: Civil Rights and Constitutional Implications (Sept. 2017).

20. Kelly v. Robinson, 479 U.S. 36 (1986).

21. *Kelly* interpretation: Abbye Atkinson, "Consumer Bankruptcy, Nondischargeability, and Penal Debt," 70 *Vand. L. Rev.* 917, 936 (2017).

22. Kassas v. State Bar of California, 49 F.4th 1158 (9th Cir. 2022); 11 U.S.C. § 1328(a)(2), (a)(4).

23. Pamela Foohey, "Fines, Fees, and Filing Bankruptcy," 98 *N.C. L. Rev.* 419, 421 (2020).

24. *See* Anthony v. Baker (*In re* Baker), 86 B.R. 234, 238–39 (D. Colo. 1988) (withdrawing reference of adversary proceeding based on malicious prosecution from bankruptcy court); *In re* Nifong, No. 8-80034C-7D, 2008 WL 2203149, at *4 (Bankr. M.D.N.C. May 27, 2008) (creditors pursuing

exception to discharge for willful and malicious injury based in part on civil rights claims and finding that a bankruptcy judge lacks authority to adjudicate those claims under 28 U.S.C. § 157(b)(5)).

25. Bruner v. Taylor (*In re* Taylor), 72 B.R. 696, 698, 699-700 (Bankr. E.D. Tenn. 1987).

26. *In re* Todd, 65 B.R. 249, 254–56 (Bankr. N.D. Ill. 1986).

27. Kawaauhau v. Geiger, 523 U.S. 57, 63–64 (1998).

28. *See* Voluntary Petition at 19, *In re* Kovach, 13-15340 (Bankr. N.D. Ohio July 29, 2013); Discharge of Debtor in a Chapter 7 Case at 1, *In re* Kovach, 13-15340 (Bankr. N.D. Ohio Nov. 6, 2013), docket #15; Kyle Swenson, "How Cleveland's Trying to Get Out of Paying $18.7 Million in Judgments Against Two Cleveland Police Officers," *Cleveland Scene*, Jan. 13, 2016.

29. Complaint to Revoke Discharge, Ayers v. Kovach (*In re* Kovach), No. 13-15340, at 6 (Bankr. N.D. Ohio Nov. 5, 2014), docket #18; Agreed Order at 2, *In re* Kovach, No. 13-15340 (Bankr. N.D. Ohio Feb. 19, 2015) (pursuit of a state court action against the debtor in name only, for the purpose of seeking indemnification, would not violate the discharge injunction).

30. Gabriel Thompson, "My Brother, the White Nationalist," *Pacific Standard*, Nov. 26, 2018, psmag.com/magazine/the-red-pill-my-brother-the-white-nationalist; Shane Bauer, "I Met the White Nationalist Who 'Falcon Punched' a 95-Pound Female Protestor," *Mother Jones*, May 9, 2017.

31. Complaint & Demand for Jury Trial at 25, 85, 17-72, Sines v. Kessler, 17-00072 (W.D.Va. Oct. 12, 2017); Voluntary Petition for Individuals Filing for Bankruptcy at 6-7, *In re* Damigo, 19-90003 (Bankr. E.D. Cal. Jan. 2, 2019), docket #1.

32. Status Report by Sines Plaintiffs, Sines et al. v. Damigo (*In re* Damigo), 19-9006 (Bankr. E.D. Cal. Oct. 3, 2019), docket #12; Status Report by Sines Plaintiffs, Sines et al. v. Damigo (*In re* Damigo), 19-9006 (Bankr. E.D. Cal. Apr. 17, 2023), docket #49 (further delay due to 4th Circuit appeal); Order, *In re* Damigo, 19-90003 (Bankr. E.D. Cal. Feb. 15, 2019), docket #23 (granting motion to modify automatic stay to permit continuation of Charlottesville action, docket #12).

33. Order of Discharge, *In re* Damigo, 19-90003 (Bankr. E.D. Cal. Apr. 16, 2019), docket #27; Civil Minutes, Sines et al. v. Damigo (*In re* Damigo), 19-9006 (Bankr. E.D. Cal. Oct. 17, 2019), docket #13.

3. Bankruptcy for Fake People

1. Scope of discharge: 11 U.S.C. § 1141(d) (providing only two narrow exceptions to discharge for "a corporation"). The scope of the discharge for very small businesses under the new subchapter V of the Bankruptcy Code is contested. Cantwell-Cleary Co. v. Cleary Packaging, LLC (*In re* Cleary Packaging, LLC), 36 F.4th 509 (4th Cir. 2022) (interpreting section 11 U.S.C. § 1192).

2. Creation of new LLCs: Delaware Division of Corporations 2020 Annual Report.

3. *In re* A.H. Robins Co., Inc., 59 B.R. 99, 102, 104 (Bankr. E.D. Va. 1986), upheld by Beard v. A.H. Robins Co., Inc., 828 F.2d 1029, 1031 (4th Cir. 1987).

4. United States v. Apex Oil Co., 579 F.3d 734 (7th Cir. 2009). Context for decision: Daniel J. Bussel, "Doing Equity in Bankruptcy," 34 *Emory Bankr. Dev. J.* 13, 46 (2017).

5. Notice of Trustee's Settlement, Messer v. Jenner (*In re* Fyre Festival), 17-11883 (Bankr. S.D.N.Y. May 19, 2020), docket #183; Complaint Seeking the Avoidance and Recovery of Fraudulent Transfers at 4, Messer v. Jenner (*In re* Fyre Festival), 17-11883 (Bankr. S.D.N.Y. Aug. 28, 2019), docket #88.

6. Chapter 7 Trustee's Final Account, *In re* Fyre Festival LLC, 17-11883 (Bankr. S.D.N.Y. Nov. 1, 2021), docket #264 ($7.6 million in allowed claims took pro rata shares of $300,000). Ticket holders in a class action seeking $100,000,000 in damages signed on to a settlement agreeing to a collective claim of $2 million, also subject to a 4 percent recovery. Trustee's Motion . . . for an Order Approving a Stipulation of Settlement Between the Trustee and Ticketholder Claimants at 3, 9, *In re* Fyre Festival, 17-11883 (Bankr. S.D.N.Y. April 13, 2021) docket #250.

7. Transcript of Proceedings of March 20, 2018 at 43–46, *In re* Bikram's Yoga College of India LP, 17-12045 (Bankr. C.D. Cal. Mar. 30, 2018), docket #112 (court granting motion to appoint a Chapter 11 trustee). Results of trustee work: Notice of Asset Case and Possible Dividend Distribution, *In re* Bikram's Yoga College of India, LA, 17-12045 (Bankr. C.D. Cal. July 7, 2021), docket #513.

8. "Harvey's behavior:" Transcript of Hearing on First-Day Motions at 12, *In re* the Weinstein Company, 18-10601 (Bankr. D. Del. Mar. 22, 2018), docket #86. State attorney general investigation: Complaint at 24, People of the State of New York v. The Weinstein Company LLC et al., 450293 (N.Y. Sup. Ct. 2018), docket #1.

9. Transcript of Hearing on First Day Motions Mar. 20, 2018, at 12, *In re* the Weinstein Company, 18-10601 (Bankr. D. Del. Mar. 22, 2018), docket #86; *id.* at 18 ("[B]oard has done everything in its power to steer this ship in the right direction since the revelations of October 2017[.]").

10. Decision and Order, Rehal v. Weinstein et al., 151738 (N.Y. Sup. Ct. May 13, 2019), docket #38.

11. Path to bankruptcy: Declaration of Robert Del Genio at 16–19, *In re* the Weinstein Company, 18-10601 (Bankr. D. Del. Mar. 20, 2018), docket #7; buyer's account: Barry Shlachter, "The Real Story of How a Dallas Investor Bought the Weinstein Co.," *D Magazine*, Aug. 8, 2019.

12. Debtors' Reply in Support of the Debtors' Motion to Reconsider Ruling Granting U.S. Trustee's Motion to Convert at 9, *In re* Forever 21, Inc., 19-12122 (Bankr. D. Del. Oct. 12, 2020), docket #1603.

13. Transcript of Telephonic Hearing on Reconsideration Motion at 7, *In re* Forever 21, Inc., 19-12122 (Bankr. D. Del. Oct. 26, 2020), docket #1631.

14. Transcript of Motions Hearing on August 27, 2020 at 29, *In re* Remington Outdoor Company, 20-81688 (Bankr. N.D. Ala. Aug. 28, 2020), docket #502.

15. Statement of Stephen H. Case at 31–32, Business Bankruptcy Issues in Review: Hearings Before the Subcommittee on Administrative Oversight and the Courts of the Committee on the Judiciary, on S. 1914 (May 19 and June 1, 1998).

16. 11 U.S.C. §§ 308, 362(n), 1106, 1121(e), 1125(f); 28 U.S.C. § 586(a)(7).

17. Small Business Reorganization Act of 2019, Pub. L. 116-54.

4. Civil Rights in a Bankrupt City

1. Town Hall Meeting on Detroit Bankruptcy, Sept. 7, 2013, www.c-span.org/video/?314907-1/rep-conyers-hosts-town-hall-detroit-bankruptcy.

2. Streetlights and ambulances: Declaration of Kevyn D. Orr at 24, *In re* City of Detroit, 13-53846 (Bankr. E.D. Mich. July 18, 2013), docket #11. Soda-can alert system: Nathan Bomey, *Detroit Resurrected: To Bankruptcy and Back* 50 (W. W. Norton & Co. 2016).

3. In Detroit, the police force in 2013, the year the city filed for bankruptcy, underrepresented minority residents by over 24 percent. The San Bernardino, California, police force underrepresented minority residents by 43 percent. "Special Report: Diversity on the Force: Where Police Don't Mirror Communities," at 7, 11, *Governing*, Sept. 2015. *See generally* John Kelly, "Police Diversity Lags in Many Cities," *USA Today*, Dec. 15, 2016

(high frequency of larger cities having over 10 percent disparity for representation of Black and Hispanic people and the gap was not narrowing over time); Jeremy Askenas and Haeyoun Park, "The Race Gap in America's Police Departments," *N.Y. Times*, Apr. 8, 2015.

4. Monell v. Dept. of Social Services of City of New York, 436 U.S. 658, 690 (1978).

5. *Owen* quote: Owen v. City of Independence, Missouri, 445 U.S. 622, 649 (1980). Legal standard: Monell, 436 U.S. at 683, 694 (overruling *Monroe v. Pape*, which had held that municipalities were not persons for purposes of section 1983 litigation); Los Angeles County, Cal. v. Humphries, 562 U.S. 29, 35–36 (2010) (referring to a city's "own violations"); Joanna C. Schwartz, "Backdoor Municipal Immunity," *Yale L. J. F.* 136, 137 (Oct. 14, 2022) (Court requires "evidence of nearly identical past misconduct to prove policymakers' deliberate indifference.").

6. Owen, 445 U.S. at 671 (Powell, J., dissenting). Justice Powell was not the only justice who worried about the financial impact of civil rights liability on cities. Joanna Schwartz, *Shielded: How the Police Became Untouchable* 200 (Viking 2023) (discussing *Monell* dissent).

7. Owen, 445 U.S. at 651–52 ("the threat that damages might be levied against the city may encourage those in a policymaking position to institute internal rules and programs designed to minimize the likelihood of unintentional infringements on constitutional rights."); Schwartz, *Shielded* at 165, 177.

8. Joanna C. Schwartz, "Police Indemnification," 89 *N.Y.U. L. Rev.* 885, 889–90 (2014); Joanna C. Schwartz, "How Governments Pay: Lawsuits, Budgets, and Police Reform," 63 *UCLA L. Rev.* 1144, 1148 (2016) (majority pay from jurisdictions' general funds rather than from agency); Theodore Eisenberg and Stewart Schwab, "The Reality of Constitutional Tort Litigation," 72 *Cornell L. Rev.* 641, 686 (1987).

9. Schwartz, "How Governments Pay," at 1165 ("[I]n the jurisdictions in my study, law enforcement liability accounts for significantly less than one percent of most jurisdictions' expenditures.").

10. O'Loghlin v. County of Orange, 229 F.3d 871 (9th Cir. 2000).

11. *Silver Sage Partners, Ltd. v. City of Desert Hot Springs*, 339 F.3d 782, 787 (9th Cir. 2003).

12. Detroit is "the most densely concentrated Black city in the country" and has a history of police brutality and violence. Kate Hamaji, Kumar Rao, Marbre Stahly-Butts, Janaé Bonsu, Charlene A. Carruthers, Roselyn Berry, and Denzel McCampbell, *Freedom to Thrive: Reimagining Safety and*

Security in Our Communities 31–32 (Center for Popular Democracy 2017) (citing 2011–15 data and historical examples); Thomas Sugrue, *The Origins of the Urban Crisis: Race and Inequality in Postwar Detroit* (Princeton U. Press 2014). Midwestern city ranking: Scott Calvert and Dan Frosch, "Police Rethink Policies as Cities Pay Millions to Settle Misconduct Claims," *Wall St. J.* Oct. 22, 2020 (data from 2015–20).

13. David Bjerk, "Does Greater Police Funding Help Catch More Murderers?," 19 *J. Empirical Leg. Stud.* 528, 530 (2022) ("I find no evidence that such variation [in per capita police budget] has any significant empirical relationship with homicide clearance rates."). *See also* Hassan Kanu, "Police Are Not Primarily Crime Fighters, According to the Data," *Reuters*, Nov. 2, 2021 (how police officers spend their time).

14. Melissa Jacoby, "Settling Detroit; Remembering General Unsecured Creditors," *Credit Slips*, Sept. 12, 2014 (reporting on civil rights claimants' request for special committee); Order Denying Motion to Appoint Committee of Creditors with Claims Under 42 U.S.C. § 1983, *In re* City of Detroit, 13-53846 (Bankr. E.D. Mich. Mar. 11, 2014), docket #2993. When the government watchdog appointed a committee to represent miscellaneous creditors that would have included civil rights claimants, the court accepted the city's request to dissolve the committee, deeming it unnecessary. *In re* City of Detroit, 519 B.R. 673 (Bankr. E.D. Mich. 2014).

15. Lyda v. City of Detroit, 2014 WL 6474081 at *5 (Bankr. E.D. Mich., Nov. 19, 2014), affirmed by Lyda v. City of Detroit, 2015 WL 5461463 (E.D. Mich. Sept. 16, 2015); *In re* City of Detroit, Mich., 841 F.3d 684, 696, 698 n.6 (6th Cir. 2016); *id.* at 698 ("Plaintiffs' constitutional rights are inviolable; but the remedies available to them in the chapter 9 setting are not."); Melissa Jacoby, "Chapter 9's Cabinet of Constitutional Curiosities: Ongoing Constitutional Violations," *Credit Slips*, November 22, 2016.

16. Tresa Baldas, "Lawsuits Against Detroit in Limbo Because of Bankruptcy," *Detroit Free Press*, Aug. 4, 2013 (ACLU lawyer: "Our No. 1 priority is to vindicate the constitutional rights of our clients and for policy change.").

17. Parties' Joint Motion for Decertification at 2, Brown v. City of Detroit, 10-12162 (E.D. Mich. Oct. 12, 2018), docket #126 (case stayed until Oct. 1, 2014).

18. *In re* City of Detroit, 548 B.R. 748, 754–55 (Bankr. E.D. Mich. 2016) (discussing Hughes dispute).

19. Melissa Jacoby, "Detroit's Managerial Milestones," *Credit Slips*, Oct. 9, 2013.

20. 11 U.S.C. § 901 (extending Chapter 11 voting and plan confirmation

rules to Chapter 9); *id.* § 1129(a)(10) (requiring majority support of at least one impaired class of claims); *id.* § 943 (listing additional plan confirmation requirements including feasibility and a finding that the plan is in the best interest of creditors). Plan can provide a debt is not canceled: *id.* § 944(c)(1).

21. Civil right claimant arguments: Objections of Creditors Deborah Ryan et al. to Amended Plan, *In re* City of Detroit, 13-53846 (Bankr. E.D. Mich. Apr. 15, 2014), docket #4099; Brief in Concurrence of Creditors, *In re* City of Detroit, 13-53846 (Bankr. E.D. Mich. June 30, 2014), docket #5693; Second Supplemental Brief of Ryan et al. at 4, *In re* City of Detroit, 13-53846 (Bankr. E.D. Mich. Aug. 15, 2014), docket #6764. Takings Clause claims in bankruptcy: *In re* Financial Oversight and Management Board, 41 F.4th 29, 41 (1st Cir. 2022) (In Puerto Rico restructuring case akin to municipal bankruptcy, upholding district court finding that the Fifth Amendment precludes the impairment or discharge of claims for just compensation.).

22. City of Detroit, 524 B.R. at 266. Whether the city would be obliged to indemnify these third parties would depend on other factors, such as the city's collective bargaining agreements. The scope of indemnification also might depend on when the obligation arose.

23. Nathan Bomey and Mark Stryker, "Historic Detroit Bankruptcy Doodle to Be Donated to DIA," *Detroit Free Press*, Mar. 18, 2015 ("Rosen, who served as lead mediator in the city's bankruptcy, is the honored guest at a private April 10 event at the DIA to enshrine his 'historic doodle,' according to an invitation distributed by the museum."); Daniel Howes, Chad Livengood, and David Shepardson, "Bankruptcy and Beyond: The Inside Story of the Deals That Brought Detroit Back from the Brink in Fifteen Months," *Detroit News*, Dec. 13, 2014.

24. Media blitz: Nathan Bomey, *Detroit Resurrected* at 200.

25. Parties' Joint Motion for Decertification at 4, Brown v. Detroit, 10-12162 (E.D. Mich. Oct. 12, 2018), docket #126 ("[I]t will be several more years before class 14 notes will be issued."). Holders of claims in Class 14 initially were told they would receive a pro rata share of $16.48 million in new B Notes. Eighth Amended Plan for Adjustment of Debts of the City of Detroit at 51, *In re* City of Detroit, 13-53846 (Bankr. E.D. Mich. Oct. 22, 2014), docket #8045. As of September 2019, Class 14 contained 115 allowed claims of $200 million in the aggregate. City of Detroit's Motion to Implement Distributions of B Notes to Holders of Allowed Class 14 Claims at 7, *In re* City of Detroit, 13-53846 (Bankr. E.D. Mich. Sept. 17, 2019), docket #13126.

26. City of Detroit's Motion to Implement Distributions of B Notes to

Holders of Allowed Class 14 Claims at 8, *In re* City of Detroit, 13-53846 (Bankr. E.D. Mich. Sept. 17, 2019), docket #13126 (giving claimants six months after receiving notice to provide brokerage and tax information, and thereafter interest would revert to city); Order Granting the City of Detroit's Motion, *In re* City of Detroit, 13-53846 (Bankr. E.D. Mich. Nov. 13, 2019), docket #13173 (approving Detroit's proposed method of distribution). Difficulties reporting updated information necessary for payment: Exhibit A to Certificate of Service of Correction Letter, *In re* City of Detroit, 13-53846 (May 21, 2020), docket #13287. Brokerage account data: Board of Governors of the Federal Reserve System, *Report of the Economic Well-Being of U.S. Households in 2017* 26 (May 2018). According to the 2013 Survey of Consumer Finance, 17 million American households owned a brokerage account, but only 2.8 percent of those in the bottom quartile of income had such an account, and 6.7 percent of those in the second-lowest income quartile. Constantijn W.A. Panis and Michael J. Brien, *Brokerage Accounts in the United States* 3 (Advanced Analytical Consulting Group Nov. 30, 2015). African American households have investment accounts at dramatically lower rates than white households do. *A Snapshot of Investor Households in America* (FINRA Investor Education Foundation Sept. 2015).

27. Tax inequality: Andrew Van Dam, "Black Families Pay Significantly Higher Property Taxes than White Families, New Analysis Shows," *Wash. Post*, July 2, 2020 (citing research by Troup Howard and Carlos Avenancio-Leon). Detroit tax disparities: Christine MacDonald and Mark Betancourt, "Detroit Homeowners Overtaxed $600 million," *Detroit News*, Jan. 9, 2020; Bernadette Atuahene, "Predatory Cities," 108 *Calif. L. Rev.* 107, 109–10 (2020)(one in four residential properties in Detroit were subject to tax foreclosure between 2011 and 2015, a period that spans the city's bankruptcy, a far higher rate of foreclosure than one would find in other cities, as well as higher than in other parts of Wayne County, Michigan, with predominantly white residents); Bernadette Atuahene and Timothy Hodge, "Stategraft," 91 *S. Cal. L. Rev.* 263 (2018) (at least half and perhaps more than 80 percent of recent Detroit assessments were conducted in violation of the state constitution, substantially contributing to tax foreclosures). *See generally* Dorothy Brown, *The Whiteness of Wealth* (Crown 2021).

28. Sanford v. Detroit, 17-13062, 2018 WL 6331342 (E.D. Mich. Dec. 4, 2018).

29. Complaint and Jury Demand, Johnson v. Adams, 19-12331 (E.D. Mich. Aug. 6, 2019), docket #1. Oralandar Brand-Williams, "Man Exonerated in '99 Slaying Sues 2 Detroit Cops," *Detroit News*, Aug. 6, 2019.

30. Jim Christie, "San Bernardino Still Contesting Civil Rights Claims to Chapter 9 Plan," *Reuters*, Mar. 16, 2017 (Banuelos); Ryan Hagen, "San Bernardino Seeks Final Confirmation of Bankruptcy Plan Friday," *San Bernardino County Sun*, Jan. 27, 2017 (Banuelos); Ryan Hagen, "Attorneys File Notice to Appeal San Bernardino Bankruptcy Confirmation," *San Bernardino County Sun*, Feb. 23, 2017 (Triplett); Joyce E. Cutler, "San Bernardino Shielded from Police-Related Court Awards," *BNA Bankruptcy Law Reporter*, Mar. 10, 2017 (Triplett); Katy Stech, "San Bernardino Bankruptcy Leaves Little for Police-Brutality Payouts," *Wall St. J.*, Jan. 7, 2016 (city did not honor its promise to pay $686,000 to the mother of slain resident by July 15, 2012, and filed for bankruptcy two weeks after that). *See also* Ryan Hagen, "Why Two Attorneys Are Appealing San Bernardino's Bankruptcy Decision," *San Bernardino County Sun*, May 28, 2017 (Rovinski Renter had at least eight surgeries after police encounter and may lose her home). San Bernardino statistics: California Department of Justice and California Department of Finance data; Annie Gilbertson and Aaron Mendelson, "California Police Use Force at a Higher Rate Against Blacks, Data Shows," KPCC.org, Aug. 17, 2017.

31. Voting: Ryan Hagen, "Attorneys File Notice to Appeal San Bernardino Bankruptcy Confirmation," *San Bernardino County Sun*, Feb. 23, 2017 (43 creditors out of the 983 creditors voted against the plan in the relevant class). Potential for greater recovery: Civil rights claimants of San Bernardino or its police officers may receive more than 1 percent if their judgments exceed $1 million due to an Excess Liability Insurance contract between San Bernardino and the Big Independent Cities Excess Pool Joint Powers Authority (BICEP). This contract requires the city to self-insure for the first $1 million of costs, settlements, and judgments per claim but provides for any claim exceeding that $1 million and up to $9 million of coverage per claim. The applicable policy has exclusions that could be pertinent in police misconduct cases, including in which the covered party is found to have acted with "actual fraud, corruption, and actual malice" or "engaged in a willful act" or for certain types of events, including the "[p]olice use of mace, oleoresin capsicum (O.C. or pepper gas), or tear gas," BICEP Policy and the Reinsurance Contracts, Appendix of Exhibits in Support of Third Amended Plan, *In re* San Bernardino, 12-28006 (Bankr. C.D. Cal. July 29, 2016), docket #1882-5.

32. Objection to Third Amended Plan for the Adjustment of Debts of the City of San Bernardino, California (July 29, 2016) at 3, *In re* City of San Bernardino, 12-28006 (Bankr. C.D. Cal. Sept. 2, 2016), docket #1924

(objections of six civil rights claimants); Notice of Joinder and Joinder in Objection to Confirmation of Debtor's Third Amended Plan Filed on Behalf of Michael Wade and Others at 1, *In re* City of San Bernardino, 12-28006 (Bankr. C.D. Cal. Sept. 2, 2016), docket #1925; Notice of Joinder and Joinder in Objection to Confirmation of Debtor's Third Amended Plan Filed on Behalf of Michael Wade and Others at 2–3, *In re* City of San Bernardino, 12-28006 (Bankr. C.D. Cal. Sept. 20, 2016), docket #1951 (objections of seven civil rights claimants in post-petition wrongful death action brought against two police officers); Memorandum to the Court re: Civil Rights Claims of Creditor Javier Banuelos at 2, *In re* City of San Bernardino, No. 12-28006 (Bankr. C.D. Cal. Sept. 20, 2016), docket #2013 ("The plan is a great injustice. In violation of precedent it destroys most civil rights claims."); Amended Formal Objection to Third Amended Plan to Adjustment of Debts of the City of San Bernardino, California at 2, *In re* City of San Bernardino, No. 12-28006 (Bankr. C.D. Cal. Sept. 2, 2016), docket #1913 (noting objection of Paul Triplett); Chapter 9 Objection to Confirmation of the Third Amended Plan at 1, *In re* City of San Bernardino, 12-28006 (Bankr. C.D. Cal. Sept. 1, 2016), docket #1906 (objection of civil rights claimant William Schmart).

33. Deocampo v. Potts, 836 F.3d 1134, 1141, 1143, 1146 (9th Cir. 2016). Vallejo police problems: Shane Bauer, "How a Deadly Police Force Ruled a City," *New Yorker*, Nov. 16, 2020; Otis R. Taylor, "In Vallejo, Police Encounters Often Turn Violent," *S.F. Chronicle*, Sept. 13, 2020.

34. *In re* City of San Bernardino, 566 B.R. 46, 48 (Bankr. C.D. Cal. 2017) ("A lynchpin of the Plan was payment of 1% on the dollar on the allowed claims of Class 13, the class of general unsecured creditors"). *Id*. at 49 (recognizing civil rights claims as significant component of Class 13 and the need to protect employees because under California law the city had an obligation to indemnify them). *Id*. at 50 ("the primary purpose of the Plan Injunction was to shield the City's employees, specifically its police officers" from civil rights liability). *Id*. at 54–56 (explaining reasoning for approving plan and police officer protection, including the lack of funds to both pay the judgments against city employees and invest in a police resources plan). *Id*. at 57–59 (citing *Deocampo v. Potts* and other sources for authority to protect police officers through San Bernardino bankruptcy).

35. Treva Lindsey, *America, Goddam: Violence, Black Women, and the Struggle for Justice* 38 (U. California Press 2022).

36. Destin Jenkins, "What Does It Really Mean to Invest in Black Communities?," *The Nation*, June 29, 2020. *See generally* Destin Jenkins, "The

Fed Could Undo Decades of Damage to Cities. Here's How," *Wash. Post*, Apr. 27, 2020.

37. Schwartz, *Shielded*, at 21, 193; Joanna C. Schwartz, "Civil Rights Ecosystems," 118 *Mich. L. Rev.* 1539 (2020).

38. Kenny Cooper, "Civil Rights on Hold? Chester's Bankruptcy Freezes All Litigation Against the City," WHYY, Apr. 21, 2023.

5. My Money, My Rules

1. Lawsuit: Soto et al. v. Bushmaster Firearms Int'l a/k/a Remington Outdoor Company et al., UWY-CV15 6050025S (Conn. Super. Ct. Dec. 13, 2014). Families' lawsuit objectives: Peg Brickley, "Sandy Hook Families Question Remington's Plan for Speedy Sale," *Wall St. J.*, Aug. 10, 2020; Peg Brickley, "Remington Won't Have to Answer Questions from Sandy Hook Families," *Wall St. J.*, Aug. 27, 2020.

2. Supreme Court's denial of certiorari: Remington Arms Co., LLC v. Soto, 140 S.Ct. 513 (Nov. 12, 2019). A key issue was whether the Protection of Lawful Commerce in Arms Act, passed in 2005, blocked this suit. *See generally* Linda S. Mullenix, "Outgunned No More?: Reviving a Firearms Industry Mass Tort Litigation," 49 *S.W. L. Rev.* 390 (2020). State court discovery: Melissa Angell, "Sandy Hook Families Fight Remington's School Records Bid," *Law 360*, Sept. 2, 2021; Plaintiffs' Motion to Compel, Soto v. Bushmaster Firearms Int'l, UWY-CV15 6050025S (Conn. Super. Ct. July 2, 2021), docket # BL-309 (reporting receipt of images of Santa Claus, the Minions character, videos of go-carting, and the ice bucket challenge as a result of their request for documents relevant to Sandy Hook families' lawsuit for wrongful death, and arguing "Remington has treated discovery as a game.").

3. Government watchdog position: Transcript of Emergency Status Conference on August 6, 2020, at 13–14, *In re* Remington Outdoor Co., 20-81688 (Bankr. N.D. Ala. Aug. 10, 2020), docket #265. Continued Sandy Hook family objections: Objection to Confirmation at 2–3, *In re* Remington Outdoor Co., 20-81688 (Bankr. N.D. Ala. Mar. 1, 2021), docket #1546. Notice of Filing Revisions, *In re* Remington Outdoor Co., 20-81688 (Bankr. N.D. Ala. Mar. 10, 2021), docket #1635. Confirmation of plan and resolution: Transcript of Confirmation Order on Mar. 11, 2021, at 9, *In re* Remington Outdoor Co., 20-81688 (Bankr. N.D. Ala. Mar. 12, 2021), docket #1659 ("Court found that cause existed . . . to confirm the plan after the resolution of the Sandy Hook Families and other tort claimant's

objections."); *id*. at 22 (court expressing appreciation to the Sandy Hook families for settling, "I think it is in the best interest of all parties."); Order Approving Settlement Payment to the Sandy Hook Families, *In re* Remington Outdoor Company, 20-81688 (Bankr. N.D. Ala. Mar. 29, 2022), docket #2453; Michael Steinberger, "The Lawyer Trying to Hold Gunmakers Responsible for Mass Shootings," *N.Y. Times*, Sept. 29, 2023 (insurers negotiated the agreement with the families, which includes an obligation to make litigation materials public, although that had not yet happened).

4. George W. Kuney, "Hijacking Chapter 11," 21 *Emory Bankr. Dev. J.* 19, 57 (2004) (expense of DIP loans and likely windfalls given that loans are nearly always repaid in full); Report of the American Bankruptcy Institute Commission to Study the Reform of Chapter 11 at 75 (2014); B. Espen Eckbo, Kai Li, and Wei Wang, *Do Lenders Extract Rents When Financing Bankrupt Firms?* (working paper last revised Oct. 7, 2021).

5. Chesapeake Energy: Transcript of Emergency Motion Hearing on July 31, 2020, at 177–78, *In re* Chesapeake Energy Corp., 20-33233 (Bankr. S.D. Tex. Aug. 4, 2020), docket #615. GNC bankruptcy: Objection of Noteholders at 6, *In re* GNC Holdings, Inc. et al., 20-11662 (Bankr. D. Del June 25, 2020), docket #102 (calling relief "unnecessary and disproportionate" and "improper"); Rose Krebs, "GNC Can Tap into Chapter 11 Funds Despite Creditor Opposition," *Law360*, June 25, 2020 (court approved financing in light of "unprecedented and uncertain" times in the retail industry due to COVID-19).

6. Jacqueline Palank, "Firms in Chapter 11 Face Fast Trip to Auction Block," *Wall St. J.*, Jan. 13, 2013. Lender leverage in Chapter 11 generally: Melissa B. Jacoby and Edward J. Janger, "Ice Cube Bonds: Allocating the Price of Process in Chapter 11 Bankruptcy," 123 *Yale L. J.* 865 (2014); Melissa B. Jacoby and Edward J. Janger, Tracing Equity: "Tracing Equity: Realizing and Allocating Value in Chapter 11," 96 *Tex. L. Rev.* 673–735 (2018).

7. Weinstein Company details: Melissa B. Jacoby, "Unbundling Business Bankruptcy Law," 101 *N.C. L. Rev.* 1703, 1739 (2023). Remington: Alexander Gladstone and Peg Brickley, "Remington Layoffs Roil Ilion, NY, One of America's Oldest Factory Towns," *Wall St. J.*, Oct. 29, 2020.

8. ABI Commission Report on Chapter 11 at 87, 201, 204, 206.

9. Brief for the Federal Appellants at 15, *In re* TWA Airlines, 01-1788, 2001 WL 34113536 (3d. Cir. Mar. 25, 2002). For decades, the U.S. Supreme Court and intermediate appellate courts, including the Third Circuit that would rule on TWA, had not looked fondly on efforts outside of bankruptcy

to use sales to strip off labor law or antidiscrimination obligations. John Wiley & Sons, Inc. v. Livingston, 376 U.S. 543, 544, 548 (1964); Einhorn v. M.L. Ruberton Construction Co., 632 F.3d 89, 94–95 (3d Cir. 2011) (courts go beyond common law rule "when necessary to protect important employment-related policies" . . ."[t]his court . . . has extended the labor law successorship doctrine to employment discrimination claims under Title VII.").

10. *In re* Trans World Airlines, 322 F.3d 283, 293 (3d Cir. 2003).

11. Details of sale and limitations on responsibility: Asset Purchase Agreement at 114, ¶ 6.2, *In re* the Weinstein Company, 18-10601 (Bankr. D. Del. Mar. 20, 2018), docket # 8.

12. *In re* Leckie Smokeless Coal Co., 99 F.3d 573, 577, 585 (4th Cir. 1996).

13. Joshua Macey and Jackson Salovaara, "Bankruptcy as Bailout: Coal Company Insolvency and the Erosion of Federal Law," 71 *Stan. L. Rev.* 879, 886, 945 (2019).

14. Spewed lead: California Dep't of Toxic Substances Control's Preliminary Objection, *In re* Exide Holdings, Inc., 20-11157 (Bankr. D. Del. Oct. 7, 2020), docket #917. Just another reminder: Tony Barboza, "Court Allows Exide to Abandon a Toxic Site in Vernon. Taxpayers Will Fund the Cleanup," *L.A. Times*, Oct. 16, 2020 (quoting Assemblywoman Cristina Garcia).

15. Not all contracts restrict assignments to third parties to the same extent. Kenneth Ayotte and Henry Hansmann, "Legal Entities as Transferrable Bundles of Contracts," 111 *Mich. L. Rev.* 715 (2013); Kenneth Ayotte, "Leases and Executory Contracts in Chapter 11," 12 *J. Emp. Leg. Stud.* 637, 649, 660 (2015).

16. Weinstein Company contract issues in detail: Jacoby, "Unbundling Business Bankruptcy Law," at 1730–31, 1745–52.

17. Czyzewski v. Jevic Holding Corp., 137 S. Ct. 973 (2017).

18. Jobs and health insurance: United States Trustee's Objection to Debtors' Motion for Order Authorizing Implementation of and Performance Under Employee Incentive Plan at 2, *In re* Jevic Holding Corp., 08-11006 (Bankr. D. Del. June 20, 2008), docket #117 ("Because the Debtors terminated their health insurance plan, terminated employees were not offered the opportunity to acquire replacement insurance coverage under COBRA."). End of operating business: Debtors' Emergency Motion for Interim and Final Orders, at *4, *6, *In re* Jevic Holding Corp., 08-11006 (Bankr. D. Del. May 20, 2008), docket #11.

19. Restriction on how money could be spent: Interim Financing Order, at 23–24, *In re* Jevic Holding Corp., 08-11006 (Bankr. D. Del. May 22, 2008), docket #32; Debtors' Emergency Motion for Interim and Final Orders, at 7, 12, *In re* Jevic Holding Corp., 08-11006 (Bankr. D. Del. May 20, 2008), docket #11. Bonuses to executives: Motion of Debtors . . . for an Order Authorizing the Implementation of and Performance Under Employee Incentive Plan, at 9, *In re* Jevic Holding Corp. at 5, 08-11006 (Bankr. D. Del. May 30, 2008), docket #60; Order Authorizing . . . Incentive Plan at 2, *In re* Jevic Holding Corp., 08-11006 (Bankr. D. Del. July 10, 2008), docket #159 (authorizing lower payout).

20. Order Authorizing the Debtors to Sell at Auction Substantially All of the Debtors' Personal Property Free and Clear of All Liens, Claims, Interests, and Encumbrances . . . , *In re* Jevic Holding Corp., 08-11006 (Bankr. D. Del. July 10, 2008), docket #158.

21. Lawsuit: Complaint and Objection to Claims, Official Committee of Unsecured Creditors v. CIT Group/Business Credit Inc. (*In re* Jevic Holding Corp.), 08-11006 (Bankr. D. Del. Dec. 31, 2008), docket #372. Merit of lawsuits: *In re* Jevic Holding Corp., 2011 WL 4345204 at *14 (Bankr. D. Del. Sept. 15, 2011) ("CIT has not established that dismissal is warranted with respect to . . . claims . . . under 11 U.S.C. §§ 547, 548, and 550."). Defendants' intent to fight at every turn: Transcript regarding Hearing Held November 13, 2012, at 106, Official Committee of Unsecured Creditors v. CIT Group/Business Credit Inc. (*In re* Jevic Holding Corp.), 08-11006 (Bankr. D. Del. Nov. 27, 2012), docket #1514.

22. Joint Motion . . . for Entry of an Order Approving Settlement at 19-20, Official Committee v. CIT Group, 08-11006 (Bankr. D. Del. June 27, 2012), docket #1346 (Sun's lawyer explaining exclusion of WARN Act claimants from distribution to keep funds from party suing Sun).

23. Transcript regarding Hearing Held 11/13/2012 at 112, Official Committee of Unsecured Creditors v. CIT Group/Business Credit Inc. (*In re* Jevic Holding Corp.), 08-11006 (Bankr. D. Del. Nov. 27, 2012), docket #1514. Order Granting Joint Motion . . . for Entry of Order Approving Settlement, Official Committee v. CIT Group, 08-11006 (Bankr. D. Del. Dec. 4, 2012), docket #1520 (vacated).

24. Jevic, 137 S. Ct. at 985.

6. From Overindebtedness to Liability Management

1. Money in bank: Declaration of Jon Lowne in Support of the Debtors' Chapter 11 Petitions and First Day Pleadings at 14, *In re* Purdue Pharma, 19-23649 (Bankr. S.D.N.Y. Sept. 16, 2019), docket #3. No debt: Debtors' Informational Brief at 1, *In re* Purdue Pharma, 19-23649 (Bankr. S.D.N.Y. Sept. 16, 2019) ("unlike most debtors, the Debtors have no funded debt and no material past due trade obligations. Nor do they have any judgment creditors."); Brief for the Petitioner at 3–4, Harrington v. Purdue Pharma, 23–124, 2023 WL 6220089 (U.S. Sept. 20, 2023) [hereinafter Solicitor General brief]. At the time of the bankruptcy, almost 3,000 actions were pending against Purdue Pharma and over 400 opioid-related actions against the Sacklers directly. *Id*. at 4.

2. Statement of the United States Regarding the Shareholder Release at 4–5, *In re* Purdue Pharma L.P., 19-23649 (Bankr. S.D.N.Y. July 19, 2021), docket #3268 ("[T]he set of Releasing Parties is specifically not limited to only creditors of the bankruptcy estate who are receiving some measure of compensation under the plan."); Solicitor General brief, at 4–6, 33.

3. Solicitor General brief at 5 (payments to survivors receiving more than the minimum payout will be spread over up to ten years); Jonathan C. Lipson, "The Rule of the Deal: Bankruptcy Bargains and Other Misnomers," 97 *Am. Bankr. L. J.* 41, 99–100 (2023) (in settlement with last objecting states, Sacklers' contribution period lengthened from nine to eighteen years.). The Purdue Pharma plan does include a complicated "snapback" procedure that could renew claimants' legal rights in the event that the Sacklers default. Plan Support Letter from the Official Committee of Unsecured Creditors, in Joint Appendix, at 85, Harrington v. Purdue Pharma, 23–124, 2023 WL 6220126 (U.S. Sept. 20, 2023).

4. Harrington v. Purdue Pharma, 23–124, 2023 WL 5116031 (U.S. August 10, 2023). Briefs by former solicitors general and others are filed in Supreme Court case 23-124.

5. Brief for Ad Hoc Group of Individual Victims of Purdue Pharma, Harrington v. Purdue Pharma, 23–124, 2023 WL 7042396 (Oct. 20, 2023); Brief of Cheryl Juaire, Tiffinee Scott, Dede Yoder, Kathleen Scarpone, Stephanie Lubinski, Lynn Wencus, Gary Carter, Wendy Petrowsky, Kara Trainor, Kathleen Strain, Lindsey Arrington, Shannie Jenkins, Kerri Morales, C.R. Foster, and Robert Prochno as Amici Curiae in Support of Respondents, Harrington v. Purdue Pharma, 23–124, 2023 WL 7184144 (Oct. 27, 2023).

6. Brief for Ellen Isaacs Supporting Petitioner 2, Harrington v. Purdue Pharma, 23–124, 2023 WL 6220096 (Sept. 20, 2023) (special protection for billionaires); John Seewer & Geoff Mulvihill, "Families of Opioid Victims Outraged by OxyContin Makers' 'Sweetheart Deal,' " *Associated Press*, Sept. 3, 2021; Meryl Kornfield, "Opioid Victims Confront Purdue Pharma's Sackler Family: 'It Will Never End for Me,' " *Wash. Post*, March 10, 2022 (scam).

7. Purdue Pharma assertions about bankruptcy as the best forum: Debtors' Informational Brief at 4, *In re* Purdue Pharma, 19-23649 (Bankr. S.D.N.Y. Sept. 16, 2019), docket #17. *See also* Complaint for Injunctive Relief at 38, Purdue Pharma v. Commonwealth of MA et al., 19-0289 (Bankr. S.D.N.Y. Sept. 18, 2019), docket #1 ("[D]ecades of experience demonstrates that bankruptcy is a proven and efficient vehicle to successfully, rationally, and equitably resolve such mass tort liability."). Quote from bankruptcy court: Transcript of June 16, 2021 at 141, *In re* Purdue Pharma, 19-23649 (Bankr. S.D.N.Y. June 17, 2021), docket #3094.

8. Written Statement of Erik Haas, World Wide Vice President, Litigation, Johnson & Johnson at 6, U.S. Senate Committee on the Judiciary, Hearing on Evading Accountability: Corporate Manipulation of Chapter 11 Bankruptcy (Sept. 19, 2023).

9. "Magic Mineral" comes from Paul Brodeur's 1968 *New Yorker* article. Harrison Smith, "Paul Brodeur, Journalist, Who Exposed Asbestos Hazards, Dies at 92," *N.Y. Times*, Aug. 10, 2023.

10. Latency period: James S. Kakalik et al., "Costs of Asbestos Litigation," RAND Institute for Civil Justice 2–3 (1983). Multiple potential sources of exposure: Stephen J. Carroll et al., "Asbestos Litigation Cost and Compensation: An Interim Report," Rand Institute for Civil Justice 5 (2002) (typical plaintiff names several dozen defendants). Large numbers of claimants without functional impairment: *id.* at vi, 17.

11. Lloyd Dixon, Geoffrey McGovern, and Amy Coombe, "Asbestos Bankruptcy Trusts," RAND Institute for Civil Justice 1–2 (2010); Anita Bernstein, "Fellow-Feeling and Gender in the Law of Personal Injury," 18 *J. L. & Policy* 295, 304, 331, 374 (2009) ("A court can be confident that asbestos causes mesothelioma, but it cannot know how."); Michelle J. White, "Asbestos and the Future of Mass Torts," 18 *J. Econ. Perspectives* 183, 186–87 (2004).

12. Technically, the first asbestos-company bankruptcy was North American Asbestos, filed in 1976. Carroll et al., at 110, fn 4.

13. 100 percent promise: *Id.* at 114. Funding of Manville trust: *Id.*, at 113,

table 6.4. 95 percent approval rate among voting claimants: Kane v. Johns-Manville Corp., 843 F.2d 636, 641 (2d Cir. 1988). Channeling injunction: *Id*. at 640.

14. Impact of compensation rates on future asbestos lawsuits and bankruptcies: Carroll et al., at xxix, 102.

15. Chronological list of asbestos bankruptcies: the law firm Crowell & Moring, which represents insurance carriers, has long tracked and reported on these bankruptcies and, as of 2023, continues to keep an up-to-date list on its website. Crowell & Moring, *History of Asbestos Bankruptcies*, https://www.crowell.com/en/services/practices/insurance-reinsurance /history-of-asbestos-bankruptcies.

16. Final Report of the National Bankruptcy Review Commission 315–50 (1997).

17. Examples of asbestos bankruptcy recovery inconsistencies are documented in the Written Statement of Melissa B. Jacoby at 6–8, U.S. Senate Committee on the Judiciary, Hearing on Evading Accountability: Corporate Manipulation of Chapter 11 Bankruptcy (Sept. 19, 2023), drawing largely, although not exclusively, on Dixon et al. (reporting on disease values and variable payment percentages in asbestos personal injury trusts through 2009) and other studies by the RAND Institute for Civil Justice cited therein.

18. Senate Judiciary Committee Report 109-97 to accompany S. 852, "The Fairness in Asbestos Injury Resolution Act of 2005," (109th Congress, June 30, 2005) (Democrats Kennedy, Biden, Feingold, and Durbin concerned about capping the contribution of defendants even if more funds prove necessary, while Republican senators Kyl and Coburn worried that the FAIR Act was based too much on a bankruptcy model that had failed to deliver what it promised.).

19. "A human tragedy of overwhelming proportions:" Petition for a Writ of Certiorari, Mabey v. Official Committee of Equity Security Holders of A.H. Robins, 87-1267, 1998 WL 1093566 (U.S. Jan. 29, 1988).

20. Clare L. Roepke and Eric A. Schaff, "Long Tail Strings: Impact of the Dalkon Shield 40 Years Later," 4 *Open J. of Obstetrics and Gynecology* 996 (2014).

21. Lawsuits filed before bankruptcy: Mary F. Hawkins, *Unshielded: The Human Cost of the Dalkon Shield* 28 (U. Toronto Press 1997); Karen M. Hicks, *Surviving the Dalkon Shield IUD: Women Versus the Pharmaceutical Industry* 50 (Teachers College Press 1994). Evidence of concealment of harm and shortcomings of studies: Hicks at 5, 33, Hawkins at 3, 17–21.

22. Financial condition of Manville: Hicks, at 6, 58. Controversy of A.H. Robins filing and lawsuit of National Women's Health Network: Morton Mintz, *At Any Cost: Corporate Greed, Women, and the Dalkon Shield* 245 (Pantheon Books 1985).

23. Scope of permanent protection of third parties provided by A.H. Robins bankruptcy: Ralph Brubaker, "Nondebtor Releases and Injunctions in Chapter 11: Revisiting Jurisdictional Precepts and the Forgotten Callaway v. Benton Case," 72 *Am. Bankr. L. J.* 1 (1998); Hicks at 10. Court approval: *In re* A.H. Robins, 788 F.2d 994 (4th Cir. 1986); *In re* A.H. Robins, 880 F.2d 694 (4th Cir. 1989).

24. Lawsuits preceding bankruptcy: *In re* Drexel Burnham Lambert Group, Inc., 130 B.R. 910, 913 (S.D.N.Y. 1991). Milken: Thomas E. Ricks, "Milken Refuses to Testify in House Probe of Drexel Burnham's Junk Bond Activity," *Wall St. J.*, April 28, 1988 ("Mr. Milken . . . credited with almost single-handedly creating the huge market for junk bonds, which fueled the unprecedented takeover boom of the 1980s, and in the process helped transform Drexel into one of the nation's most profitable and powerful investment banks.") Temporary protection provided by Drexel bankruptcy: Wade Lambert, "Judge Bars Suits Against Employees of Drexel Burnham," *Wall St. J.*, Oct. 19, 1990.

25. Details about settlement and plan's protection of non-debtors, including Milken: Brubaker, "Revisiting Jurisdictional Precepts," at 4 fn.11 (documenting protection of approximately 200 former Drexel employees for alleged individual misdeeds). Brubaker noted that, even after contributing to the Drexel plan, "Milken retained personal worth of approximately $125 million, as well as control of family assets held in the names of his wife and children, reportedly worth another $350 million." *Id.* Citation of A.H. Robins and Manville as support for action in Drexel district court approval: Drexel, 130 B.R. at 928, fn 49.

26. *In re* Drexel Burnham Lambert Group, 960 F.2d 285, 293 (2d Cir. 1992).

27. *In re* Continental Airlines, 203 F.3d 203, 211, 212, 214 (3d Cir. 2000).

28. Billion-dollar pill: Transcript of March 10, 2022, hearing at 74, *In re* Purdue Pharma, 19-23659 (Bankr. S.D.N.Y. Mar. 17, 2022), docket #4539 (Kristy Nelson: "With Brian, like many others, his abuse began not by choice, rather innocently after he was prescribed your billion-dollar pill as a result of a car accident."). Singlehandedly created new generation: Ryan Hampton, *American Fix: Inside the Opioid Addiction Crisis and How to End It* 126 (All Points Books 2018). Sell sell sell: Shraddha Chakradhar and

Casey Ross, "The History of OxyContin, Told Through Unsealed Purdue Documents," *STAT News*, Dec. 3, 2019 (discussing Purdue Pharma sales bulletin to the prescription sales force, Jan. 25, 1999).

29. Key information revealed: Lipson, at 61. Opioid settlements: Brendan Pierson & Disha Raychaudhuri, "For Groups Fighting U.S. Opioid Crisis, Settlement Money Can Be Hard to Come By," *Reuters*, June 17, 2023 (settlements since 2021 set compensation at more than $50 billion).

30. Extraction of assets: Disclosure Statement at 164–65, *In re* Purdue Pharma, 19-23649 (Bankr. S.D.N.Y. June 3, 2021), docket #2983; Solicitor General brief at 5.

31. Vision coming into the bankruptcy: Purdue Pharma Informational Brief at 44–45.

32. Jonathan Randles, "Companies Lease Offices in New York Suburb to Pick Bankruptcy Judge," *Wall St. J.*, Aug. 13, 2020. New York's Department of State received Purdue Pharma's certificate of change on March 1, 2019. Joint Appendix (Volume 1), Harrington v. Purdue Pharma, 23–124, 2023 WL 6220126 (U.S. Sept. 20, 2023).

33. Emergency relief fund efforts, proliferation of lawyers and professional fees: Ryan Hampton, *Unsettled: How the Purdue Pharma Bankruptcy Failed the Victims of the American Overdose Crisis* (St. Martin's Press 2021). Limited recovery for individuals and families: Solicitor General brief at 5 (payout between $3,500 and $48,000, for those who can document use of a Purdue Pharma-branded opioid, before deducting lawyers' fees and cost of administering the trust).

34. Marshall Huebner quote: Transcript from July 23, 2020, at 50, *In re* Purdue Pharma, 19-23649 (Bankr. S.D.N.Y. Aug. 5, 2020), docket #1549.

35. Injunction protecting Sacklers and corresponding obligations: *In re* Purdue Pharma, 633 B.R. 53, 86 (Bankr. S.D.N.Y. 2021).

36. Complaint for Injunctive Relief at 25, 28, Purdue Pharma v. Commonwealth of Massachusetts, et al., 19-8289 (Bankr. S.D.N.Y. Sept. 18, 2019), docket #1.

37. United States Department of Justice Plea Agreement with Purdue Pharma L.P., Oct. 20, 2020. Details of the DOJ complaint and settlement analyzed in Lipson, at 77–78.

38. Published opinion following oral ruling: *In re* Purdue Pharma, 633 B.R. 53 (Bankr. S.D.N.Y. 2021). Most complex case: *id.* at 106.

39. Court reasoning: *id.* at 88–90.

40. Over 95 percent among voting personal injury claimants: *id.* at 107. Vote tally: Final Declaration at 10, Exhibit A, *In re* Purdue Pharma,

19-23649 (Bankr. S.D.N.Y. Aug. 2, 2021), docket #3372 (130,488 claims, 58,196 voting yes, 2,600 voting no). Large undervote: Solicitor General brief at 6 (out of 618,194 claimants in Purdue Pharma bankruptcy in all classes, fewer than 20 percent entitled to vote did so).

41. *In re* Purdue Pharma L.P., 635 B.R. 26 (S.D.N.Y. 2021).

42. Terms of settlement and recommendation to permit opioid crisis survivors to speak at hearing: Mediator's Fourth Interim Report at 5–7, 8, *In re* Purdue Pharma, 19-23649 (Bankr. S.D.N.Y. Mar. 3, 2022), docket #4409. Hearing featuring twenty-six individuals and families: Transcript of March 10, 2022 hearing at 9, *In re* Purdue Pharma, 19-23649 (Bankr. S.D.N.Y. March 17, 2022), docket #4539.

43. *In re* Purdue Pharma, 69 F.4th 45 (2nd Cir. 2023).

44. *Id.* at 85–91.

45. Brief of Amicus Curiae U.S. Conference of Catholic Bishops in Support of Debtor Respondents at 2, 5, Harrington v. Purdue Pharma, 23–124 (Oct. 27, 2023).

46. Pamela Foohey, "Bankrupting the Faith," 78 *Mo. L. Rev.* 719, 721, 724–26 (2013); Pamela Foohey, "When Churches Reorganize," 88 *Am. Bankr. L. J.* 277, 284 (2014).

47. USA Gymnastics details, including prohibition on punitive damages: Lindsey D. Simon, "Bankruptcy Grifters," 131 *Yale L. J.* 1154, 1157, 1195 (2022). Testimony: Written Statement of Tasha Schwikert Moser, Esq. Bronze-Medal Olympian Gymnast, Attorney, Sex Abuse Survivor at 3, Hearing on Oversight of the Bankruptcy Code, Part 1: Confronting Abuses of the Chapter 11 System, Subcommittee on Antitrust, Commercial and Administrative Law, Committee on the Judiciary, U.S. House of Representatives, July 28, 2021. Athlete protections: Rachel Martin and Tom Goldman, "USA Gymnastics Settles Abuse Claims Involving Former Team Doctor Larry Nassar," *NPR Morning Edition*, Dec. 14, 2021.

48. Debtors' Informational Brief at 46, *In re* Boy Scouts of America, 20-10343 (Bankr. D. Del. Feb. 18, 2020), docket #4 (Cases present "unique, historic, and complex challenges."). Professional fees: Mike Baker, "Staggering Legal Fees in Boy Scouts Bankruptcy Case," *N.Y. Times*, May 11, 2021 (cites presiding judge as calling the cost "staggering"); Omnibus Order Granting Final Allowance of Certain Fees and Expenses for Certain Professionals, *In re* Boy Scouts of America, 20-10343 (Bankr. D. Del. Oct. 17, 2023), docket #11541 (over $157 million for debtor's professionals, $54 million for survivor committee professionals, nearly $13 million for professionals of committee representing other

non-abuse claimants, and nearly $21 million for future claims representative and his professionals).

49. Thirty years: Debtor's Informational Brief at 3. Recent abuse claims: Transcript of Boy Scouts of America Official Tort Claimants Committee Town Hall at 7, Oct. 14, 2021 ("over 18,000 claims of the 82,000 claims that happened after youth protection was in place. That's 22%, folks."). Delay in survivors coming forward: Marci A. Hamilton et al., "History of Child Abuse Statutes of Limitation Reform in the United States 2002 to 2021" at 2, *Child USA* (June 21, 2022).

50. Financial profile of new Delaware subsidiary: Schedules of assets and liabilities for Delaware BSA, LLC at 4, 17, *In re* Boy Scouts of America, 20-10343 (Bankr. D. Del. April 8, 2020), docket #377. Bright future: Transcript of Hearing on Feb. 19, 2020, at 11–13, *In re* Boy Scouts of America, 20-10343 (Bankr. D. Del. Feb. 20, 2020), docket #76 (after explaining the organization's history "in the fabric of America," and the inclusion of girls in scouting, asserting that "it's a pretty exciting time for this organization").

51. Chartered organization information: Boy Scouts of America Informational Brief at 22.

52. Tort Claimants Committee Recommends That Survivors Vote to Reject the Boy Scouts Plan, Oct. 1, 2021 (Local Councils will be left with over a billion dollars in cash and property in excess of assets needed to fulfill scouting mission).

53. Payment in full: exhibit 1 at 6–7 to Notice of Filing of Unsealed Version of Joint FCR and Coalition Motion, *In re* Boy Scouts of America, 20-10343 (Bankr. D. Del. Feb. 14, 2022), docket #8811-1 (identifying downward valuation of abuse claims to support Boy Scouts' "pivot to a 'full pay' strategy").

54. Plan confirmation: *In re* Boy Scouts of America, 642 B.R. 504, 560–62, 586, 602, 607 (Bankr. D. Del. 2022).

55. Plan approval on appeal: *In re* Boy Scouts of America, 650 B.R. 87 (D. Del. 2023). Effective date of bankruptcy plan: Associated Press: "Boy Scouts Bankruptcy Plan in Effect; Appeals Likely Go On," *Associated Press*, April 19, 2023.

56. Historically employed: Brief for Mortimer-Side Initial Covered Sackler Respondents at 1–2, Harrington v. Purdue Pharma, 23–124, 2023 WL 7042562 (Oct. 20, 2023). Almost every mass tort crisis: Brief of Respondent Ad Hoc Committee of Governmental and Other Contingent Litigation Claimants at 45 fn 12, Harrington v. Purdue Pharma, 23–124, 2023 WL 7042626 (Oct. 20, 2023).

7. Beyond the Victory Lap

1. First Mallinckrodt bankruptcy: *In re* Mallinckrodt, 639 B.R. 837, 865, 868, 871, 874, 902 (Bankr. D. Del. 2022).

2. Jonathan Randles, "A $1.7 Billion Opioid Settlement Is at Risk of Falling Apart," *Bloomberg*, June 16, 2023; Alexander Saeedy, Alexander Gladstone, and Akiko Matsuda, "Hedge Funds Seek to Cut Off $1 Billion Meant for Opioid Victims," *Wall St. J. Pro Bankruptcy*, July 26, 2023.

3. Alexander Gladstone, "Mallinckrodt Pays Executives $3.4 Million in Bonuses After Skipping Interest, Opioid Payments," *Wall St. J.*, June 21, 2023; Alexander Gladstone and Andrew Scurria, "Mallinckrodt Pays Executives $5 Million in Bonuses Ahead of Possible Bankruptcy," *Wall St. J. Pro. Bankruptcy*, Sept. 8, 2020; Alexander Gladstone, "Mallinckrodt Sued for Allegedly Misleading Investors: Shareholders Accuse Pharmaceutical Company of Misrepresenting Its Financial Strength Before Missing Payments to Opioid Victims and Bondholders," *Wall St. J. Pro. Bankruptcy*, July 11, 2023.

4. "Gruesome:" Audio recording of First-Day Hearing at 0:19:52, *In re* Mallinckrodt, 23-11258 (Aug. 30, 2023), docket #158 (statement of David Molton); Sujeet Indap, "A Toxic Mix: Opioid Victims' $1bn Hit from Repeat Pharma Bankruptcy," *Fin. Times*, Oct. 4, 2023.

5. Mallinckrodt, 639 B.R. at 893–96.

6. Predictions not guaranteed: Lindsey D. Simon, "Bankruptcy Grifters," 131 *Yale L. J.* 1154, 1204 (2022).

7. Calculations from Florida-UCLA-LoPucki Bankruptcy Research Database. www.lopucki.law.ufl.edu.

8. Marc C. Scarcella and Peter R. Kelso, "A Reorganized Mess: The Current State of the Asbestos Bankruptcy Trust System," 30:4 *Mealey's Litigation Report* 1, Mar. 18, 2015. *Id.* at 3 (twenty-three trusts paying less today than in 2008; nine trusts paying more). Insolvency of Manville and other asbestos trusts: *Id.* at 16; Lloyd Dixon, Geoffrey McGovern, and Amy Coombe, "Asbestos Bankruptcy Trusts," RAND Institute for Civil Justice (2010).

9. Dueling estimates: Rebuttal Expert Report of Charles E. Bates at 3, Exhibit C to Notice of Filing of Unsealed Version of Joint FCR and Coalition Motion, *In re* Boy Scouts of America, 20-10343 (Bankr. D. Del. Feb. 14, 2022), docket #8811-1 (reporting Claro Report estimating low end of reasonable range of claim value for abuse claims in the aggregate at between $24.76 and $30.41 billion). Estimate put forward by Boy Scouts of America

at plan confirmation hearing: *In re* Boy Scouts of America, 642 B.R. 504, 557 (Bankr. D. Del. 2022) (between $2.4 and $3.6 billion).

10. Scouting Settlement Town Hall, Nov. 1, 2023; Brief for the Boy Scouts of America as Amicus Curiae in Support of Respondent at 3–4, Harrington v. Purdue Pharma, 23-124 (Oct. 27, 2023) (emphasis in original).

11. Motion . . . for Approval of Amendment of Trust Distribution Procedures at 2, *In re* Boy Scouts of America, 20-10343 (Bankr. D. Del. Oct. 2, 2023), docket #11514 (survivors unable to access key information); Response of Dumas & Vaughn Claimants at 2, 5, *In re* Boy Scouts of America, 20-10343 (Bankr. D. Del. Oct. 9, 2023), docket #11528 (survivors have not had the months of access to documents promised by the Boy Scouts' plan to determine whether to pay for and pursue the individual review option, and giving specific examples of shortcoming of document production and search functionality); Order Granting Motion . . . for Approval of Amendment of Trust Distribution Procedures, *In re* Boy Scouts of America, 20-10343 (Bankr. D. Del. Oct. 16, 2023), docket #11537.

12. Missing forms and lawyers: Transcript of Scouting Settlement Townhall—Tuesday September 26, 2023 (Randi Roth: "of the universe of more than 7,000 claimants who chose this expedited or quick pay option more than 4,500 of them have not signed or submitted their expedited form yet. . . . If you do not file a claim on time, you cannot receive compensation.") Difficulty connecting with lawyers: *Id.* (Aaron Curtis: "we've got quite a few claimants asking how do they get their lawyer to call them back because their lawyer is not responding.") Update on submissions: Scouting Settlement Town Hall, Nov. 1, 2023; Logistical challenges with ballot: Transcript of Boy Scouts of America Official Tort Claimants Committee Town Hall at 3, 16–17 (Oct. 28, 2021).

13. Number of requests and lack of discretion to change: Consolidated Response of the Honorable Barbara J. Houser (Ret.) in Her Capacity as Trustee at 2, 5, *In re* Boy Scouts of America, 20-10343 (Bankr. D. Del. Oct. 27, 2023), docket #11565. Survivor who had voted against plan: Motion to Change Election, *In re* Boy Scouts of America, 20-10343 (Bankr. D. Del. Oct. 11, 2023), docket #11532.

14. 64 percent: Georgene M. Vairo, "The Dalkon Shield Claimants Trust: Paradise Lost (or Found?)," 61 *Fordham L Rev.* 617, 633, 654 (1992). 50–60 percent contingency fees: Mary F. Hawkins, *Unshielded: The Human Cost of the Dalkon Shield* 79 (U. Toronto Press 1997); Karen M. Hicks, *Surviving the Dalkon Shield IUD: Women Versus the Pharmaceutical Industry*

102 (Teachers College Press 1994). Revictimization: *id.* at 8, 101 (replication of greed and pathologies that contributed to harm from Dalkon Shield and related cover-ups); Hawkins at 33 ("the reorganization plan resulted in a legal maze that left claimants feeling isolated from a process that was intended to provide some kind of compensation for their losses."). Encouragement to take expedited payment: Hawkins at 66, 84. Inconsistent and undercompensatory recoveries: "Dalkon Shield Users Seek More Money," *Tampa Bay Times*, Nov. 14, 2001; Hawkins at 66–67 (variable outcomes for similar injuries, lack of clarity how compensation offers were calculated). Role model: Brief for Respondent the Official Committee of Unsecured Creditors at 48, Harrington v. Purdue Pharma, 23-124, 2023 WL 7042630 (Oct. 20, 2023).

15. Treatment of punitive damages in mass tort bankruptcies: Simon at 1196.

16. Fourth Circuit disapproval of emergency treatment fund: Official Committee of Equity Security Holders v. Mabey, 832 F.2d 299, 301, 303 (4th Cir. 1987). The U.S. Supreme Court denied review.

17. Humphrey: Transcript of Boy Scouts of America Official Tort Claimants Committee Town Hall at 27, Oct. 7, 2021. Definition of abuse claim: Form of Abuse Claims Bar Date Notice at 2, Exhibit 2 to Order . . . Establishing Deadlines for Filing Proofs of Claim et seq., *In re* Boy Scouts of America, 20-10343 (Bankr. D. Del. May 26, 2020), docket #695-2 (abuse claim occurring on or before February 18, 2020, with respect to a child under the age of eighteen (18) at the time of the abuse, given a broad substantive scope).

18. Fourth Circuit analysis: *In re* A.H. Robins, 880 F.2d 694, 698 (4th Cir. 1989).

19. Informational Brief of LTL Management LLC at 48, 118, 120, *In re* LTL Management, 21-30589 (Bankr. W.D.N.C. Oct. 14, 2021), docket #3.

20. Dismissal of second case: *In re* LTL Management, 652 B.R. 433 (2023). Professional fees: Evan Ochsner, J&J Unit's Failed 'Two-Step' Talc Bankruptcies Cost $178 Million," *Bloomberg Bankruptcy Law*, Oct. 4, 2023.

21. Informational Brief of Aearo Technologies at 42, 43, *In re* Aearo Technologies, 22-2890 (S.D. Ind. July 26, 2022), docket #12. Dismissal: In re Aearo Technologies LLC at *22, 2023 WL 3938436 (Bankr. S.D. Ind. June 9, 2023). Aearo filed an appeal on June 29, 2023.

22. Delayed disclosure of abuse and documentation of statute of

limitation changes: Marci A. Hamilton et al., 2021 "Annual Report: A National Overview of the Movement to Prevent Child Sex Abuse and to Empower Victims Through Statutes of Limitation Reform Since 2002" at 3, Child USA (June 21, 2022). Baltimore bankruptcy in advance of legal changes: Lee O. Sanderlin, "Church Moves to Limit Liability; Archdiocese Announces Its Bankruptcy Ahead of Child Victims Act Becoming Law," *Baltimore Sun*, Sept. 30, 2023, A1.

23. State court preparation: New York law: Child Victims Act, C.P.L. R. sec. 214-g, signed into law Feb. 14, 2019; NY Comp. Codes R. & Regs. Title 22 sec. 202.72; *In re* Child Victims Act Cases Removed from State Court at *4, —F. Supp.3d —, 2023 WL 5123396 (E.D.N.Y. Aug. 10, 2023) (describing initiatives). Bankruptcy courts: Marci A. Hamilton, Andrew J. Ortiz, and Carter E. Timon, "Roman Catholic Dioceses in Bankruptcy: An Exploratory Study of Victims' Experiences," 30 *J. Bankr. L. & Prac.* (2021) ("our findings suggest that federal bankruptcy judges should receive training on child sexual abuse and the longstanding effects of childhood trauma.... Furthermore, courts should give victims the right to appear and read a victim-impact statement prior to the finalization of a reorganization plan.").

24. Brief of Amicus Curiae U.S. Conference of Catholic Bishops in Support of Debtor Respondents, Harrington v. Purdue Pharma, 23–124 (Oct. 27, 2023).

25. Legislative history example: *In re* Child Victims Act Cases Removed from State Court at *2. Academic research: Alexandra Lahav, *In Praise of Litigation* (Oxford U. Press 2017); Gillian K. Hadfield, "Framing the Choice Between Cash and the Courthouse: Experiences with the 9/11 Victim Compensation Fund," 42 *Law & Soc'y Rev.* 645, 648 (2008).

26. Kennedy quote: Kristina Cooke, Mike Spector, Benjamin Lesser, Dan Levine, and Diha Raychaudhuri, "Boy Scouts, Catholic Dioceses Find Haven from Sex Abuse Suits in Bankruptcy," *Reuters*, Dec. 30, 2022.

27. Elizabeth Chamblee Burch, "Procedural Justice in Nonclass Aggregation," 44 *Wake Forest L. Rev.* 1 (2009).

28. Victimized: Georgene M. Vairo, "The Dalkon Shield Claimants Trust: Paradise Lost (or Found?)," 61 *Fordham L. Rev.* 617, 618 (1992). Negative reactions to bankruptcy: Hicks at 7 (secrecy of trust operations); 9 (inadequacy of distribution of notice to affected women); 10, 57, 101 (perceptions of how the Robins family and many Richmond lawyers profited from the case); 37 (concerns that many of 135,000 claim forms that were outright rejected in bankruptcy process were filed by women of color and women from other countries); 51 (receiving postcard from court discouraging

women from contacting the court); 116 (perception that bankruptcy did not hold people accountable for the harm they caused); Hawkins at 3 (deep emotional wounds, minimal compensation for many women); 30–31 (request to recuse district court judge for his personal friendship with head of Robins family and with lawyers was denied); 62, 78 (impact on women with carefully developed cases that had been ready for trial when stopped by the bankruptcy); 76 (lack of public access to help women understand operation of trust); Barnaby J. Feder, "What A.H. Robins Has Wrought," *N.Y. Times*, Dec. 13, 1987, at A1 (estimating more than 150,000 women whose rights were being affected by the bankruptcy have heard little or nothing about what is happening in the case).

29. Lesley Wexler, Jennifer K. Robbennolt, and Colleen Murphy, "#MeToo, Time's Up, and Theories of Justice," *U. Ill. L. Rev.* 45, 71 (2019); Jennifer K. Robbennolt, "Apologies and Settlement Levers," 3 *J. Empirical Legal Stud.* 333 (2006); Leslie Bender, "Feminist (Re)Torts: Thoughts on the Liability Crisis, Mass Torts, Power, and Responsibilities," *Duke L. J.* 848, 905–6 (1990).

30. Rachel Greenwald Smith, *On Compromise: Art, Politics, and the Fate of an American Ideal* 184 (Greywolf Press 2021).

Conclusion

1. Credit card debt: Press Release, "Total Household Debt Reaches $17.06 Trillion in Q2 2023; Credit Card Debt Exceeds $1 Trillion," Federal Reserve Bank of New York, Aug. 8, 2023. Consumer credit as bankruptcy indicator: Robert M. Lawless, "The Paradox of Consumer Credit," 2007 *U. Ill. L. Rev.* 347, 362 n 80, 370 (2007). Business filings: Press Release, "Year-to-Date Commercial Chapter 11 Filings Increased 61 Percent Compared to Same Period Last Year," American Bankruptcy Institute and Epiq Global, Oct. 3, 2023; Sarah Chaney Cambon, "Big-Company Bankruptcies Hang Over Economy," *Wall St. J.*, Oct. 8, 2023.

2. Labor union with no debt: Declaration of William E. Adams, *In re* International Longshore and Warehouse Union, 23-30662 (Bankr. Oct. 2, 2023), docket #9.

3. Richard Hynes and Nathaniel Pattison, "A Modern Poor Debtor's Oath," 108 *Va. L. Rev.* 915 (2022); The Consumer Bankruptcy Reform Act of 2022, S.4980 (117th Congress).

4. Research collected in Melissa B. Jacoby, "Corporate Bankruptcy Hybridity," 166 *U. Pa. L. Rev.* 1715, 1744 (2018).

5. Judge Bailey testimony: Statement of the Honorable Frank J. Bailey, The Importance of Diversity on the Federal Bench, Subcommittee on Courts, Intellectual Property, and the Internet, Committee on the Judiciary, U.S. House of Representatives, Mar. 25, 2021 ("In most districts, those serving on the bench do not at all reflect the people that work, live, and seek bankruptcy relief in those locations."); *id.* ("I am here to tell you that the NCBJ [National Conference of Bankruptcy Judges] believes that systemic change in our society must include racial and ethnic diversity among bankruptcy judges and lawyers."). Demography of federal judges: Administrative Office of the U.S. Courts, The Judiciary Fair Employment Practices Annual Report Fiscal Year 2019, at 3, 5–6 ("bankruptcy judges continue to reflect the least diversity with respect to race and ethnic composition" relative to other federal judges).

6. Karen Gross, "Taking Community Interests into Account in Bankruptcy: An Essay," 72 *Wash. U. L. Q.* 1031, 1036 (1994).

Glossary

1. Huebner quote: Hearing Transcript for Sept. 17, 2019, at 9–10, *In re* Purdue Pharma, 19-23649 (Bankr. S.D.N.Y. Sept. 18, 2019), docket #324.

2. Sheelah Kolhatkar, *Black Edge: Inside Information, Dirty Money, and the Quest to Bring Down the Most Wanted Man on Wall Street* Prologue (Random House 2017).

3. Frequency of priority debts in personal bankruptcy cases: Pamela Foohey, Robert M. Lawless, and Deborah Thorne, "Portraits of Bankruptcy Filers," 56 *Ga. L. Rev.* 573, 611 (2022).

4. Eileen Appelbaum and Rosemary Batt, *Private Equity at Work: When Wall Street Manages Main Street* 3 (Russell Sage Foundation 2014).

5. Professional fees of personal bankruptcy lawyers: Foohey, Lawless, and Thorne, "Portraits of Bankruptcy Filers," at 573, 589.

ABOUT THE AUTHOR

Melissa B. Jacoby is the Graham Kenan Professor of Law at the University of North Carolina at Chapel Hill. A frequent commentator on bankruptcy and debt in national media outlets, she has published over fifty articles, book chapters, and op-eds. She lives in Chapel Hill, North Carolina, and Brooklyn, New York. *Unjust Debts* is her first book. Find her at mbjacoby.org.

PUBLISHING IN THE PUBLIC INTEREST

Thank you for reading this book published by The New Press; we hope you enjoyed it. New Press books and authors play a crucial role in sparking conversations about the key political and social issues of our day.

We hope that you will stay in touch with us. Here are a few ways to keep up to date with our books, events, and the issues we cover:

- Sign up at www.thenewpress.com/subscribe to receive updates on New Press authors and issues and to be notified about local events
- www.facebook.com/newpressbooks
- www.twitter.com/thenewpress
- www.instagram.com/thenewpress

Please consider buying New Press books not only for yourself, but also for friends and family and to donate to schools, libraries, community centers, prison libraries, and other organizations involved with the issues our authors write about.

The New Press is a 501(c)(3) nonprofit organization; if you wish to support our work with a tax-deductible gift, please visit www.thenewpress.com/donate or use the QR code below.